Advancing Inclusive Excellence in Higher Education

A volume in
Contemporary Perspectives on Access, Equity, and Achievement
Chance W. Lewis, *Series Editor*

Contemporary Perspectives on Access, Equity, and Achievement

Chance W. Lewis, *Series Editor*

Unveiling the Cloak of Invisibility: Why Black Males are Absent in STEM Disciplines (2023)
   Anthony G. Robins, Locksley Knibbs, Ted N. Ingram, Michael N. Weaver Jr., and Adriel A. Hilton

Economic, Political, and Legal Solutions to Critical Issues in Urban Education and Implications for Teacher Preparation (2022)
   Stephanie Thomas, Shanique J. Lee, and Chance W. Lewis

Imagining the Future: Historically Black Colleges and Universities—A Matter of Survival (2022)
   Gary B. Crosby, Khalid A. White, Marcus A. Chanay, and Adriel A. Hilton

Un-Silencing Youth Trauma: Transformative School-Based Strategies for Students Exposed to Violence & Adversity (2022)
   Laurie A. Garo, Bettie Ray Butler, and Chance W. Lewis

Dissertating During a Pandemic: Narratives of Success From Scholars of Color (2022)
   Ramon B. Goings, Sherella Cupid, Montia D. Gardner, and Antione D. Tomlin

Purposeful Teaching and Learning in Diverse Contexts: Implications for Access, Equity and Achievement (2022)
   Darrell Hucks, Yolanda Sealey-Ruiz, Victoria Showunmi, Suzanne C. Carothers, and Chance W. Lewis

Reimagining School Discipline for the 21st Century Student: Engaging Students, Practitioners, and Community Members (2022)
   John A. Williams III, and Chance W. Lewis

Black Mother Educators: Advancing Praxis for Access, Equity, and Achievement (2021)
   Tambra O. Jackson

The Impact of Classroom Practices: Teacher Educators' Reflections on Culturally Relevant Teachers (2021)
   Antonio L. Ellis, Nathaniel Bryan, Yolanda Sealey-Ruiz, Ivory Toldson, and Christopher Emdin

Seeing The HiddEn Minority: Increasing the Talent Pool through Identity, Socialization, and Mentoring Constructs (2020)
   Andrea L. Tyler, Stephen Hancock, and Sonyia C. Richardson

Multiculturalism in Higher Education: Increasing Access and Improving Equity in the 21st Century (2020)
   C. Spencer Platt, Adriel A. Hilton, Christopher Newman, and Brandi Hinnant-Crawford

Conquering Academia: Transparent Experiences of Diverse Female Doctoral Students (2019)
    Sonyia C. Richardson, and Chance W. Lewis

Community College Teacher Preparation for Diverse Geographies: Implications for Access and Equity for Preparing a Diverse Teacher Workforce (2019)
    Mark M. D'Amico, and Chance W. Lewis

Comprehensive Multicultural Education in the 21st Century: Increasing Access in the Age of Retrenchment (2019)
    Brandi Hinnant-Crawford, C. Spencer Platt, Christopher Newman, and Adriel A. Hilton

Global Perspectives on Issues and Solutions in Urban Education (2019)
    Petra A. Robinson, Ayana Allen-Handy, Amber Bryant, and Chance W. Lewis

Let's Stop Calling it an Achievement Gap: How Public Education in the United States Maintains Disparate Educational Experiences for Students of Color (2019)
    Autumn A. Arnett

Responding to the Call for Educational Justice: Transformative Catholic-Led Initiatives in Urban Education (2018)
    L. Mickey Fenzel and Melodie Wyttenbach

Recruiting, Retaining, and Engaging African-American Males at Selective Public Research Universities: Challenges and Opportunities in Academics and Sports (2018)
    Louis A. Castenel, Tarek C. Grantham, and Billy J. Hawkins

Engaging African American Males in Community Colleges (2018)
    Ted N. Ingram, and James Coaxum III

Advancing Equity and Diversity in Student Affairs: A Festschrift in Honor of Melvin C. Terrell (2017)
    Jerlando F. L. Jackson, LaVar J. Charleston, and Cornelius Gilbert

Cultivating Achievement, Respect, and Empowerment (CARE) for African American Girls in PreK–12 Settings: Implications for Access, Equity and Achievement (2016)
    Patricia J. Larke, Gwendolyn Webb-Hasan, and Jemimah L. Young

R.A.C.E. Mentoring Through Social Media: Black and Hispanic Scholars Share Their Journey in the Academy (2016)
    Donna Y. Ford, Michelle Trotman Scott, Ramon B. Goings, Tuwana T. Wingfield, and Malik S. Henfield

White Women's Work: Examining the Intersectionality of Teaching, Identity, and Race (2016)
    Stephen Hancock, and Chezare A. Warren

Reaching the Mountaintop of the Academy: Personal Narratives, Advice and Strategies From Black Distinguished and Endowed Professors (2015)
    Gail L. Thompson, Fred A. Bonner II, and Chance W. Lewis

School Counseling for Black Male Student Success in 21st Century Urban Schools (2015)
    Malik S. Henfield and Ahmad R. Washington

Exploring Issues of Diversity within HBCUs (2015)
    Ted N. Ingram, Derek Greenfield, Joelle D. Carter, and Adriel A. Hilton

Priorities of the Professoriate: Engaging Multiple Forms of Scholarship Across Rural and Urban Institutions (2015)
    Fred A. Bonner II, Rosa M. Banda, Petra A. Robinson, Chance W. Lewis, and Barbara Lofton

Autoethnography as a Lighthouse: Illuminating Race, Research, and the Politics of Schooling (2015)
    Stephen Hancock, Ayana Allen, and Chance W. Lewis

Teacher Education and Black Communities: Implications for Access, Equity and Achievement (2014)
    Yolanda Sealey-Ruiz, Chance W. Lewis, and Ivory Toldson

Improving Urban Schools: Equity and Access in K–16 STEM Education (2013)
    Mary Margaret Capraro, Robert M. Capraro, and Chance W. Lewis

Black Males in Postsecondary Education: Examining their Experiences in Diverse Institutional Contexts (2012)
    Adriel A. Hilton, J. Luke Wood, and Chance W. Lewis

Yes We Can! Improving Urban Schools through Innovative Educational Reform (2011)
    Leanne L. Howell, Chance W. Lewis, and Norvella Carter

Advancing Inclusive Excellence in Higher Education

Practical Approaches to Promoting Diversity, Equity, Inclusion, and Belonging

edited by

Shawna Patterson-Stephens
Central Michigan University

Tamara Bertrand Jones
Florida State University

INFORMATION AGE PUBLISHING, INC.
Charlotte, NC • www.infoagepub.com

Library of Congress Cataloging-in-Publication Data

A CIP record for this book is available from the Library of Congress
http://www.loc.gov

ISBN: 979-8-88730-308-6 (Paperback)
       979-8-88730-309-3 (Hardcover)
       979-8-88730-310-9 (E-Book)

Copyright © 2023 Information Age Publishing Inc.

All rights reserved. No part of this publication may be reproduced, stored in a retrieval system, or transmitted, in any form or by any means, electronic, mechanical, photocopying, microfilming, recording or otherwise, without written permission from the publisher.

Printed in the United States of America

CONTENTS

Foreword ix
Eboni M. Zamani-Gallaher

1 Advancing Diversity, Equity, Inclusion, and Belonging
   in Higher Education: Praxis, Pedagogy, and Research 1
   Shawna Patterson-Stephens and Tamara Bertrand Jones

2 Feeding Fish to the Tiger to Survive: Interrogating Structures
   of Oppression in Higher Education 9
   Kakali Bhattacharya, Jia "Grace" Liang, and Teara Lander

3 Problematizing Diversity: Imagining Inclusion Through a
   Liberated Lens 29
   Charee Dee Mosby-Holloway and Sara C. Furr

4 Moving Towards Greatness: Implementing a Diversity Plan
   at an Urban Research Institution 49
   Alicia W. Davis, Chance W. Lewis, and John A. Williams III

5 Recognizing and Addressing Implicit Bias in Adjudication and
   Title IX Procedures: A Case Study Approach 63
   Shawna Patterson-Stephens

6 Building a Social Justice-Centered Higher Education and
   Student Affairs Program in California's Central Valley 97
   Varaxy Yi, Susana Hernández, Ignacio Hernández, and Jonathan T. Pryor

7   The Black Male Research BootCamp: Intentionally Shaping
    Black Men's Doctoral Student Socialization 133
    Jesse Ford and Tamara Bertrand Jones

8   Meet Them in the Center: A Model for Embedded Sexual
    Misconduct Survivor Advocacy and Support Services 151
    Sarah Colomé

9   Challenging Intersectional Marginalization in Identity Based
    Centers 175
    *Jonathan A. McElderry, Stephanie Hernandez Rivera,
    and Shannon Ashford*

10 Resisting Interlocking Structures and Relations Through
    Social Justice Praxis: Insights From a Dialogic Exchange
    Between Three Black Women Academics 193
    Talia R. Esnard, Deirdre Cobb-Roberts, and Devona F. Pierre

11 The Journey Matters: Examining the Paths and Lived
    Experiences of African American Males for STEM Success 215
    *Latara O. Lampkin, Adrienne Stephenson, Andria Cole,
    Jonathan Townes. and Marquise L. Kessee*

12 "Not a Thing That We Talk About": Recommendations for
    Supporting and Engaging LGBQ+ Identified Caribbean
    Heritage Students 243
    Louise Michelle Vital and Mike Hoffshire

13 Conclusion 265
    Tamara Bertrand Jones and Shawna Patterson-Stephens

    Epilogue—Advancing Inclusive Excellence in Higher
    Education: Implications for Moving Beyond Diversity
    to Create Equitable and Anti-Racist Institutions 269
    Frank A. Tuitt

    About the Contributors 275

FOREWORD

In many ways, I am still the wishful child at heart that I was during my formative years growing up on Chicago's Southside. As a girl, I noticed how racially segregated the City of Chicago was as I would traverse going back and forth to school. Daily I would see the intersections of race, gender, age, social classes, disability, and religion. Whether it was riding the CTA bus across town, or going to my mother's job at the University of Chicago Hospital, I could openly see marginality, oppression, discrimination, and differential mattering dependent on one's social group.

By my adolescent years, it wasn't just my awareness of racism, sexism, and classism that was heightened, but for the first time, I experienced anti-Blackness and overt racial discrimination in and out of school. I witnessed unreasoned and outright antipathy toward those experienced as "different" and "othered" due to religious beliefs, nationality, and sexuality. Hence, during this period, I saw how much race permeated everything. That race was complex and it mattered—as it does—does not mitigate other aspects of self but can exacerbate what is considered a subordinated, oppressed identity. That was nearly 4 decades ago.

I share part of my backstory as a means of underscoring that then and now—egalitarian values are elusive. Institutions of higher learning are slowly coming to grips with the reprisal of vitriol in contemporary identity politics that eviscerate equity and empowerment for members of minoritized groups. The perils, paradox, and promise of upending formalized inequities requires more than reimagining but instead a rebooting that actually dismantles the systematizing of prejudice across the spectrum of difference on campuses and in general.

As a society, we are still failing at fairness, inclusion, equity, and justice. In these troubling times, dehumanization and systemic oppression are deeply rooted in the fabric of American life. We need more than just openness to change, we are in dire need of radical transformative change. *Advancing Inclusive Excellence in Higher Education: Practical Approaches to Promoting Diversity, Equity, Inclusion, and Belonging* is a well-crafted book that advances discussion among experts in the field that serves as a clarion call to understand—and to more importantly—ACT in our rethinking and redesigning postsecondary educational spaces to be equitable. Edited by Shawna M. Patterson-Stephens and Tamara Bertrand Jones, this volume has breadth and depth across a myriad of theories, research, policy, and praxis. The throughline across the chapters is elevating the necessity of consciously creating intersectional spaces, equity-centered conversations, fostering agency, and challenging anti-identity sentiments.

This text blends theoretically rich contributions alongside empirical work, and interlocks practical recommendations. While it is a read that can benefit scholars in training in graduate programs and features interdisciplinarity, it also summons seasoned educators to actively subvert structures of oppression for marginalized communities to bolster inclusion, belonging, and actualize institutional social justice efforts. In short, this is a timely and important collection that offers an authentic assessment of age-old concerns and current issues that reflect the perennial dilemma in difference. It begs us to right-size our rhetoric with our institutional realities relative to equity, diversity, inclusion, and belonging.

—Eboni M. Zamani-Gallaher
University of Pittsburgh

CHAPTER 1

ADVANCING DIVERSITY, EQUITY, INCLUSION, AND BELONGING IN HIGHER EDUCATION

Praxis, Pedagogy, and Research

Shawna Patterson-Stephens
Tamara Bertrand Jones

> *You can play a shoestring if you're sincere.*
> —John Coltrane

Diversity work is a labor of passion and love. It requires sincerity. The labor associated with advancing diversity, equity, inclusion, and belonging (DEIB) in higher education occurs around the clock and involves a comprehensive approach that touches upon emotional, psychological, social, professional, and spiritual domains. It is the acknowledgement of these overlapping domains that prompted the development of this text. The successful implementation and integration of DEIB at colleges and universities reaches across identity, and fills gaps in curricula, service, and policy

---

Advancing Inclusive Excellence in Higher Education, pages 1–8
Copyright © 2023 by Information Age Publishing
www.infoagepub.com
All rights of reproduction in any form reserved.

with intentionality and purpose. For those committed to the task of *doing* the work, knowing where to begin and what to do is often the preeminent challenge. Still, with some effort, we can all learn to create quality educational experiences, even if the most readily available instrument is simply a "shoestring."

The core themes of this volume center on DEIB in higher education. While some educators use these terms interchangeably, we define diversity as a concept that envelopes several modes of social identity, including race, ethnicity, gender, citizenship status, Indigeneity, ability, sexual orientation, faith/secular identities, size, veteran's status, and so on. The practice of fortifying representation amongst marginalized populations without making considerations for structure and support has been the primary model for diversifying higher education for the past 30 years. Within the context of higher education and diversity, our conversations are shifting beyond ensuring people from historically underserved backgrounds are represented.

Inclusion is now increasingly intertwined in postsecondary diversification efforts, where we aim to guarantee different types of people have access to higher education, and that the environment is one where community members are holistically included upon arrival to campus. Inclusion entails ensuring a diverse range of voices and perspectives are present in curricula and pedagogies, course materials, in the physical structure, within policy, procedure, infrastructure, and in the professional and social opportunities made available on campus.

When differentiating the dichotomy between equality and equity, we hope to highlight how everyone's experiences are unique, and while equality works towards supplying communities with similar resources, equity works to ensure the resources are adequately identified to the scale representative of the unique circumstances and needs emergent from said community. Specifically, historically underserved people, communities, and societies demonstrate different needs connected to the relationship between cultural histories and social location, with cycles of oppression and White supremacy.

For the purposes of this text, belonging is an extension of inclusion. In addition to providing community members ample space to realize an educational landscape that encompasses all aspects of one's lived experience, belonging infiltrates psychological barriers, where the expectations of faculty, staff, and students reflect their actual encounters on campus. Instituting a sense of belonging across all rungs of the academy reinforces a collective connectivity to the ideological spirit of a postsecondary education.

The foundational underpinning of these themes is the framework for inclusive excellence and change (Williams et al., 2005). Institutions seeking to achieve inclusive excellence are those which identify systemic issues that permeate infrastructure, policies, practices, and curricula in a manner that propagates bias, prejudice, and exclusion. Rather than remaining reliant on isolated programs, campus leadership that requires holistic, wraparound DEIB efforts are better situated to embed inclusive excellence within the fabric of their institution. In total, this framework sets the stage for how each contributing author examined issues of diversity, equity, inclusion, and belonging in higher education.

Oftentimes, students, faculty, and staff seeking to actively engage in DEIB concepts, pedagogies, and praxis encounter readings that examine research problems and provide discussion on these themes. However, it is a rare occurrence to encounter works that delve into the content while simultaneously offering readers with tangible techniques they can rework to address concerns on their respective campuses. Current issues emanating from college campuses include, but are not limited to: (a) supporting campus DEIB efforts in the face of an antagonistic political climate, (b) mitigating disparate resource stratifications persistent among minoritized communities, (c) implementing trauma-informed praxis within conflict resolution and campus safety procedures, (d) creating culturally relevant socialization structures for faculty of color, and (e) managing implicit bias prevalent in recruitment and hiring practices, conduct hearings, tenure and promotion, course grading, evaluations, and Title IX procedures. With accessibility in mind, contributors in this volume provide readers with practical responses to addressing contemporary DEIB issues in higher education.

We include the perspectives of faculty and staff with a range of experiences and expertise in order to provide a multidimensional approach to addressing concerns across various levels and functional areas in the academy. Rather than replicate findings and recommendations established in extant literature, we provide faculty, staff, and graduate students with insight and tools they will require to transform established recommendations into actionable solutions and promising practices.

We seek to advance findings and recommendations into action. For instance, according to extant research, our readers should think more critically about mentorship, especially as it relates to the recruitment and retention of minoritized students, faculty, and staff. We can point to several publications which center the importance of mentorship, however, How does one become an effective mentor? How would a chair successfully implement a culturally significant mentoring framework within their department, particularly one that centers the experiences of faculty of color? How could one appropriately assess their level of effectiveness in teaching others how to mentor in culturally responsive ways?

Within each chapter, the contributing authors address a wide range of DEIB issues that are unique to their positionality as educators in the postsecondary sector. As editors, we intentionally identified authors with diverse professional backgrounds who could provide various methods for contending with DEIB trends in their respective areas in higher education. Thus, the questions we seek to answer are equally as diverse. For instance, Alicia Davis and Chance Lewis share ways to cultivate and implement DEIB strategic plans on campus. Jonathan McElderry, Stephanie Hernandez Rivera, and Shannon Ashford explore what it means to navigate the complexity of supporting students, uplifting institutional expectations, and practicing self-care as both intercultural center and marginalized staff members in higher education. Each author's contribution is individualized, but collectively, they demonstrate the multifaceted technique that is required in effectively advancing DEIB at colleges and universities. While it is the role of institutional diversity offices to create synergy across campus initiatives, DEIB efforts must surface from all sectors of campus, within each functional area, and led by faculty, staff, and executive administrators.

This volume is designed to focus on higher education structures and functional areas rather than identity-based praxis. While our contributors may elect to center a particular identity or form of oppression in their writing, the intention of each overall chapter is to examine DEIB issues within units on college campuses, such as academic departments and student development and support service offices. This text is distinctive because it does not focus on one aspect of DEIB work. Our book offers readers accessible theory and practical applications for complex issues across a range of foci. Our text serves as an exemplar for manuscripts to follow, as we address a variety of subject matter.

Though researchers and practitioners offer several suggestions on how these issues could be addressed through scholarship, it is rare to encounter step-by-step strategies for effectively implementing proposed recommendations. This text emerges as a handbook that aptly examines contemporary challenges in higher education through an emulsion of research and praxis. We have compiled our volume with adult learners in mind, and we have proceeded in the hope that it will encourage further scholarly discussion about the continually changing but always meaningful ways in which DEIB are addressed in the postsecondary sector.

This text provides graduate students with preemptive techniques and professional standards, which will help to shape their scholarship and praxis upon entry into the field. Further, this volume targets faculty and researchers who are engaged in examining matters of DEIB in the postsecondary sector, as well as individuals who seek assistance in enacting these themes in their pedagogy, research, and practice. Finally, higher education practitioners are often seeking supplemental resources to inform their work. This book provides intercollegiate staff with key concepts and strategies aimed at enhancing their skill sets within the realm of DEIB work.

Many, if not all, graduate preparation programs offer a required diversity or social justice oriented course. What does it mean for educators who do not elect to take these courses? Or further still, how many opportunities do educators have to conduct self-guided development in DEIB after graduation? Within the context of tightened budgets, inadequate professional development funding, and reduced access to course matriculation benefits, texts such as this provides faculty and staff with the opportunity to engage in the praxis of continued skill-building in a manner that is high-touch and economical.

Chapter 2 follows three women of color, who are trained by and work in predominantly White institutions. They explore how hidden and overt structures of higher education continue to sustain and proliferate oppression, silencing, and deficit narratives through curriculum design, training of educational leaders, and mentoring. Bhattacharya's (2016) framework of being in higher education as a marginalized group is akin to riding the boat with Richard Parker—the tiger from the movie, *Life of Pi*. Using this framework and the Richard Parker analogy, the authors discuss the materiality of the oppression faced by women of color in higher education and their negotiation and coping strategies. The authors conclude the chapter by making recommendations relevant for leadership in higher education to have difficult equity-centered conversations, subvert structures of oppression, and create agentic spaces for marginalized communities in higher education.

Chapter 3 traces the evolution of institutional diversity efforts from access, diversity, and student success to futuristic notions of inclusion and liberation. The progressive narrative has largely shaped historical institutional diversity efforts. Colleges and universities perform diversity because it is just and is the right thing to do; and while there has been tremendous movement towards creating more diverse and inclusive college campuses, there is rarely discussion around systemic change or dismantling dominant power structures. Diversity is ultimately dictated by the institution. This chapter proposes that the narratives of those doing diversity work are crucial in reimagining what diversity and inclusion can and should look like on college and university campuses. Using visionary fiction as a model to create liberated narratives, the authors share their own experiences of doing diversity work on campus and call for others to do the same.

Chapter 4 acknowledges that increasing diversity at postsecondary institutions remains a constant focus for higher education leaders. The use of diversity plans to hold universities and colleges accountable in providing access, equity, and inclusivity in student and faculty recruitment and instructional practices has caused higher education administrators to reflect upon their procedures by engaging with America's multicultural communities. This chapter outlines how an urban research institution created and implemented their diversity plan to shift the diversity infrastructure on campus. Student and faculty recruitment, student retention rates, graduation rates, and creating a diverse curriculum are highlighted throughout the chapter. The expected outcome of this chapter is for postsecondary institutions to develop and implement strategic diversity plans at their institutions.

Chapter 5 examines some of the ways implicit bias exists, emerges, and develops in conduct hearings and Title IX proceedings on college campuses. Title IX procedures have emerged as a way to correct gender discrimination in higher education, and universities—particularly public institutions—must demonstrate strict accordance with the due process clause of the 14th Amendment. Similarly, investigative procedures and conduct hearings must afford due process as outlined by an institution's respective code of conduct and hearing policy. Still, concealed assumptions continue to influence the manner in which faculty and staff engage with reporting, investigations, hearings, ancillary procedures, and sanctioning. This chapter addresses the ways educators could seek to reduce instances of bias and harm in conduct and Title IX proceedings.

In Chapter 6, the authors contextualize their efforts as higher education student affairs graduate preparation faculty to build a graduate preparation program that incorporates social justice frameworks in California's Central Valley. They briefly explore national and local educational contexts that shape the need for a graduate preparation program at California State University, Fresno (Fresno State); underscore their efforts to integrate social justice and equity-oriented values into the graduate curriculum; and offer reflections on the process of (re)designing curriculum, programs, and services to support diverse students and emerging professionals in the Central Valley. The authors provide context-specific strategies and recommendations for building a social-justice oriented higher education and student affairs graduate preparation program.

Chapter 7 examines how socialization activities have focused on discipline-based knowledge and skills required for professional success. Still, these socialization activities do not address the nuances of identity, particularly race and gender socialization issues are especially acute for Black men faculty given their limited representation in academia. The Black Male Research BootCamp (BMRBC) represents a socialization intervention for Black men doctoral students, where Black men doctoral student participants identified the importance of Black male spaces in which to learn, grow, and engage with other Black men scholars. The authors offer suggestions for Black men doctoral students and faculty, and institutions interested in supporting Black men doctoral students.

In Chapter 8, the author positions the University of Illinois Urbana-Champaign as a case study for exploring new considerations for liberatory sexual misconduct prevention and response work. Grounded in Black and Latinx feminist thought, this chapter explores how Illinois was working to pivot from a cultural competence paradigm to one of community-driven innovation and service. The first two sections of the chapter examine the current state of sexual misconduct on college campuses, the need for specialized programs and services to meet diverse student needs, and provide an explanation of the role and scope of work provided by a confidential advisor. The chapter then provides practical examples of how Illinois engaged campus and community partners to enact a social justice framework in the procurement, recruitment, hiring, onboarding, operationalization, and daily practice of an embedded confidential advisor.

Chapter 9 uses theoretical concepts and frameworks to provide recommendations and ways that practitioners can be more intentional in considering students who experience multiple-marginality on their campuses and how they can be more conscious of creating an intersectional space and programming. Additionally, the authors address issues that emerge in serving multiple communities and explore how practitioners can serve their communities from an equitable place. They also address the anti-identity sentiments that exist within different spaces and how practitioners can challenge these sentiments as well. The aim of this chapter is to support practitioners working in identity centers. This work invites practitioners to reflect on the ways their spaces also perpetuate ideologies of dominance through their support services, and at times disempower and invisibilize students with multiple-marginalized identities.

Chapter 10 illuminates the role that Black women faculty and administrators bring to bear on being social justice advocates. It further demonstrates the potential for collaborative autoethnography to unpack the complexities and risks embedded in working towards social justice within an environment of systemic and structural inequalities. The authors' discourse provides a foundation for discussing critical social justice incidents, the situated and politicized nature of being and working within higher education, and the prospects for social justice agendas. Further, their dialogue works through their attempts to serve as advocates for institutional change, and the extent to which activism places them in vulnerable positions. Such work creates a necessary space where shared stories around social justice advocacy in higher education can be situated in structural and relational terms, where critical reflection on the realities of these experiences can exist, and where exploring the implications for ushering diversity, equity, and inclusion from a critical standpoint is examined.

In Chapter 11, the authors share insights from African American male students matriculating through STEM pathway programs, as well as from those who have successfully completed their academic programs. Specifically, they share findings from a case study in which they explore factors that enhance the success of African American males pursuing STEM degrees at one of the few community colleges designated as a historically Black college and university. The authors provide considerations that can potentially enhance the recruitment, persistence, and success of African American males pursuing STEM degrees.

Chapter 12 sheds light on the fact that LGBQ+ people in the Caribbean have long struggled for social, cultural, and legal acceptance and tolerance. While some countries have legalized same-sex marriage, some islands across the Caribbean region criminalize acts related to homosexual identities. This chapter provides a contextual understanding of the LGBQ+ experience in U.S. higher education and the Caribbean, as well as the framework and methods used by the authors to conduct this research. The authors discuss the conceptual model of students as partners in learning and teaching in higher education, and conclude by suggesting strategies, interventions, and initiatives that can be utilized in higher education settings.

Chapter 13 offers summative analyses of the broader systematic issues that continue to act as barriers to the successful cultivation of pluralistic learning environments in higher education. The authors discuss next steps and recommendations for further research and creating change in the academy. The text concludes with an insightful epilogue written by Frank A. Tuitt.

REFERENCE

Williams, D. A., Berger, J. B., & McClendon, S. A. (2005). Toward a model of inclusive excellence and change in postsecondary institutions. *Making Excellence Inclusive*. AAC&U.

CHAPTER 2

FEEDING FISH TO THE TIGER TO SURVIVE

Interrogating Structures of Oppression in Higher Education

Kakali Bhattacharya
Jia "Grace" Liang
Teara Lander

ABSTRACT

Authored by three women of color who are trained by and work in predominantly White institutions, this chapter explores the ways in which hidden and overt structures of higher education continue to sustain and proliferate structures of oppression, silencing, and deficit narratives through curriculum design, training of educational leaders, and mentoring. Using Bhattacharya's (2016) framework, being in higher education as a marginalized group is akin to riding the boat with Richard Parker (tiger from the movie *Life of Pi*). The authors discuss the materiality of oppression faced by women of color in higher education, as well as negotiation and coping strategies. The authors conclude the chapter by making recommendations relevant for leadership in higher education in order to have difficult equity-centered conversations,

Advancing Inclusive Excellence in Higher Education, pages 9–28
Copyright © 2023 by Information Age Publishing
www.infoagepub.com
All rights of reproduction in any form reserved.

subvert structures of oppression, and create agentic spaces for marginalized communities in higher education. Supplementary materials for this chapter will include interactive strategies and guidelines for conducting difficult conversations, brainstorming exercises of imagination of freedom and agentic space making, and strategies for creating inclusive curriculum.

The three authors of this chapter identify as belonging to multiple-minoritized groups, including diasporic and transnational communities, while navigating a career in higher education. Thus, it is essential to understand how our experiences can be juxtaposed against transnationalism and higher education in the United States. In this chapter, we explore the relationship between otherness, as well as intersectional issues of oppression and anti-Blackness within the overt and hidden curriculum. We offer situated narratives of ourselves and participants with whom we are in community as we explore and interrogate our positions in higher education. We analyze our narratives to raise issues about inclusivity and survivance (survival and resistance). Finally, we share our recommendations for engaging in difficult conversations for those in positions of privilege and those who are acrobatically managing multiple forms of intersected oppression.

FEEDING FISH TO THE TIGER FOR SURVIVANCE

Bhattacharya (2016) documented that the experiences of multiple-marginalized people in academia are similar to being in the boat with a tiger named Richard Parker, seen in the movie *Life of Pi*. Using personal narratives from her decade-long experience in academia, Bhattacharya discussed the various ways the metaphor of being in a boat with a tiger applies to how she had negotiated her place and survivance in academia. Here, the tiger represents White supremacy and multiple intersected forms of oppression such as xenophobia, anti-Blackness, racism, patriarchy, homophobia, ableism, transphobia, and much more. Thus, as women of color, we negotiated with the tigers to share a boat for our survival and resistance. These negotiations included dealing with the tiger, being vigilant of the tiger, feeding fish to the tiger, and finding ways to uncomfortably coexist with the tiger until one discovers land (or a tiger-free destination). Because this relationship with the tiger creates a set of complicated complicities, Bhattacharya (2016), who situated herself in a hybridized space of decolonizing ontoepistemologies, shared:

> For me, a hybridized state of existence implies never situating myself firmly in either oppressive or liberatory discourses. Knowing that I shuttle between multiple subject positions and competing discourses, I choose to author myself in ways that might appear to accommodate oppressive structures and how

that might appear to celebrate agentic power through resistance. Shunning all of the subject positions informed by colonizing discourses would be akin to shunning a part of me. At the same time, rejecting subject positions forwarded by decolonizing discourses would represent a denial of the authenticity with which I always strive to author myself. Yet, I would be dishonest as well if I failed to acknowledge explicitly that colonizing discourses and pervasive microaggression have material effects, and oppressive imperialistic practices materially harm those whom they colonize. (p. 314)

In other words, we cannot claim a pure space devoid of external forms of oppression or the internalization of dominant oppressive narratives. Therefore, even while we are in the boat with Richard Parker (the tiger from the movie *Life of Pi*) feeding him fish, we understand our complicity for survival while secretly plotting, planning, and executing an escape route for liberation. But we are inextricably entangled because our existence depends on not falling prey to the predatory structures of higher education. Still, we inevitably become complicit with oppressive forces while trying to execute survival and resistance strategies. We still have to remind ourselves that Richard Parker is always a tiger, even when we have cultivated some understanding of coexistence, established our territories, and regularly fulfilled our obligations to feed Richard Parker's insatiable hunger. Richard Parker will never love us back and/or be completely harmless, even when he sleeps and appears cute and cuddly. These structures of oppression are always violent no matter what metamorphosed, cloaked form it takes. Additionally, knowing many of us are in a boat with some version of Richard Parker, we present a collective threat to the status quo. Therefore, even as we coexist in the boat with Richard Parker, we continue to forge solidarities with other vulnerable boat dwellers and draw strength from those connections so that our collective resilience would unmatch everything Richard Parker can throw at us.

This chapter is written in narrative, personalized voices, honoring that our bodies, consciousness, and awareness are empirical sources of information. Our voices are different, requiring us to situate and write with our individualized styles and compulsion. We have intentionally walked away from creating a homogenous structure in how we represent our narratives. We offer these narratives as contemporary critical historicities, writing ourselves and our participants into existence.

KAKALI'S NARRATIVE: FROM HERE, THERE, AND A THIRD PLACE

I identify as a Desi woman in U.S. academia. Desi refers to people who identify with heritage from South Asia. I migrated to Canada in my early teens and to the United States in my twenties to pursue graduate studies. Currently, I am a qualitative research methodologist at the University of Florida. Substantively, I am interested in the social context of higher education as it pertains to race, class, gender, and migration issues. One cannot dismiss the material consequences of crossing oceans, migrating to a new world, trading in old ways of knowing and living, for being minoritized across interlocked, intersected social structures of oppression. One learns the deficit narratives written for them and their cultures, but in many instances, fails to recognize themselves through those narratives, as they represent the colonial imagination of the subaltern.

In this section, I share the findings of an ethnographic case study I conducted with two Desi women from India during their first year of graduate education in the United States. I wanted to explore their relations and practices as they learned to negotiate the overt and hidden curriculum in higher education and beyond, that racialized, minoritized, and exoticized them. Data collection lasted about a year and a half, where I engaged the participants in informal conversations, photo and object elicitations, and conducted participant observations in formal and informal contexts. I represented the data in an ethno-dramatic format to highlight the performativity of their actions in varied informal academic and social environments.

Both Neerada and Yamini came to the United States from Mumbai, India. Neerada and Yamini were pursuing master's degrees in computer science and business administration, respectively. They enjoyed privileges of caste, class, location, religion, and social visibility. When they came to the United States, they lost those privileges and had to deal with various types of minoritization to which they were previously unexposed. Desiring to belong within peer groups within their programs, both went out of their comfort zones to engage in activities they considered would create social desirability. I present these negotiations within their informal academic contexts in the scenes below.

* * *

ACT 1, SCENE 1

A university computer lab. Neerada is seen with Chang, a Chinese student, and Gina, a Black student from Kenya, both in their mid-to-late twenties. In the corner, Anthony, a Black American technician, is working on a computer.

> *Neerada:* Are you coming to the departmental potluck tonight, Chang?
> *Chang:* No. I don't belong there. Sorry, Neerada, but people hardly ever talk to me except to ask about *China* and Chinese food. Like, I'm supposed to be some kind of expert! I feel like there's a divide amongst Whites and internationals in this program. Nothing bad,

but I've been here for 2 years, and they still treat me like an outsider.

Gina: You just have to learn to ignore that. The other day Katya and I went to the dining hall and sat at the end of this long table. There were plenty of spaces, but the White people walked around and sat in the corner at another table. Katya was upset, but I told her we're here to study, so ignore those things.

Neerada: Me too, Gina! When I'm on the bus, and there's an empty seat beside me, people don't sit right away. Some stand, and some sit elsewhere. Even if the bus is crowded. First, I didn't notice, but I began to pay attention when it happened more than once.

Anthony: That's exactly why I live in the city. I'd rather drive 2 hours every day than live somewhere where people only see me as Black and not as a person.

Chang: Yes! That's exactly it, Anthony. I'm always made to be Chinese before I can be Chang.

Anthony: I've even seen them like that with professors. You know Dr. Riley? He's like the only Black professor in the department.

Chang: Yeah, but he's so good at what he does that no one messes with him, even if they don't like his race.

Gina: That's what you have to do to survive. Be twice as good as everyone and concentrate on your studies.

Neerada: Even if all that race stuff is going on, it's hard for me to think that people are that way towards me. I never had to face it before I came here, and I mostly try to ignore it. That's why I'm going to this potluck. Besides, I find this concept of potluck very interesting. You invite people over for dinner, and then you tell them to bring their food and drinks (*laughs*), and then people can take their leftovers back as well (*laughs*). It's too bad you can't come. Please think about it, Chang. How can you be an insider unless you try?

Chang: No, thank you. I'd rather stay in the lab.

Anthony: I am with Chang on this one.

* * *

ACT 1: SCENE 2

Neerada is in her apartment in Hickory Towers on a Friday night. It is a modest space with a living, dining, and kitchen area, a card table for a dining table, and a bean bag chair. A bookshelf is beside the table with university-related paraphernalia and pictures of people taking multiple trips in various locations in the United States. The phone rings. The audience hears only Neerada's side of the conversation.

Neerada: Hi Maa. I'm alright. How are you and Papa? And the dogs? Do Fluffy and Toffee miss me? Yes, Maa, I'm NOT eating out; I'm cooking at home. There's not that much vegetarian options here to eat out anyway. What am I doing tonight? Nothing. Just in my flat. My roommates are at a conference, so I'm just by myself here (*voice quivers*). No, Maa, I can't just call people to come over to my place. It's not like India. I've to give them advance notice, they check their schedules, and then decide if they'd come over. Plus, I don't know if people would come to my place and eat Indian food with my department. But wait. I could do this thing they call a potluck. Maybe I'll invite them next Friday.

(The audience sees Neerada talking for a few more minutes without sound as the light fades on stage.)

The stage lights up. Eight people gradually come into Neerada's apartment. Besides Julie and Kevin, everyone appears to be of non-White heritage, including one Indian student, Bharat. The card table is crowded with dishes, Tupperware, and a prominently placed bag of potato chips. Neerada puts a plate of red tandoori chicken and a dish of saag paneer on the table.

Neerada: Okay, I think we're ready to eat now.

Julie and Kevin move to the table. Kevin closely examines the tandoori chicken and other international dishes, grimaces, and serves himself a plateful of chips. Julie advises the other student about the other dishes, and both load up their plates. After Julie and Kevin have gotten their food, the international students follow, except for Neerada and Bharat, who hang back.

Bharat: (*Whispers*) Neerada, there's nothing vegetarian here except for the potato chips and your *saag* paneer, which is now mostly gone.
Neerada: I know.
Bharat: I thought you were a vegetarian. And you still cooked chicken?
Neerada: Yes, I did. Amrus[1] know of tandoori chicken, so I thought I'd try if they believe the *saag* paneer is too weird.
Bharat: But what are you going to eat?
Neerada: I don't care. I'd rather not eat dinner if I could have people from my department in my apartment doing normal American things and not have to be lonely on a Friday night. (Both look around and see that Julie and Kevin are eating alone.) I'm just tired of feeling like an outsider and trying to fit in. I hate thinking that I'm different because of my race. I guess I don't want to accept the international and domestic divide.

ACT 2: SCENE 1

Yamini and eight other students are in Noku's (identifies as South Korean) apartment hanging out. The people present are primarily international students except for Katie, Ron, and Maggie.

Feeding Fish to the Tiger to Survive • 15

Katie: Yamini, we love Indian food so much! Why don't you do an Indian luncheon?

Noku: I love Indian food. My boss at my last job was Indian. She'd always feed me and teach me swear words *(laughs).* *(Shouting)* Chutiya! Gandu! Benchod!

Yamini: *(To Noku)* Shhhh! We don't say those things out loud *(laughs).* *(To Katie)* Listen, I don't even know how to cook. I can download some recipes and try them first. But I can't invite the whole class. Sally and her group think I'm invisible and don't even say hi. I'll ask the nine of us here and the rest some other time.

Ron: Yeah, Sally and her mean girl group is like that with Maggie, Katie, and me too. I guess they don't like that we hang out with international students.

Maggie: *(irritated)* People need to grow up. This is not high school.

ACT 2, SCENE 2

Yamini is hosting an Indian luncheon for nine friends from her program. Ron, Maggie, and Katie are the only White, domestic students; the rest are non-White international students. People served themselves and seemed to be having friendly conversations with each other. Flash the pictures from Figure 2.1 in the background.

Katie: Yamini, the other day, I read a report on the Internet that some monkeys in India attacked some children at a temple. I was so shocked. I didn't know that monkeys roam around freely like that. I always thought monkeys belonged in zoos.

Everyone laughs.

Figure 2.1 Yamini's Indian luncheon: Using cuisine to create relationalities.

>   *Ron:* How can a perfectly intelligent person doing her master's ask that? Do you think the zoo grows the monkeys from the ground?
>   *Katie:* I'm just not used to seeing monkeys like that. That's all.
>
> *Everyone laughs again.*
>
>   *Maggie:* Yamini, the food is delicious. Do you have recipes?
>   *Yamini:* Yes, I can share. I was nervous about cooking for so many people for the first time.
>   *Ron:* If you don't mind me asking, don't women have to be in the kitchen in India and learn all household duties like cooking, cleaning?
>   *Yamini:* Not me. We had servants who cooked and cleaned and a driver.
>   *Katie:* (*singsong voice*) Chauffeur-driven princess Yamini!
>   *Yamini:* Hardly. Everyone I knew had servants and a driver.
>   *Maggie:* You know Yamini, before you came, I never thought of Indians as Asians until you pointed out that India was in Asia.
>   *Yamini:* It's an American issue, I think. When I visit my cousins in the United Kingdom or Australia, people there understand Asians include Indians too, not just Southeast Asians.
>   *Maggie:* It must be weird always to have to teach people here why you're Asian too.
>   *Katie:* Sally was asking why she and her friends were not invited to your luncheon. She almost invited herself, saying, "Yamini won't mind, would she?"
>   *Yamini:* I can invite them later. Cooking is hard for me. I can't cook for a large group of people all at once.
>   *Maggie:* It's okay, don't worry about inviting them. Why should you? It's your house, your luncheon, your efforts, and it shouldn't be wasted on people who don't appreciate you. I'm proud of you for cooking so well for us. Thank you for doing this.

JIA'S NARRATIVE: EXOCITIZING THE UNFAMILIAR

The first time I entered Mrs. Leighton's office, I immediately recognized a familiar smell: the incense of my grandma, *nai-nai* [奶奶]'s, burned at the altar where she kept a Buddha statue. Growing up, she always had me beside her while praying. Mrs. Leighton had a Buddha statue on her desk too. I enthusiastically asked,

"Mrs. Leighton, are you a Buddhist too?"

"No, honey. One of the international students gave that to me. She's from your part of the world, where was it? Japan, China, you know, from there. You know what I mean."

I work for Mrs. Leighton's boss, an administrator of the college of education, as a graduate assistant, and Mrs. Leighton is the secretary. She is kind of my boss or at least my supervisor. If *Nai-nai* were still alive, she would be about the same age as Mrs. Leighton. The last time I remember talking to *Nai-nai* was during the last summer break. *Nai-nai* was noticeably pale and could no longer kneel as she wanted when praying. She shrank so much; every time she coughed, her whole body shook. Decades of smoking had damaged her lung, and we had been told that her heart was failing too. Mrs. Leighton had never smoked in her life.

"*xiao-jia-zi* [小佳子]," *Nai-nai* caressed my face—she always called me by my nickname, "What's wrong? What's going through your little mind? You know I always want you to be happy."

"*Nai-nai*, I'm gonna be so far away from you. It's not even in the same country." I burst into tears, "I don't wanna go."

"Oh, silly child." *Nai-nai* hugged me into her chest, rocking gently as she always did, "*Nai-nai* is going nowhere. I will be right here for you. Just like now, we see each other during your school breaks and holidays. You love *Nai-nai's* food, don't you?"

I was the only grandchild raised by *Nai-nai* until my parents relocated me to live with them when I was about 10 years old. *Nai-nai* carried me on her back everywhere she went when I was little. When I was old enough, she had this little bench next to her that I would stand on top of and watch when she cooked. I was her sous chef, getting the first tastes and bites of everything coming out of *Nai-nai's* kitchen. *Nai-nai* was a fantastic cook; everything she brought to the table was a treat to my eyes and belly.

"Yes, *Nai-nai*." I mumbled, "But it's not the same. It's the United States. I can't just take a train and come. It's gonna take hours, even flying." Secretly I knew what I feared.

"Did *Nai-nai* promise you that I would see you get into graduate school?" *Nai-nai* wiped the tears from my face, "I didn't break the promise, did I? Oh, my little girl, I'm so proud of you, so proud." *Nai-nai* kissed my forehead and put her head on top of mine.

"The moment the semester ends, I'm on my way back to see you." I wrapped my arms around *Nai-nai* even tighter as if she would disappear from me the next minute.

Nai-nai passed away in the middle of the semester. Mother hid the news from me and said she didn't want to interrupt my schoolwork. I was in a rage.

"How could you do this to me?!" I yell on the phone.

"You wouldn't have made it. *Nai-nai* couldn't swallow; she could barely sip. She was in and out." Mother sobs on the other end, "We didn't want you to see her that way. We knew she wouldn't want you to."

"That's not your decision to make!" I bawl. My heart is being ripped apart.

People say that a broken heart can never be mended. It broke my heart not to have been able to say goodbye to *Nai-nai*. Still today, I keep longing for a different ending, for forgiveness. I guess that's why I don't mind running errands for Mrs. Leighton—even after my work hours.

Mrs. Leighton has a much bigger frame than my *Nai-nai*. But she always smiles as if she is in a good mood; *Nai-nai* smiled a lot, too. *Nai-nai* never raised her voice at me. She packed homemade snacks for me for school, and every meal was homemade. When I was sick, she made rice porridge mixed with my favorite condiments like cinnamon or honey. Nancy and Ramia, the other graduate assistants, said Mrs. Leighton loves to cook for her grandchildren. I imagine that Mrs. Leighton likes homemade food too.

Mrs. Leighton looks at me on this particular day while enjoying some sushi. "Hey, Jia. Look, Keiko brought this for me." Mrs. Leighton says. She held a Tupperware dish of some unfamiliar spiced beef. "She made this herself. I had other international students bring their country's food as well. When am I gonna have your country's food? General Tso's chicken sounds good."

"I . . . I will. Maybe next week." I respond. I did not tell Mrs. Leighton that I had never heard of this dish before coming to the United States. I search for a recipe online during the weekend and try to make it after failing three times. Finally, I bring the food to Mrs. Leighton on Monday. She seems to like it, which makes me happy.

This is my second semester in graduate school. The front office where I work is Mrs. Leighton's domain. Mrs. Leighton looks up and smiles when I arrive.

"Look who's here," she says as she does every day.

"Hi, Mrs. Leighton," I respond. "How's your day today?"

"Not bad, not bad," she says.

Nancy and Ramia are there already. Both girls hear me speaking with Mrs. Leighton and come out to greet me. Ramia is a journalism major from India. I like her because she knows what it's like to speak English as a second language and makes me feel comfortable not speaking ideally. On the other hand, Nancy was born and raised in the United States. Though she is well-intentioned, she sometimes says inconsiderate or insensitive things without meaning to.

"Hey, Jia."

"Hello, Nancy; hello, Ramia," I respond. "Have you had lunch yet?"

"Yeah, we went to the student center a couple of hours ago."

"Silly girl," Mrs. Leighton jumps in. "It's already 2 o'clock. Who eats lunch this late?"

Before I explain that asking if someone has eaten is a standard greeting in Chinese culture, Mrs. Leighton stands and moves around her desk with a speed that one wouldn't expect from someone so old. She grabs my arm gently and looks into my eyes.

"Do you ever eat?" she asks. "Look at you! You're so skinny! Put some meat on your bones. The difference between you and those refugees from Africa is that your skin is lighter."

The next second before I realize what's happening, Mrs. Leighton turns me like I were on a Lazy Susan—my front, back, and sides. I am caught off guard. I let her.

"Nancy, Ramia, wouldn't you two agree? Right? Look at her; she is so

> flat." Mrs. Leighton waits, confident that she will get positive responses.
> "Well, at least she doesn't need to worry about losing weight," Nancy jokes back. Nancy has been trying out new diets monthly and talks a lot about how many pounds she plans on losing.
> Ramia only looks at me and shrugs her shoulders.
> "But, let's just say it's no secret that Jia is Leighton's favorite. She'd feed you every day if she could." Nancy makes spoon-feeding motions with her hands. There are laughs from Mrs. Leighton and Ramia.
> I stand there, smiling awkwardly and wondering why they think it's okay to joke about my body? Or anyone's skin color? Am I expected to live a certain way because I look different? In China, I was Han, the largest ethnicity, and everywhere I went, there were people just like me. It wasn't until I moved to the United States that I learned what race meant, mainly what my race meant. We were supposed to be the model minority and the perpetual foreigner.
> A series of questions flood my mind. Why did I go along with being a spectacle? Is it because I don't want to cause a scene? Or would I be labeled over-sensitive and problematic if I told them I felt hurt and dismissed? I quietly retreat to the small back office, relegated to graduate students.

This year would mark my eleventh year in educational leadership, first as a graduate student and then as a faculty member. Educational leadership has not been a welcoming or safe place for Asian Americans, not when they are leadership candidates in preparation programs, not after they become school administrators, and not when they are part of the faculty of educational leadership (Endo, 2015; Liang & Peters, 2017; Mansfield et al., 2010; Wrushen & Sherman, 2008). While Asian American students accounted for 6% of the K–12 public school student population, Asian, Native Hawaiian or other Pacific Islanders, American Indians/Alaska Natives, and multiracial groups accounted for 1% of the nation's school principals (National Center for Education Statistics, 2020a, 2020b). The experiences, views, and contributions of Asian Americans in educational leadership are primarily under-studied and under-theorized (Poon et al., 2016). For instance, for over 2 decades (1995–2015), out of all the articles published in the three leading journals in the field of educational leadership, *Educational Administration Quarterly*, *Journal of School Leadership*, and *Journal of Educational Administration*, there was no article specifically focused on Asian Americans (Liang et al., 2018). It is particularly troubling given that the field and its professional outlets are increasingly showing an apparent effort to bring critical perspectives on diversity, equity, and justice into educational leadership.

It is not my intention to question the substantial progress the field of educational leadership has made scholarly and in practice or the contribution or influence these leading journals (and others) have garnered by publishing works that have challenged the field to move forward for diversity, equity, and social justice. Nonetheless, I posit that such an absence is problematic as it signals and echoes the invisibility of Asian Americans within social sciences and in the U.S. society at large, as a result of discrimination and injustice rooted in the racialized discourses of the model minority and perpetual foreigner and stereotypes associated with Asian Americans. Like Venegas-Garcia (2013) noted, the absence of Latina/Chicana voices in educational leadership, the lack of Asian American women and men's voices in educational leadership, as well, "leaves an immeasurable void open to many misconceptions, negative assumptions, and stereotypes about who is or can be a leader and where, how, and why they lead" (p. 687).

Functioning like a self-fulfilled prophet, the disproportional underrepresentation of Asian Americans in educational leadership contributes to the lack of research which in turn feeds the invisibility of the group; people do not tend to associate Asian Americans with educational leadership, nor see and acknowledge their limited, if not absent, representation (Museus & Kiang, 2009; Somer, 2007). For the Asian Americans who are in educational leadership positions, this lack of attention and void of knowledge render their needs and contributions invisible and perpetuate, if not promote isolation and self-doubt; it makes leadership a domain beyond reachable for the Asian Americans who aspire to leadership because they see no role models—a desert, seeing no legitimacy if one is Asian American (Liang, 2020; Poon et al., 2016).

TEARA'S NARRATIVE: ANTI-BLACKNESS WITH LIMITED SAFE SPACES

I am a Black American woman administrator at the University of Oklahoma. I self-identify as a Black feminist and mother scholar. I have attended and worked in predominately White institutions and have experienced racism, microaggressions, and othering at every university I worked or attended. As an undergraduate student, I pursued various leadership positions in spaces created for Black students and other mainstream spaces. While in the Black spaces, I was often welcomed and supported, but my leadership aspirations were questioned in mainstream spaces. Similar to my coauthors, I experienced discrimination as an adult. However, I was conditioned to understand race, racism, and anti-Blackness early as a domestic student.

The following narrative is from my 2017 dissertation, demonstrating the daily racialized experiences Black women and girls experience (Lander, 2017). I used a combination of Black feminist thought (Collins, 1990), intersectionality (Crenshaw, 1991), and critical race theory (Delgado &

Stefancic, 2012) to inform a narrative inquiry study. I created composite narratives of four participants based on my interactions with them.

The participants were undergraduate women student leaders at predominately White institutions making decisions to lead or were placed in positions of influence. They spoke about various experiences, from learning about racism and how they would be treated because of their identity or physical appearance. In the next section, I share one participant, Janelle's recollection of the first time she understood the effects of race and skin color and how she carried that with her in higher education.

> I've always had a strong work ethic, and I learned what and who to prioritize very early. My mother, Lisa, was my first role model and instilled a strong work ethic in me. I was born and raised in Kansas City, Kansas, in a predominately Black neighborhood. I still remember when my classmates and I were completing a census form that included race, gender, number of people living in the home, and other demographic questions. I began completing the form when my teacher, Ms. Quigley, announced to me, Laila, and Kalel not to fill in the African-American/Black bubble on the form.
>
> "I'll come around to tell you what to mark," she said.
>
> I immediately protested, "But... I'm Black!"
>
> "Hold on, Janelle, I'll come to your desk when I finish with Kalel," Ms. Quigley said.
>
> When she reached my desk, I stopped completing the form and waited for her.
>
> "I'm African-American, Ms. Quigley," I say, thinking that maybe that is the correct answer.
>
> Ms. Quigley turned to face me, looking annoyed, and said, "Janelle, you need to select mulatto."
>
> "But..." hesitantly, I asked, "Why can't I select Black?"
>
> "Just select mulatto; that's the correct selection you need to make." She snapped.
>
> I had taken the time on the bus on my way home to think about what would happen if I told my mom about this incident. I grew increasingly anxious with each stop that brought me closer to my bus stop. When I walked into the kitchen, mom was cooking dinner. Thankfully, her back was to me because she'd know something was wrong if she saw my face. She asked her usual question when I came home from school. "How was your day, baby?" Before I could convince myself not to tell her, I hurriedly asked,
>
> "Mom, am I Black?"
>
> She hesitated but said, "Of course you are baby. Why would you ask that?" I was surprised she didn't turn around, but then she stopped chopping vegetables to take a deep breath.

As she inhaled and exhaled outwardly, I told her what had happened. "Well, today in class, all of us were filling out a form, and my teacher told me to mark a word that started with an 'm,' like mulata or mullato. I'd never seen it before. I told her I was Black, but she didn't listen and told me to mark that "m" word. I thought I was Black, but after she told me to mark the m-word, I wasn't sure what it meant, and maybe it was another word for Black that I didn't know."

I couldn't see my mom's face as I told her what had happened. She had begun chopping again, but with much more force and speed, and from time to time, she would wipe her face with the back of her hands as if she was wiping away tears. But she wasn't chopping onions.

"Mom, are you okay? Am I in trouble?" I asked cautiously.

She turned to face me, her eyes slightly red and the knife no longer in her hands. "Janelle, you are Black, and your teacher had no right to tell you anything otherwise. The word she had you marked is mulatto, an old term to define someone mixed or biracial."

'But why would she think I'm not Black? I'm Black, right?"

"Yes, you are... it's just, it's just that your skin is light, and she thought you were biracial, don't worry, I'm going to go to your school tomorrow to straighten this out because this is unacceptable. She shouldn't tell anyone what to put on a form, especially after you told her you were Black." Her voice was calm, but I know it was only to reassure me that she wasn't upset. I felt terrible for the fate of my teacher tomorrow, but I had to tell my mom what she had me do. Mom straightened out Ms. Quigley the next day.

While I matriculated through K–12 education and into college, I found myself involved in various activities. As I moved into my major courses, I focused more on school and student organizations. I continued to volunteer for a local children's cheerleading squad through my commitment to the Anderson Leadership Fellows program, but collegiate cheering was too much of a time commitment. The Anderson Leadership Fellows program was fantastic. Like cheerleading, the diversity of members within the leadership fellows program was low. I was one of four Black students out of 60 chosen to be a fellow. I often felt I needed to be a voice for *all* Black people within Anderson Leadership Fellows. Although the fellowship is supposed to help bridge the gap about race, it is also frustrating to always have to explain why racism is happening and that it still hurts.

As a junior, I was also heavily involved in the Black Voices United (BVU), and I was once again "voluntold" to run for office. I was currently serving as the social media chair and had done well. I helped with a few controversial issues BVU had to handle, like the racist comments that were made on Yik Yak, an anonymous social media network, after we did a silent protest that involved us laying down in the student union for 4 minutes to call attention to the Michael Brown murder in 2015. Someone said, "Somebody call the KKK," while another said, "Just go feed them watermelon." It was yet another

> time that reminded me of my Blackness on campus and that I needed to be as unified as possible with the Black students and the Black community on campus. After the racial incidents, I decided I needed to run for office. I approached the Black faculty advisor, Thomas, at the next BVU meeting, excited. I told him I would run, and he was happy and genuinely believed I would be a great VP. The one thing I liked about Thomas was his support of his students. I always knew he loved his students, but if I forgot, he showed us daily. He appreciated and praised us for our hard work, which was refreshing, and I think it kept some students here.
>
> I feel like I have grown up so much already, and I also know there is so much further to go. From being told I was a mulato to being comfortable in my skin, being a leader, and realizing how other people see me as Black in White spaces, as a Black sister with other Black sisters, I feel like I am continuously learning and growing.

DISCUSSION AND RECOMMENDATIONS

Through personal, autoethnographic, and participants' narratives, we share the myriad ways higher education and society have thrust forces of oppression toward us, targeting us for our various minoritized positions. Yet, we are not the minority. We are the global majority. But when we are in a boat with a tiger in the middle of the ocean, which in these cases are predominantly White spaces, we are isolated. Our survival requires compliance, and our resistance requires community, subversiveness, and at times full-on overt forms of protests. In Kakali's narrative, her participants could not figure out what kind of fish to feed to Richard Parker to mitigate the anticipated harm. They gathered within their community to decode the hidden curriculum, create solidarities, and bring certain familiarities of being in a foreign country. At the same time, they learned the various ways they lost their privileges from their home country to reconfigure minoritized, exoticized, essentialized identities to forge some community with their academic peers.

Both Jia and the participants in Kakali's narrative were entangled in complicated complicities associated with the exoticization of their cuisine and using their cuisine to create relationalities. This act of offering food to those with an imperialistic gaze on Jia, Neerada, and Yamini, was feeding Richard Parker some fish to minimize harm. Yet, the harm was not fully minimized and came in a package wrapped in a façade of sweetness with internalized prejudice and bigotry. Jia's experience also demonstrated a betrayal of someone she compared to her grandmother, whom she was mourning because Jia could not see her when she passed. The grief made her equalize Mrs. Leighton to her grandmother, and she offered her the same respect and dignity that she'd offer her grandmother, only to realize that grandmother metamorphosed into the tiger. The tiger sees her as the exotic Other for her amusement and awe and to appease her hunger, literally. Amid such violence, Jia learned some form of coexistence, although it was not without a deep psychological cost.

In Teara's narrative, Janelle was thrust into anti-Blackness from a young age and continued to carry that with her as she entered higher education. In a predominantly White space, Janelle faced all the known forms of anti-Blackness, ranging from speaking for all Black people to dealing with overt racialized attacks. While Janelle was exhausted and continued to find safe, liberatory spaces within a university campus, her safety came from predominantly Black spaces, where she began cultivating her leadership skills. In this way, while Janelle was also feeding fish to the tiger via her accommodations and complicities, she was also seeking and building liberatory spaces to mitigate harm from the beast while being vigilant of the beast's activities. The narratives confirm that no matter which forms the beast takes, as those of us who are passengers on the boat with the beast, we must never see the beast as anything but a greedy hungry predator.

Recommendations

While we offer recommendations, as of this writing, we have endured 2 years of a global pandemic, unmitigated racism by a threatened White supremacy, and a humanitarian crisis with multiple deaths and illnesses of our loved ones. In the midst of this exhaustion, it is challenging to offer recommendations knowing oppressive gazes are upon us. Thus, these recommendations are what we share publicly, while we invite like-minded readers to engage us privately to share more sacred insights that we do not offer for the public gaze.

Create Complex Frameworks of Solidarities

Given that multiply-marginalized communities are affected by similar, interlocked structures of oppression, we must create complex forms of connectivity within different communities to create solidarities of resistance. Of course, no one cultural group is monolithic, and frameworks of solidarities will evolve as structures of oppression mutate. However, without complex frameworks of solidarities, we are limited in how we come together to resist. The global majority is more in number, talent, and strategic possibilities than those who create, increase, and maintain structures that oppress us. Bhattacharya (2019) identified such a framework within her community with concretized tenets: critical interrogation of positionality, healing-centered communal dialogues, interrogation of internalized discourses of prejudice, and unsubscribing from dominant master narratives to cultivate our own personal and scholarly identities. Through such frameworks of solidarities, we can dismiss the trappings of an oppressor/oppressed relationship and remind ourselves of other nurturing relationships that sustain us. We are more than a co-passenger with a tiger in the boat. We have ancestral wisdom, literature, music, and connection with nature, animals, and more that nurture us. Our complex frameworks of solidarities can become a reminder and a healing agent for the pain we endure daily.

We have intentionally kept these recommendations broad, understanding that some conversations around solidarity and resistance need to occur privately, including locations in which such solidarities thrive. Once identified as an exemplar, such identification could create vulnerabilities for those highlighted in exemplars. However, creating complex frameworks of solidarities require that we understand each other's location in the world in a multifaceted way while rejecting a binary racialization of Black and White.

Educate, Interrogate, and Challenge Anti-Blackness

Anti-Blackness is a pervasive and vile force of oppression nationally and globally. We must continue to learn how this force shows up overtly and stealthily in our actions, thoughts, and disposition. There are existing refereed, non-refereed literature, talks, podcasts, music, and movies that offer opportunities to learn about anti-Blackness in addition to resource sharing by various social media accounts. Because even if it is that one time we engaged in anti-Blackness without knowing that we were doing it, for the person at the receiving end, it was likely not the first experience. For that person, it may have been the thousandth time they were experiencing this painful minimization.

Using these spaces and resources will reduce the task that often falls on Black folx to continuously explain how an act, policy, law, arrest, or classroom discipline is anti-Black. We have an obligation to do this work ourselves and remain aware of how we show up in higher education spaces where anti-Blackness is normalized, sometimes in coded and at other times in overt ways. This is evident in how few Black academics are hired into tenured track positions and then subsequently tenured. This lack of representation allows for anti-Black ontoepistemologies to flourish without being challenged. Using frameworks of complex solidarities and our internal ethical benchmarks, we have to raise our voices when we witness anti-Blackness and leverage our positions, privileges, and spheres of influence to continuously interrogate internalized and normalized anti-Blackness and develop equitable approaches and practices.

Amplify Respect and Dignity Individual and Collective Re-Memorying and Healing

Being fluid in our work for solidarity also means we need to recognize the unique—and yet shared—minoritized histories and embodied experiences of our ancestors, the generations before us, our generation, and even those after ours. While suppressing certain memories is for survival, individual and collective healing journeys often take us to these buried, lingering wounds and pains. Such wounds and pains are paths to memories of dark days *and* paths to resilience and hope; attending them can be opportunities for recreating and redefining so that the narratives are no longer solely overshadowed by the dominant discourse—re-memorying (Espiritu & Duong, 2018; Um, 2012) for liberating and reclaiming what was lost in suppressing what is part of who we are. Such individual and collective healing is a process that calls for courage, patience, and empathy—all demand genuine respect for human dignity that allows us to see through and break the divisions and antagonisms set up by Richard Parker. To that end, we invite readers to consider building communities within and outside our institutions and programs—and even outside of academia—to align with the idea that knowledge democracy is essential for developing solidarities. Creating a purpose-driven research, teaching, and service agenda aligned with one's passion can build a sacredness or a sanctuary around one's work. And most importantly, cultivating practices of inner journeying for individual and collective community work.

NOTE

1. Indian slang for Americans.

REFERENCES

Bhattacharya, K. (2016). The vulnerable academic: Personal narratives and strategic de/colonizing of academic structures. *Qualitative Inquiry, 22*(5), 309–321. https://doi.org/10.1177/1077800415615619

Bhattacharya, K. (2019). (Un)settling imagined lands: A par/des(i) approach to de/colonizing methodologies. In P. Leavy (Ed.), *The Oxford handbook of methods for public scholarship* (pp. 175–215). Oxford University Press.

Collins, P. H. (1990). "Defining Black feminist thought." In *Black feminist thought: Knowledge, consciousness, and the politics of empowerment* (pp. 19–40). Routledge.

Crenshaw, K. (1991). Mapping the margins: Intersectionality, identity politics, and violence against women of color. *Stanford Law Review, 42*(July), 1241–1299. https://doi.org/10.2307/1229039

Delgado, R., & Stefancic, J. (2012). *Critical race theory* (2nd ed.). New York University Press.

Endo, R. (2015). How Asian American female teachers experience racial microaggression from pre-service preparation to their professional careers. *The Urban Review, 47*(4), 601–625. https://doi.org/10.1007/s11256-015-0326-9

Espiritu, Y., & Duong, L. (2018). Feminist refugee epistemology: Reading displacement in Vietnamese and Syrian refugee art. *Signs, 14*(3), 587–615. https://doi.org/10.1086/695300

Lander, T. F. (2017). *She just did: A narrative case study of Black women student leaders at a predominantly White midwestern institution* [Doctoral dissertation]. Kansas State University. ProQuest Dissertation and Theses #10272538.

Liang, J. G. (2020). Vietnamese American women public school administrators leading for social justice and equity. *Journal of Southeast Asian American Education and Advancement, 15*(2), Article 5. https://doi.org/10.7771/2153-8999

Liang, J. G., & Peters, A. (2017). "I am more than what I look alike": Asian American women in public school administration. *Educational Administration Quarterly, 53*(1), 40–69. https://doi.org/10.1177/0013161X16652219

Liang, J. G., Turner, J., & Sottile, J. (2018, November). *Look for our voice: Asian American women in educational leadership* [Paper presentation]. Annual Conference of the University Council for Educational Administration (UCEA), Houston, TX.

Mansfield, K. C., Welton, A., Lee, P., & Young, M. D. (2010). The lived experiences of female educational leadership doctoral students. *Journal of Educational Administration, 48*(6), 727–740. https://doi.org/10.1108/09578231011079584

Museus, S., & Kiang, P. (2009). Deconstructing the model minority myth and how it contributes to the invisible minority reality in higher education research. In S. D. Museus (Ed.), *Conducting research on Asian Americans in higher education: New Directions for Institutional Research* (no. 142, pp. 5–15). Jossey-Bass.

National Center for Education Statistics. (2020a). *The condition of education 2020: Racial/ethnic enrollment in public schools.* https://nces.ed.gov/programs/coe/pdf/coe_cge.pdf

National Center for Education Statistics. (2020b). *Annual reports and information staff (annual reports): Characteristics of public school principals.* https://nces.ed.gov/programs/coe/indicator/cls

Poon, O., Squire, D., Kodama, C., & Byrd, A. (2016). A critical review of the model minority myth in selected literature on Asian Americans and Pacific Islanders in higher education. *Review of Educational Research, 86*(2), 469–502. https://doi.org/10.3102%2F0034654315612205

Somer, M. G. (2007). *The experiences of Asian American females seeking vice president and president positions in community colleges: A view of the barriers and facilitators* [Unpublished doctoral dissertation]. Oregon State University.

Um, K. (2012). Exiled memory: History, identity, and remembering in Southeast Asia and Southeast Asian diaspora. *Positions: Asia Critique, 20*(3), 831–850. https://doi.org/10.1215/10679847-1593564

Venegas-Garcia, M. (2013). Leadership for social change: Learning from the perspectives of Latina/Chicana activist educators. *Journal of School Leadership, 23*(4), 685–709. https://doi.org/10.1177%2F105268461302300406

Wrushen, B. R., & Sherman, W. H. (2008). Women secondary school principals: Multicultural voices from the field. *International Journal of Qualitative Studies in Education, 21*(5), 457–469. https://doi.org/10.1080/09518390802297771

CHAPTER 3

PROBLEMATIZING DIVERSITY

Imagining Inclusion Through a Liberated Lens

Charee Dee Mosby-Holloway
Sara C. Furr

ABSTRACT

This chapter traces the evolution of institutional diversity efforts from access, diversity, and student success to futuristic notions of inclusion and liberation. The progressive narrative has largely shaped historical institutional diversity efforts. Colleges and universities perform diversity because it is just and is the right thing to do; and while there has been tremendous movement towards creating more diverse and inclusive college campuses, there is rarely discussion around systemic change or dismantling dominant power structures. Diversity is ultimately dictated by the institution. This chapter proposes that the narratives of those doing diversity work are crucial in reimagining what diversity and inclusion can and should look like on college and university campuses. Using visionary fiction as a model to create liberated narratives, the authors share their own experiences of doing diversity work on campus and call for others to do the same.

A hallmark of dominance and control is the continual focus on maintaining a progressive narrative; that the future one is moving towards is enlightened, good, and just (Melamed, 2006). This is a narrative that was critical to sustaining control over individuals and can also be seen in the complicated evolution of diversity and inclusion in higher education. In the late sixties and early seventies, historically White colleges and universities wrestled with how to provide marginalized peoples with access to learning spaces that had forcibly and often lawfully excluded them. Beginning in the late seventies and early eighties notions of diversity and identity politics continually shaped universities, through student protest and resistance; in many cases lead to the creation of cultural centers and other dedicated spaces for cultural exploration. More recently, campuses moved toward understandings of diversity and inclusion defined most profoundly through the lens of student success (i.e., retention and persistence). University resources channeled to aid marginalized students in being more successful in a White environment to live up to a definition of success rooted in dominance, control, and whiteness. While contemporary inclusion rhetoric is seemingly focused on social change, it equally seems to be about control.

While institutions define and use diversity, student affairs practitioners are often those responsible for doing the work of diversity. They are staffing the departments and offices, chairing the committees, developing the retention programs, advocating with students, facilitating workshops and trainings, in short they are doing diversity work. Sara Ahmed (2012) both defines diversity work and describes the experience of those that do that work:

> Diversity work can refer to work that has the explicit aim of transforming an institution; second, diversity work can be what is required, or what we do, when we do not "quite" inhabit the norms of an institution. When you don't quite inhabit the norms, or you aim to transform them, you notice them as you come up against them. The wall is what we come up against: the sedimentation of history into a barrier that is solid and tangible in the present, a barrier to change as well as to the mobility of some, a barrier that remains invisible to those who can flow into the spaces created by institutions. (p. 175)

Diversity work can be an exhausting and isolating experience. The barriers to the work are constantly changing and adapting to fit a narrative of change and progress while still protecting old ways of knowing and being (Ahmed, 2012; Ferguson, 2012).

These constant barriers and resistance combined with the apathy of those that do not encounter the same barriers and resistance, make it difficult for student affairs practitioners and others doing diversity work at colleges and universities to find the time and energy to reflect on their work or their relationship to institutions in which they work. The institution defines diversity and the diversity workers are expected to execute that particular vision. There is no room to imagine the work differently, to imagine one's relationship to that work differently. Imagination is a human experience that has been withheld, and at times forcibly removed from marginalized people (Benjamin, 2016). Histories have been intentionally rewritten and reframed to represent narratives that exclude, ignore, and pathologize people of color. Imagination is a critical tool for envisioning and reclaiming new and nonnormative definitions of diversity and inclusion (Benjamin, 2016). The liberated narratives of student affairs practitioners and diversity workers are essential to challenging the progressive narrative and institutional barriers to diversity and inclusion. Liberated narratives employ imagination and joy as tools of exploration and reflection (Benjamin, 2016). A liberated future for students, faculty and staff must be self-defined. We can define our own stories and experiences within these larger systems so we are able to show up in problematic places as our full selves. We can be pained and not broken.

THE GROWTH OF DIVERSITY AND SOCIALLY JUST EDUCATIONAL POLICY

The growth of diversity in higher education in the United States and its relationship to the development of socially just educational policies is important to understand social justice in higher education. The following section briefly outlines notable events related to the growth of diversity and social justice-related educational policy, as well as the promotion of socially just educational environments.

Notable Moments

Throughout its history, the United States government has enacted legislation to administer and regulate educational policy to create an equitable environment on college and university campuses (Chang et al., 2011). These acts of legislation outlined changes in governmental expectations—some initiated to support greater equity and accessibility for students from increasingly diverse backgrounds and some to maintain control in the hands of the privileged. In addition, colleges and universities themselves have enacted organizational and policy changes in response to the increasing diversity of the student population, which have had similar positive and negative effects related to the creation of socially just campuses.

The Morrill Acts
The Morrill Acts of 1862 and 1867 were first and foremost land grants to expand the United States westward by giving land to eligible states; higher

education was not a primary objective (Thelin, 2004). Both of the Morrill Acts, however, helped to cultivate the growth of universities, as the United States began to build for the future by spurring economic growth and expanding its western territories (Thelin, 2004). Under the 1862 Morrill Act, if a state was eligible it was given 30,000 acres of federal land to enhance or establish postsecondary institutions (Thelin, 2004). It is important to note, if a state had seceded to be a part of the Confederate rebellion against the United States during the Civil War, it was ineligible to receive the land grant (Thelin, 2004). However, as long as race was not an admission criterion, the 1867 Morrill Act extended the grant to southern states (Thelin, 2004). The United States government added an addendum in 1890 allowing these states to create a separate land grant institution for people of color (Thelin, 2004).

Many of the states awarded additional grants, however, neglected to provide funding to these Black land grant institutions, thus creating inequitable learning environments for people of color (Thelin, 2004). Many of the Black land grant institutions evolved into the historically Black colleges and universities (HBCUs) that still exist today (Thelin, 2004). The United States government may have intended to create equitable educational opportunities for people of color with the 1890 Morrill Act, but instead it divided education by allowing states to propagate segregation through poorly funded Black land grant institutions. This action is an example of how the U.S. government has authorized discriminatory acts throughout the development of higher education.

Women in Higher Education

During the last part of the 19th century, even though it was unpopular, at least 45 United States institutions of higher education began to allow the attendance of women (Graham, 1978; Thelin, 2004). Thirty-two percent of undergraduate students were women by 1880, 40% in 1910, and by 1920 "women were 47 percent of the undergraduate enrollment" (Graham, 1978, p. 764). The depression of the 1930s led to a decline in the undergraduate enrollment of women (Graham, 1978).

By 2009, however, enrollment of women increased to 57% in U.S. undergraduate institutions (U.S. Department of Education, National Center for Education Statistics, 2014). Because many of the traditionally male institutions felt uneasy having women on campus, the position of dean of women was created to nurture the needs of women students (Schwartz, 1997). While Oberlin College hired the first woman to supervise students as the "Lady Principal of the Female Department" in 1833 (Bashaw, 1999), in 1892, Alice Freeman Palmer was selected as the first dean of women in the United States (Schwartz, 1997). By 1927, there were 17 deans of women, primarily in the Midwest (NADW, 1927, as cited in Schwartz, 1997). Schwartz (1997) noted that deans of women were responsible for "the housing of women students, training in etiquette and social skills, women's self-government, leadership opportunities for women students, and women's intercollegiate athletics" (p. 421).

The deans of women also built "the foundations of practice for student affairs and higher education administration, including graduate study, the development of professional associations, research on students, college environments, and student guidance and counseling" between 1890 and 1930 (Schwartz, 1997, p. 422). However, in 1937, the deans of women began to disappear as campuses began to follow the recommendation of the American Council on Education, which was based on a proposal by William H. Cowley, to combine the activities within student personnel services (Schwartz, 1997). Generally, deans of men were given the opportunity to serve as the dean of students; whereas deans of women either retired or became full-time faculty (Schwartz, 1997). By the 1970s, the dean of women position on campus was almost completely extinct (Schwartz, 1997). While the combination of student services under a dean of students appears to enhance equitable services to all students, it also resulted in women students losing a major advocate on campus and professional women losing an important role in student affairs administration.

G.I. Bill

The Servicemen's Readjustment Act, popularly known as the G.I. Bill, was passed by Congress in 1944 (Thelin, 2004) and contributed to a thriving student population enrolling in higher education after World War II. The government, as well as society, saw college as a way to create opportunities for the average U.S. citizen, particularly veterans (Thelin, 2004). The G.I. Bill helped to open campuses to men and women who were previously unable to attend due to lower socioeconomic statuses and the perceived elitism of higher education (Thelin, 2004). College was now accessible to all veterans regardless of cost and social status (Thelin, 2004). Because of the resulting high student enrollments, institutions identified the need for improved management techniques and organizational designs (Thelin, 2004), which led to the further development of the student affairs profession (American Council on Education, 1937; American Council on Education, Committee on Student Personnel Work, 1949).

Civil Rights

Segments of society began to question who should and should not be allowed to attend college (Thelin, 2004). These arguments usually revolved around the concepts of access, equity, and excellence (Gaston-Gayles et al., 2004; Geiger, 2005). College campuses became a symbolic focus and battleground for civil rights in U.S. life due to racial segregation and other forms of discrimination (Gaston-Gayles et al., 2004; Geiger, 2005). College students across the country joined these conversations for equality and rights in higher education (Geiger, 2005). Civil rights legislation was enacted beginning with *Brown v. the Board of Education* in 1954 and continuing through the passage of the Civil Rights Act of 1964, and Title IX of the Education Amendment of 1972 to increase access to education. The intent of these equal opportunity acts was to increase accessibility for all students; however, researchers have concluded that these acts also should be considered a form of interest convergence (DeCuir & Dixson, 2004; Ladson-Billings, 1998; McCoy, 2006, as cited in Hiraldo, 2010), where White people actually benefited more than the intended equity recipients: underrepresented people. *Brown vs. the Board of Education* benefited those in power (who were White) because the decision itself made the United States seem friendly and open to all people (Bell, 1980). At the same time, the majority of White families could send their students to private schools or move out of the desegregated school districts (i.e., "White flight"; Bell, 1980, p. 518). Thus, economic and educational superiority continued for White people.

Three additional pieces of legislation addressed needs for people with disabilities: the Rehabilitation Act of 1973, which protected and provided support for people with disabilities who participated in higher education; the 1975 Education for All Handicapped Children Act, which made it easier for qualified students with disabilities to enter postsecondary education; and the Americans With Disabilities Act (ADA) in 1990 that provided additional protections in school and work settings (Geiger, 2005; Thelin, 2004). Each act helped create opportunities for students with disabilities from an environmental perspective; however, the societal construction of disability identity still needs to be deconstructed to create an equitable higher education experience since society determines what is normal or abnormal for a person (Evans et al., 2005). The creation of a socially just campus is not just about enhancing the operational and learning environment; it is also about deconstructing how society interacts, works, and learns with and from people with disabilities (Evans et al., 2005).

These notable moments are important as the field of higher education is changed by the intentional increase in diverse student identities. While many of the policy changes came out of equality efforts, they also highlighted greater needs to create inclusive environments for all students. While these efforts increased access to higher education for traditionally marginalized populations, the presence of a more diverse student body exposed how woefully unprepared institutions were and continue to be to serve all students.

CURRENT DEMOGRAPHICS ON CAMPUS

The student population on today's campus continues to diversify in the United States (U.S. Department of Education, National Center for Education

Statistics, 2017). As of 2021, full-time undergraduate student enrollment was reported as 58% women and 42% men (U.S. Department of Education, National Center for Education Statistics, 2023). Note that the U.S. government still relies on the binary construction of gender therefore providing no data related to transgender and gender nonconforming students on U.S. college campuses. Similarly, no systemic governmental data reports the proportion of lesbian, gay, bisexual, queer, asexual, plus (LGBQA+) students in college. According to the U.S. Department of Education, National Center for Education Statistics (2023b), the percentage of college students of color in the United States has been increasing. From 2004–2023, the percentage of Hispanic or Latino students doubled, increasing from 1.8 million to 3.6 million and the number of Black students rose 57% from 2.1 million to 2.3 million. During the same period, the percentage of White students decreased from 10.8 million to 9.2 million.

As the student population changes, the need for the demographics of staff and faculty to reflect the student population will continue to be of great importance. To date there is no data on the level of representation of SAPros to student populations they serve based on race, gender, sexuality, and ethnicity. Flaunting the increased racial and ethnic diversity of students as an accomplishment without looking at its relationship to staff representation presents an incomplete picture and fails to address potential issues related to staff demographics.

PROMOTING EQUITABLE EDUCATIONAL ENVIRONMENTS

According to Freire (2000), in a safe educational environment, students "come to see the world not as a static reality, but as a reality in process, in transformation" (p. 83). If higher education intends to adapt to demographic and societal changes, it will have to work towards an inclusive campus community by transforming its Eurocentric roots. To accomplish this goal, higher education will have to take steps to attract and retain a diverse student population while changing the funding paradigm (Calhoun, 2006; Griffin & Hurtado, 2011). The talents of underrepresented students will go unused unless higher education takes on the responsibility of investing in critical student support resources: staff, faculty, financial support, and programs to create equitable environments (Chang et al., 2011; Zusman, 2005). Institutions will also have to work collaboratively with the government to increase accessibility for students from socioeconomically challenged communities (Chang et al., 2011; Zusman, 2005). The creation of a safe socially just environment on campus is needed so that students will be able to explore their societal role regarding power and privilege without repercussions (Ayers, 1998; Chang et al., 2011). The profession of student affairs was originally created to help support such an environment (Dungy & Gordan, 2011; Hurtado, 2005) but the conditions necessary to support SAPros have not always been present or even explored.

RETENTION AND PERSISTENCE AS STUDENT SUCCESS

In the early 2000s the NSSE Institute for Effective Educational Practice launched Project DEEP: Documenting Effective Educational Practice. This project conducted case studies from 20 high performing colleges and universities. The high performing institutions that were chosen had higher-than-predicted scores on the five NSSE clusters of effective educational practice: level of academic challenge, active and collaborative learning, student interaction with faculty members, enriching educational experiences, and supportive campus environment, as well as higher-than-predicted graduation rates. The results of Project DEEP led to the creation of arguably a stalwart titan of higher education and student affairs literature, *Student Success in College: Creating Conditions That Matter* (Kuh et al., 2010). The research presented in the book provides a roadmap of effective programs and practices that contribute to student success. While definitions of student success may change depending on a variety of factors (i.e., the institution, the stakeholders, etc.) graduation rates have long been synonymous with student success.

Since the early 1990s, the language related to graduation rates as a marker of student success has evolved into a focus on retention and persistence (Braxton et al., 2013; Kuh et al., 2010; Pascarella & Terenzini, 2005). Retention is commonly understood as the percentage of students returning to their institution the following fall, while persistence is commonly defined as percentage of students who complete their program within 150% of the normal time for completion (i.e., graduating within 6 years for students pursuing a bachelor's degree; U.S. Department of Education & National Center for Education Statistics, 2017). There are various other domains of student success (e.g., development of cognitive and social skills, academic attainment, postgraduate employment, etc.), and individual institutions have nuanced concepts of student success, but retention and persistence are often primary factors in determining student success (Braxton et al., 2004). The question of student success has become symbiotic with retention and persistence. As colleges and universities have continued to open access to marginalized populations, the retention and persistence of underrepresented students (particularly undergraduate) has become an entire field of research unto itself (Habley et al., 2012; Tinto, 2016). However, the conflation of retention and persistence with student success has its limits.

Many U.S. colleges and universities have seen improvements in retention of students, but have they also stalled in their understanding of—and interventions for—retention and persistence? Does retention and persistence automatically equate student success? Tinto (2016) argues that in the effort to retain students, the voices and experiences of students themselves—especially those on the margins—have begun to fade; he writes,

> Colleges and universities need to listen to all their students, take seriously their voices and be sensitive to how perceptions of their experiences vary among students of different races, income levels, and cultural backgrounds. Only then can they further improve persistence and completion while addressing the continuing inequality in student outcomes that threaten the very fabric of our society. (para. 18)

It is often, and it could be argued primarily, student affairs practitioners' role to develop, execute, and maintain retention and persistence based programs and services (Hurtado, 2005). However, student affairs practitioners are not always the stakeholders driving institutional policy or decisions related to retention and persistence, particularly those efforts focused on the most marginalized and vulnerable student populations. Mauro and Mazaris (2016) argue that the responsibility for retaining diversity often lies solely with those that are tasked with doing diversity and multicultural affairs work and that our perceived beliefs about what diversity is and is not have created structural and institutional barriers to retention and persistence.

THE FALLACY OF THE PROGRESSIVE NARRATIVE

Progress is about forward movement and growth. Creation and learning. Innovation and improvement. The progressive narrative is the justification and understanding that the future one is moving towards is enlightened, good, and just. The notion of student success is inextricably linked to progress. If students are able to be retained and if they are able to persist and graduate, we call this progress. In efforts to close the education gap we argue that more college graduates benefits everyone, but especially the student. They will have a higher lifetime income, better employment opportunities, and be generally healthier adults, to name a few benefits (Vernez et al., 1999). Progressive narrative is crucial to higher education. Institutions of higher learning are where knowledge is both gained and produced. Where tough questions about morality and ethics are wrestled with. It is where the innovators and creators both hone their craft and produce their work. All of this is done in the name of progress. For many colleges and universities, diversity and inclusion is also about progress. Thus far in the chapter, we have broadly mapped out some iterations of diversity on college campuses from access to identity politics to student success conversations about diversity have shifted massively over time, but one of the most pervasive overarching themes is that diversity is good.

While the progressive narrative relies on goodness being a driving force for decision making, there is no real answer to the question of good for whom. Does everyone benefit or only a select few? Who decides who benefits? These are the questions that remain unanswered by this particular narrative. It is because of this that the progressive narrative can and has functioned as a tool of dominance, control, and oppression. The progressive narrative is an old narrative. Both the social and biological constructions of race and the practice of slavery and racism are historically rooted in the progressive narrative. Constructions of race change politically, legally, biologically, and socially according to rules that are created for the explicit purpose of reinforcing Whiteness and White supremacy. For example, in the early 1600s European, African, and Indigenous indentured servants and slaves worked side by side and in many ways occupied similar social statuses. As Whiteness became clearly defined as a thing to be valued and protected, race was reconstructed accordingly. While a White indentured servant could work off their service, enslaved people of color remained property in perpetuity. Additional laws in states like South Carolina and Virginia legally designated all enslaved Africans as less than any and all Whites. Anti-miscegenation laws made interracial relationships illegal, not solely to protect White womanhood, but to protect the inheritances and legacies of Whites and to ensure that "[Black] men, women, and children would not benefit from the privileges of a legal marriage to a [White] person" (Roberts, 2011, p. 9; Painter 2010). The construction of race was used to both define and protect Whiteness, as much as it was used to define and demonize Blackness. Slavery was as much a necessary moral practice, as it was an economical one (Daly, 2002). The progressive narrative could be used to justify slavery and racial difference as much as it could be used to rally the abolitionist movement.

On college campuses diversity is sought because it is the good, just, and enlightened thing to do. But as outlined in this chapter, there are cracks and limits to that narrative; edges where it frays and falls apart. Even in its most recent iteration of inclusion, there are few conversations that challenge the most basic assumptions of higher education as a goal; the academy as liberal; and colleges and universities as interrupters of systems of privilege and power, rather than direct beneficiaries of these systems and perpetrators of oppression. Roderick Ferguson (2012) argues that even as colleges and universities invite difference—whether in terms of people, academic disciplines, programs, or centers—these differences eventually become swallowed up by the institution itself where they can be safely identified, catalogued, and monitored. In this way, the progressive narrative functions as a smokescreen that prevents critical reflection and liberation.

As previously outlined in this chapter, diversity on college and university campuses has taken on a number of forms with one of the most current being inclusion. Colleges and universities strive to be inclusive places of learning for students; spaces where students can engage across differences and explore their own identities. Diversity and inclusion has found its way into nearly every aspect of higher education, from conversations about recruiting and retaining a diverse faculty and staff and facilities management (i.e., accessibility, inclusive restrooms), to financial aid (Zusman, 2005). True to the spirit of the progressive narrative, inclusion does not inherently demand an interest or commitment to the dismantling of dominant power structures. One can strive for diverse and inclusive without interrupting or challenging systems of power, privilege, and oppression. It may be a helpful tool in increasing student success, but does it actually transform the definition of student success itself? The progressive narrative allows for the performance of diversity and inclusion (Ahmed, 2012). Substantive programs, policy, services, and actions become secondary to the importance of appearing diverse and inclusive. The performance of diversity and inclusion can be seen in everything from documents that become measures of goodness (i.e., strategic plans, mission statements) to the equating of a diverse student body with the existence of an equitable, inclusive, and good institution. Diversity becomes yet another iteration of the progressive narrative and "provides a positive, shiny image of the organization that allows inequalities to be concealed and thus reproduced" (Ahmed, 2012, p. 72). What does this mean for the people that are called to actually do the work of diversity and inclusion? Particularly for those faculty and staff that are called upon to create and implement policy, support and mentor students, and develop, execute, and assess inclusive programming and services? It is important to note that though diversity and inclusion may, in many ways, be connected to and a part of the progressive narrative, it doesn't mean that all diversity and inclusion efforts are dubious or for nefarious gains. However, if it is acknowledged that the progressive narrative maintains old systems of power, dominance, and control, "How then can we demand and create space for liberated narratives?"; narratives that center marginalized voices and experiences, narratives that allow educators to question the most foundational assumptions about ourselves and our work.

LIBERATED NARRATIVES: A MOVEMENT TOWARDS IMAGINATION AND JOY

Liberated Narratives

There is an abundance of research that focuses on the burnout and emotional exhaustion that can come with a career in higher education and student affairs. We know that social identity and the type of work one does in student affairs impacts how we experience and process this stress (Guthrie et al., 2005; Howard-Hamilton et al., 1998). Diversity workers who happen to be student affairs practitioners have an especially complicated relationship with the institutions they work in; and even in the most inclusive of environments find themselves in a cycle of encountering, neutralizing, and encountering various forms of resistance over and over again (Ahmed, 2012). As Mariam Lam (2018) wrote in the *Chronicle of Higher Education*,

> Underrepresented faculty and staff members share the burden of diversity work in many visible and invisible forms: They often assume heavier workloads in teaching, advising, mentoring, and counseling, and spend more time on outreach, recruitment, training and workshops, and other service work. While their institutions benefit from collective gains in student success, those who do this work find it exhausting to do more than their fair share, indefinitely. (para. 4)

When conversations about stress and burnout arise, solutions like self-care and holistic well-being are often pulled forth as solutions and coping strategies (Guthrie et al., 2005). Practicing self-care and embodied well-being are both valuable (though not uncomplicated) survival methods, but often do not address underlying issues related to inequity (Squire & Dian, 2019). Liberated narratives are not a cure for systemic inequity, but are a method of processing and healing from the complex experiences, harms, and resistance that diversity workers face in their higher education and student affairs journey.

In her groundbreaking and genre eschewing work on emergent strategy, adrienne maree brown (2017) contends that "if we release the framework of failure, we can realize that we are in iterative cycles, and we can keep asking ourselves—how do I learn from this?" (p. 105). Practitioners of emergent strategy are encouraged by brown "to give each other more time to feel, to be in our humanity" (p. 143). Drawing inspiration from visionary fiction and radical healing, liberated narratives are offered as a tool to both provide a pathway for releasing frameworks that obscure growth and to give space and energy to humanness.

Visionary Fiction as Praxis

In Octavia Butler's (2000) *Lilith's Brood* an alien race, the Oankali, have deep concerns about humanity. They contend that humanity's intelligence combined with the need to create and maintain hierarchical power structures is a fatal flaw; the combination of hierarchy and intelligence is a tool for dominance and control of one another. In her novel *Kindred*, Butler (1979) imagines the protagonist Dana, a Black woman living in 1976, time traveling from her present day life to the antebellum slavery period. Dana must learn how to not only survive a life in slavery, but also ensure the survival of her own White ancestors who own the plantation. Octavia Butler changed the world of speculative fiction through her writing and the questions she asked in her writing. As a Black woman writing about racism, sexism, classism, and the environment often through the perspectives of the marginalized, she forever changed the exceptionally White male-dominated world of speculative fiction and created something wholly new and necessary. She gave voice, place, and agency to those that have been excluded and rendered invisible. Butler took ownership of her narrative and wrote herself into existing worlds and worlds that she dreamed up; she wrote herself into the past, present, and future. Butler's body of work, and the work of others such as Ursula LeGuin and N. K. Jemisin, is an example of the potential of liberated narratives.

In their book *Octavia's Brood*, Walidah Imarisha and adrienne marie brown (2015) continue Butler's legacy and offer visionary fiction as a way to keep dreaming:

> Visionary Fiction is a term we developed to distinguish science fiction that has relevance towards building new, freer worlds from the mainstream strain of science fiction, which most often reinforces dominant narratives of power. Visionary fiction encompasses all of the fantastic, with the arc always bending toward justice. We believe this space is vital for any process of decolonization, because the decolonization of the imagination is the most dangerous and subversive form there is: for it is where all other forms of decolonization are born. Once the imagination is unshackled, liberation is limitless. (p. 4)

Imagination has been crucial to the survival of the marginalized. The ability to imagine new life and ways of being that were so incredibly different from one's own oppression and pain is essential to the creation of that future. Ruha Benjamin (2016) argues, "Fictions that reimagine and rework all that is taken for granted about the current structure of the social world—alternatives to capitalism, racism, and patriarchy—are urgently needed" (p. 2). The liberated imagination opens up room for joy. Author Zadie Smith (2013) describes joy as a "strange admixture of terror, pain, and delight." Joy may not be constant, but it is the very thing that sustains us, that lives in our bones, and cocoons us in moments when we need it most. Smith distinguishes joy and pleasure as altogether separate emotions. Joy has its own rhythm moving in and out of our lives at its own pace; whereas pleasure is fleeting and fickle. In pleasure, there is no room for disappointment or struggle. Joy makes room for the difficult and the simple alike.

Radical Healing for Social Change

Radical healing for social change is redundant because radical healing involves "being or becoming whole" (Neville et al., 2019, p. 1) in the face of adversity or identity-based wounds. This includes tending to our own individual healing as well as the collective healing of our ancestors and community. Part of the healing process is challenging and changing the oppressive conditions that caused the wounds in the first place. Some actions that promote radical healing include developing a sense of pride in your identity, sharing your story, maintaining radical hope, and practicing self care as previously discussed in our discussion of visionary fiction as praxis. These are very much parallel processes that can lead to liberated narratives that promote a life of dignity and respect.

Principles and Examples of Liberated Narratives

Liberated narratives have no particular form; they can be written (as we have chosen to do in this chapter), sung aloud, and even daydreamed. The process and the practice is the work. In emergent strategy, brown (2017) writes: "The patterns of the universe repeat at scale . . . what we practice at a small scale can reverberate to the largest scale" (p. 51). As diversity workers in student affairs and across higher education are tasked with ever-evolving and aspirational mandates, no act of resilience and understanding is insignificant. Accessing clarity can be a challenge; liberated narratives provide one way to find truth and possibility in your story. The following principles exist to guide the crafting of a liberated narrative:

Recognize, Release, Re-Imagine Any Limiting Framework
Interrogation and dismantling of dominant frameworks is essential in liberated narratives. These frameworks are often based on ways of knowing and being that limit our humanity.

Reflection questions.   What is the dominant framework or frameworks at work in your narrative? Are they personal frameworks such as fear, discipline, or ego? Are they societal frameworks such as capitalism, racism, or transphobia? What does your narrative look like when the framework is released or re-imagined?

Centering Your Story

Just as Octavia Butler wrote herself into her stories; liberated narratives asks you to stay focused on your journey.

Reflection questions. What is your journey in this narrative? What are you thinking, feeling, expressing? What is your truth? What do you know? What is still a mystery?

Examples of Liberated Narratives

In the last section of this chapter we have chosen to give ourselves the space to share examples of our own liberated narratives. As women of color and student affairs practitioners, we are constantly called upon to do the work of diversity and inclusion, but so rarely have the opportunity to shape that work without the walls and barriers of institutional pushback, racism, sexism, ableism, and so on. As we overcome one form of resistance, another will arise somewhere else. We offer our liberatory narratives not as a respite from work, but as a form of resistance and a tool of transformation. These narratives reflect our own identities, experiences, apprehensions, and hopes and they are offered with imagination and joy.

Fear and freedom. Unemployed. For most of my professional career the fear of losing my job was perhaps the most dominant consideration in my work. The fear was constant and overbearing. I was constantly afraid that at the whim of a supervisor or administrator I could be let go, fired,or restructured out of a position. And what then would I do? How would I pay my bills? How would I feed myself or more importantly, my dog? How would I possibly survive the humiliation of having a job one day and not having one the next? How will I explain that gap in my resume? As a student affairs practitioner and social justice educator I have come to terms with the fact that I will always have a tenuous (at best) relationship with any institution. To do diversity and inclusion work in higher education is to be a giant, swirling mass of contradictions and confusion. I am radical, but I am also human and so very afraid. I speak up when and where I can, but I can be conservative with my voice and sharply diplomatic when the occasion calls for it. I work within the system, while simultaneously wishing and praying for the day that the system burns. I talk to my students about the importance of graduating while still begrudgingly making monthly payments on my own crushing undergraduate debt. I know that the work is vital and important, but there are days when my exhaustion and disillusionment make it hard to remember why I chose this path in the first place. I know that professionalism is a concept rooted in White supremacy and patriarchy, but I still get nervous when I say that aloud. I am more than comfortable being on the front lines of resistance, but I still get sweaty palms and the urge to curl up in a ball when eyes turn to me. The fear of losing my job made me afraid to examine these contradictions and complexities of my own experience. It kept me from knowing my own possibility. It was difficult to imagine what my work life would look like without the looming fear of being unemployed. It was even more difficult to separate my sense of self-worth from my own martyrdom. However, what I experienced and came to know intimately is that I will be fine. I was able to accept the fear as my mind trying its very best to keep me safe. That my contradictions are actually quite interesting. That my conscience and energy will lead my path. I found strength in my chosen family. I made room for growth, reflection, and resurgence. All of the things that had told me I would cease to be, that my worth would plummet, and my brain would atrophy were the mirages of my own fearful mind. I found that my existence was foretold and conjured up by those in chains and that survival was in my bones. I found that I am here. That the work continues and so do I.

Justice or just us? Capitalism promotes individualism and individualism feeds ego. I started my student affairs career in residence life and immediately began charting my path to get into multicultural affairs. After 3 years, I landed a director position at a small independent Catholic, liberal arts institution. I was a one-person office and I had arrived. I was the campus expert. I was called upon to organize cultural programming, address campus climate, and resolve bias incidents. I created social justice curriculum, supported and increased cultural student organizations, and trained students, faculty, and staff to increase critical consciousness. It was a trap but it was also what I wanted. It allowed me to feel responsible and purposeful but it also set me up to fail. I was operating within an organization that did not want actual change. And while I thought that the mere existence of my office, my position, and me was a sign of shared vision, I was wrong. It also centered me. It put the responsibility on me and marginalized students to do the work. It fed the narrative of "just us." It was designed to be just us (or me). It fed my/our ego. Therefore the work never became more than us.

Fast forward 5 years later and I found myself a director of a larger department, larger institution, larger influence, and potential for a larger ego. We spent 4 years building a team, strategy, and portfolio to create systemic and formal change. We built partnerships across campus to institutionalize the way we talk about, teach, and live social justice as a community. Each time we institutionalized initiatives that reflected our espoused mission of a socially just campus, I had to defend our existence. "Look at all the things we have in place, we don't need one dedicated office. Social justice is everyone's job." We all agreed that inclusion efforts are everyone's job but this sentiment did not come about when we were fighting for resources or justifying our existence. The sentiment that we should be striving for equitable experiences and aims for all students was not required of everyone. It fell to selective offices and positions. It is everyone's job but only some are held responsible. We worked tirelessly to dismantle the "just us" mentality that feeds our ego and positions us to hold up systems like White Supremacy and patriarchy. We fought against the fear that allowing initiatives to be formalized meant a loss to us. We reminded each other that we are still valuable and needed, even when radical acts become the norm. We centered justice, imagination, and liberation and continually reminded each other of our collective strength. And this was our downfall. The further our small team moved away from the norms of organizations, hierarchy, and exceptionalism, the more fear we incited in others. It is scary (for institutions) when people do not operate under the normative rules of engagement. These are people who cannot be controlled or influenced by usual methods. Threatening to fire a person who does not attach their worth to said job does not have the same impact. Striving for social change is about dismantling norms and when there are no norms, there's no measure for the exceptional. If we truly want to create social change, we must come to terms with being. Being about justice and not just us. And honoring our full complicated selves as valuable, all the time, without external validation or being lifted up as exceptional.

CONCLUSION

Reimagining a liberated future requires us to walk away from what we have always known. It means the university model of a chief diversity officer or singular offices leading the charge of equity and inclusion is not enough. It means tying individual accountability to collective success. It is not enough to promote collaborative efforts, we must require it. It means that leaders at our highest levels must be the most staunch advocates for social change. Imagining a future we have never known means doing what has never been done before. It means holding fear and seeing freedom on the other side. It means taking what we know and looking at it in a new light. It means removing barriers and creating space for the best among us to lead the way regardless of their title or years of experience. It means valuing what is traditionally undervalued. And it means defining success for ourselves and creating space for every individual to do the same.

REFERENCES

Ahmed, S. (2012). *On being included: Racism and diversity in institutional life.* Duke University Press.

American Council on Education. (1937). *The student personnel point of view* (American Council on Education Studies, series 1, no. 3). Retrieved from American College Personnel Association website: http://myacpa.org

American Council on Education, Committee on Student Personnel Work. (1949). *The student personnel point of view* (American Council on Education Studies, series 6, no. 13). Retrieved from American College Personnel Association website: http://myacpa.org

Ayers, W. (1998). *Teaching for social justice: A democracy and education reader.* The New Press.

Bashaw, C. (1999). *Stalwart women: A historical analysis of deans of women in the south.* Teacher's College Press.

Bell, D. (1980). *Brown v. Board of Education* and the interest-convergence dilemma. *Harvard Law Review, 93*(3), 518–533.

Benjamin, R. (2016). Racial fictions, biological facts: Expanding the sociological imagination through speculative methods. *Catalyst: Feminism, Theory, Technoscience.*

Braxton, J. M., Doyle, W. R., Hartley, H. V., III, Hirschy, A. S., Jones, W. A., & McLendon, M. K. (2013). *Rethinking college student retention.* Jossey-Bass.

Braxton, J. M., Hirschy, A. S., & McClendon, S. A. (2004). *Understanding and reducing college student departure.* Jossey-Bass.

brown, a.m. (2017). *Emergent strategy.* AK Press.

Butler, O. (1979). *Kindred.* Doubleday.

Butler, O. (2000). *Lilith's brood.* Grand Central Publishing.

Calhoun, C. (2006). The university and the public good. *Thesis Eleven, 84*(7), 7–43.

Chang, M., Milem, J., & antonio, a. (2011). Campus climate and diversity. In J. H. Schuh, S. R. Jones, & S. R. Harper (Eds.), *Student services: A handbook for the profession* (pp. 47–63). Jossey-Bass.

Daly, J. P. (2002). *When slavery was called freedom: Evangelicalism, proslavery, and the causes of the Civil War.* University Press of Kentucky.

DeCuir, J. T., & Dixson, A. D. (2004). "So when it comes out, they aren't that surprised that it is there": Using critical race theory as a tool of analysis of race and racism in education. *Educational Researcher, 33*(5), 26–31. https://doi.org/10.3102/0013189X033005026

Dungy, G., & Gordon, S. A. (2011). The development of student affairs. *Student Services: A Handbook for the Profession, 5,* 61–79.

Evans, N., Assadi, J., & Herriott, T. (2005). Encouraging the development of disability allies. In R. D. Reason, E. M. Broido, T. L. Davis & N. J. Evans (Eds.), *Developing social justice allies: New directions for student services,* no. 110 (pp. 67–79). Jossey-Bass.

Ferguson, R. A. (2012). *The reorder of things: The university and its pedagogies of minority difference.* University of Minnesota Press.

Freire, P. (2000). *Pedagogy of the oppressed* (30th ed.). Bloomsburg Press.

Gaston-Gayles, J. L., Wolf-Wendel, L. E., Nemeth Tuttle, K., Twombly, S. B., & Ward, K. (2004). From disciplinarian to change agent: How the civil rights era change the roles of student affairs professionals. *NASPA Journal, 42*(3), 263–282.

Geiger, R. L. (2005). The ten generations of American higher education. In P. G. Altbach, R. O. Berdahl, & P. J. Gumport (Eds.), *American higher education in the twenty-first century: Social, political, and economic challenges* (2nd ed., pp. 38–70). Baltimore, MD: The John Hopkins University Press.

Graham, P. A. (1978). Expansion and exclusion: A history of women in American higher education. *Signs, 3*(4), 759–773.

Griffin, K., & Hurtado, S. (2011). Institutional variety in American higher education. *Student Services: A Handbook for the Profession*, 24–42.

Guthrie, V. L., Woods, E., Cusker, C., & Gregory, M. (2005). Portrait of balance: Personal and professional balance among student affairs educators. *College Student Affairs Journal 24*(2), 110–128

Habley, W. R., Bloom, J. L., & Robbins, S. B. (2012). *Increasing persistence: Research-based strategies for college student success*. Jossey-Bass.

Hiraldo, P. (2010). The role of critical race theory in higher education. *The Vermont Connection, 31*(1), 7.

Howard-Hamilton, M. F., Richardson, B. J., & Shuford, B. (1998). Promoting multicultural education: A holistic approach. *College Student Affairs Journal, 18*(1), 5–17. https://www.proquest.com/openview/1e907625f86d7a419f31746665e28446/1?pq-origsite=gscholar&cbl=47847

Hurtado, S. (2005). The next generation of diversity and intergroup relations research. *Journal of Social Issues, 61*(3), 595–610.

Imarisha, W., & brown, a. m. (Eds.). (2015). *Octavia's brood: Science fiction stories from social justice movements*. AK Press.

Ladson-Billings, G. (1998). Just what is critical race theory and what's it doing in a nice field like education? *International Qualitative Studies in Education, 11*(1), 7–24.

Lam, M. (2019, June 1). Diversity fatigue is real. *The Chronicle of Higher Education*. https://www.chronicle.com/article/diversity-fatigue-is-real/

Mauro, A., & Mazaris, A. (2016). Student recruitment and retention at the intersections: A case for capacity building. In P. Felten & B. Barnett (Eds.), *Intersectionality in action: A guide for faculty and campus leaders for creating inclusive classrooms and institutions* (pp. 3–14). Stylus Publishing LLC.

Melamed, J. (2006). The spirit of neoliberalism: From racial liberalism to neoliberal multiculturalism. *Social Text, 24*(4), 1–24. https://doi.org/10.1215/01642472-2006-009

Neville, H. A., Adames, H. Y., Chavez-Duenas, N. Y., Chen, G. A., French, B. H., Lewis, J. A., & Mosley, D. V. (2019, March 5). The psychology of radical healing. *Psychology Today*. https://www.psychologytoday.com/us/blog/healing-through-social-justice/201903/the-psychology-radical-healing

Painter, N. I. (2010). *The history of White people*. W.W. Norton & Company.

Pascarella, E. T., & Terenzini, P. T. (2005). *How college affects students: A third decade of research*. Jossey-Bass.

Roberts, D. (2012). *Fatal invention: How science, politics, and big business re-create race in the twenty-first century*. New Press.

Schwartz, R. (1997). How deans of women became men. *The Review of Higher Education, 20*(4), 419–436.

Smith, Z. (2013, January 10). Joy [Electronic version]. *The New York Review*. https://www.nybooks.com/articles/2013/01/10/joy/

Squire, D. D., & Nicolazzo, Z. (2019). Love my naps, but stay woke: The case against self-care. *About Campus, 24*(2), 4–11. https://doi.org/10.1177/1086482219869997

Thelin, J.R. (2004). *A history of American higher education.* The Johns Hopkins University Press.

Tinto, V. (2016, September 25). From retention to persistence. *Inside HigherEd.* https://www.insidehighered.com/views/2016/09/26/how-improve-student-persistence-and-completion-essay

U.S. Department of Education, National Center for Education Statistics. (2014). *Digest of Education Statistics, 2014.* Indicator 47. Retrieved from http://nces.ed.gov

U.S. Department of Education. (2023a, June). *Number of students enrolled in postsecondary institutions in the fall by gender.* Retrieved June 28, 2023 from https://nces.ed.gov/ipeds/TrendGenerator/app/trend-table/2/3?trending=column&rid=48

U.S. Department of Education (2023b, June). *Number of students enrolled in postsecondary institutions in the fall by race/ethnicity.* Retrieved June 28, 2023 from https://nces.ed.gov/ipeds/TrendGenerator/app/trend-table/2/3?trending=column&rid=47

U.S. Department of Education & National Center for Education Statistics. (2017, May). *The Condition of Education 2017* (NCES 2017-144).

Vernez, G., Krop, R. A., & Rydell, C. P. (1999). *Closing the education gap: Benefits and costs.* RAND.

Zusman, A. (2005). Challenges facing higher education in the twenty-first century. In P. G. Altbach, R. O. Berdahl, & P. J. Gumport (Eds.), *American higher education in the twenty-first century: Social, political, and economic challenges* (2nd ed., pp.115–160). The John Hopkins University Press.

CHAPTER 4

MOVING TOWARDS GREATNESS

Implementing a Diversity Plan at an Urban Research Institution

Alicia W. Davis
Chance W. Lewis
John A. Williams III

ABSTRACT

Increasing diversity remains a constant focus for higher education leaders. This chapter outlines how an urban research institution created and implemented their diversity plan to shift the diversity infrastructure on campus. The expected outcome of this chapter is for postsecondary institutions to develop and implement strategic diversity plans.

> *Today, diversity is not a nicety but a necessity, not just for some students but for all students. The evidence that this is true is everywhere. The transformative power of diversity in education is enormous; it boosts empathy and reduces bias and increases the chances that low-income students will attend college without in any way compromising the academic outcomes of their middle class peers. It exposes students to perspectives and ideas that enlarge their world views.*
>
> —John B. King Jr., former secretary of education

An increasingly diverse society and global economy drive the need for continued diversity initiatives in higher education. University diversity plans are being created and implemented to ensure diversity is the central focus of strategic planning efforts campus-wide. As students call for engagement on a variety of ideas and perspectives, it is imperative that universities cultivate experiences that will foster culturally sustaining conversations, research, and outcomes with students, faculty, staff, and the community. A growing number of higher education institutions are implementing diversity plans that focus on inclusivity and progression, rather than tenure-track faculty or student graduation, of students of color, faculty of color, individuals with disabilities, members of the LGBTQ+ community, and so on. The continued focus on the diversity infrastructure at higher education institutions causes universities to reexamine if their approach to diversity is holistic, multidimensional, and sustaining in order to create a real change in the institution's culture (Williams, 2007).

The University of North Carolina at Charlotte (UNCC) is preparing students to become leaders in a multicultural society through the implementation of their campus-wide diversity plan. The plan was established to advance teaching, scholarship, and community engagement with a diverse faculty, staff, and student body. Under the guidance of the provost, vice chancellors, department chairs, and university leaders committed to diversity initiatives, the campus-wide plan will continue to embed diversity into the "cultural fabric of the institution" (Williams, 2007, p. 12). As universities seek to create comprehensive and inclusive environments aimed at providing instruction centered around inclusion, diversity, and equity, this chapter will provide action steps to implement a strategic diversity plan. The chapter begins with a discussion surrounding diversity issues in student enrollment and faculty recruitment at postsecondary institutions. An outline of the diversity plan implementation at UNCC will follow. Three action steps will be presented that examine how UNCC created, implemented, and revised their diversity plan.

DIVERSITY ISSUES IN HIGHER EDUCATION

When deciding which institution to attend, representation matters as students analyze a university's student body to determine their commitment to diversity (Smith & Schonfeld, 2000). According to Turner (2002), 80% of students attending postsecondary institutions in 2015 would be nonmainstream students. In 2015–2016, 26 million students were enrolled in postsecondary institutions (McFarland et al., 2018). The immediate college enrollment rate for high school graduates was 70% in 2016 with 67% of students from low-income families and 64% of students from middle-income families attending college immediately upon graduation. An estimated 16.9 million undergraduate students were enrolled in public colleges and universities in 2016 with 39% being students of color. Latinx students had the highest undergraduate enrollment followed by Black and Asian/Pacific Islander students (McFarland et al., 2018). Although Black students between 18–24 years old account for 14.8% of the population, they made up 9.8% of full-time undergraduates at public universities and colleges (Harper & Simmons, 2019). The 6-year graduation rate in 2014 for first-time, full-time undergraduates was 41% for Black students and 54% for Latinx students (Musu-Gillette et al., 2017). The statistics suggest that higher education administrators are becoming aware of the need to have their student body reflect the demographics of America, but the process is slow.

In 2016, 25% of the nation's faculty were people of color (U.S. Department of Education, Integrated Postsecondary Education Data System, 2016). That percentage has remained relatively the same (26%) in 2020 (National Center for Education Statistics, 2022). When factoring in gender, the percentage is even lower as males continue to dominate higher education faculty. According to 2016 data, females of color accounted for a small percentage of higher education faculty: 2% were Black, 1% were Latinx, and 3% were Asian/Pacific Islander (McFarland et al., 2018). Turner et al. (2008) found that recruiting students of color to attend public universities and colleges requires hiring a diverse faculty. A diverse faculty contributes to the various methods of teaching, adds to the multifaceted research and scholarship occurring, and helps students of color feel welcomed and included at postsecondary institutions and not experience isolation (Chen, 2017). Faculty of color pedagogical approaches explores societal issues and incorporates culturally sustaining practices into their curriculum, making it relevant to all students (Chen, 2017). The current lack of faculty of color in higher education creates a sense of urgency in the recruiting processes for students and faculty.

FIRST MOVE: CREATING A DIVERSITY PLAN

In 1993, UNCC created task forces to review concerns related to the advancement of campus diversity. The university was engulfed in a community with rapid population growth and it was crucial for university leaders to engage with the community to create a more inclusive learning and research environment. Between 1993 and 2004, Mecklenburg County grew by 36% (U.S. Census Bureau, 2010), causing the university to revise their recruiting efforts and initiatives. In 2004, the provost was appointed to lead the charge of the diversity plan committee with a specific goal to "enhance opportunities for learning in a culturally rich environment" (UNCC, 2016, p. 1).

The committee focused on four key areas to advance campus diversity efforts: faculty, staff, students, and curriculum. Through the university's and student body's call for more inclusive applications of teaching, leading, and hiring, the committee's focus on key campus diversity efforts led to the first diversity plan for access and inclusion in 2008 (UNCC, 2016). Led by the provost and a council, consisting of members of the chancellor's cabinet, the initial diversity plan outlined six objectives for the university (UNCC, 2013a):

- Create a broad understanding of goals for diversity and inclusion for the university through active outreach to the campus community.
- Recruit and graduate a diverse student body that reflects community diversity and address the state's need to increase access to higher education for historically underrepresented and economically disadvantaged students.
- Increase the recruitment of underrepresented faculty and advance their progression through the faculty ranks.
- Increase the representation of staff from underrepresented groups.
- Ensure the presence of institutional environments and course development that enhance learning and appreciation for the full diversity.
- Develop external relationships with the community to enhance diversity off and on campus.

The council collaborated to implement workshops, programs, and initiatives to promote the university's commitment to diversity, access, and inclusion through the diversity plan.

SECOND MOVE: IMPLEMENTING A DIVERSITY PLAN

Diversity Fund

A major initiative implemented throughout all six objectives was the creation of a chancellor's diversity challenge fund (CDCF). Faculty, staff, and students interested in showcasing diversity at UNCC were awarded the opportunity to submit proposals that advocated for diversity on the campus. The proposals included activities that engaged the campus community in diversity, access, and inclusion efforts while simultaneously addressing issues connected to the multiple facets of diversity including culture, ethnicity, gender equity, race, religion, learning abilities, and so on. Deans and senior level administrators were prompted to share this funding possibility with their faculty, staff, and students. A CDCF committee was established to vote upon the proposals and grant recipients were given a monetary award to fund their projects. Grant recipients held diversity programs such as the (a) Anita Hill Speaking Engagement: Women's and Gender Studies, (b) diversity workshop for criminal justice learning community, (c) Engaging Community Members in Action Research: An Inclusive Evaluation Initiative, (d) We Are the Lowest of the 99%: Poverty Series, and so on. Through the creation of the CDCF, faculty, staff, and students were able to exercise their passion for diversity and stimulate intellectual conversations surrounding numerous topics related to equity and inclusion on the campus.

In addition to establishing the CDCF to create and implement a broad understanding of goals for diversity and inclusion, faculty and staff participated in diversity workshops held on campus. Partnering with community-based organizations, UNCC conducted numerous workshops on equity, inclusion, and social justice as leaders within every college met with their colleagues to assess the needs and evaluate what faculty, staff, and students needed and what workshops should offer. From 2013 to 2018, the CDCF awarded over 160 grants totaling approximately $750,000.

Student Recruitment, Retention, and Graduation Rates

UNCC maintains one of the most diverse student bodies in the UNC system as a tremendous effort has been placed on diversifying the student body. In Fall 2008, 28% of the student body were students of color and 54% were women (UNCC, 2018a). In order to increase minority representation on campus, recruiting measures were set in place that required creating a campus brochure to highlight information and services for students of all backgrounds, discussing financial aid and financial planning through outreach programs for applicants from marginalized populations, and hosting events such as AVID and GEAR-UP in collaboration with multicultural services to attract first-year and transfer students (UNCC, 2013a). Graduate admissions set out to recruit students into their programs through targeting merit scholarship databases to inform students of the programs offered at UNCC, partnering with organizations that focus on diverse communities to recruit talent into graduate school, and conducting graduate recruitment fairs at historically Black colleges and universities (HBCUs).

In Fall 2018, 37% of UNCC's student population identified as members of racial/ethnic minority groups (UNCC, 2018a). The growth in Latinx undergraduate student enrollment increased from 4.7% in 2009 to 10.3% in 2018 (UNCC, 2018a). Similarly, the percentages of undergraduate students identifying as Asian/Pacific Islander and two or more races also increased (UNCC, 2018a). The percentages of undergraduate and graduate students identifying as White declined during this time period while students identifying as African American remained consistent (UNCC, 2018a). Tables 4.1 and 4.2 display the undergraduate and graduate enrollment at UNCC in Fall 2009 and Fall 2018 (UNCC, 2018a).

TABLE 4.1 Undergraduate Student Enrollment at UNCC, Fall 2009 and Fall 2018

	Fall 2009 %	Fall 2009 N	Fall 2018 %	Fall 2018 N
White	65.1	12,651	57.60	13,772
Black/African American	15.9	3,097	16.70	3,996
Latinx	4.7	910	10.30	2,473
American Indian	0.4	82	0.32	77
Asian/Pacific Islander	5.0	962	7.40	1,780
Non-Resident Alien	2.7	524	2.70	649
Two or More Races	0.6	124	4.70	1,124
Women	50.6	9,829	46.90	11,201
Men	49.4	9,590	53.10	12,696

TABLE 4.2 Graduate Student Enrollment at UNCC, Fall 2009 and Fall 2018

	Fall 2009 %	Fall 2009 N	Fall 2018 %	Fall 2018 N
White	65.0	3,435	47.1	2,465
Black/African American	12.8	676	13.9	728
Latinx	2.4	127	5.2	275
American Indian	0.4	19	0.13	7
Asian/Pacific Islander	2.9	152	4.2	219
Non-Resident Alien	14.7	777	27.2	1,422
Two or More Races	0.2	11	2.1	111
Women	60.8	3,211	56.9	2,975
Men	39.2	2,071	43.1	2,254

In addition to diversifying student recruitment, UNCC's diversity plan set out to improve retention and graduation rates. With 49.8% of all students graduating in 6 years in 2000, UNCC collaborated with university and community organizations to create programs that targeted minority males and marginalized students. Through the University Transition Opportunity Program (UTOP), students from diverse backgrounds are able to participate in a summer bridge experience that exposes them to college classes and community service prior to the start of their freshmen year (UNCC, 2013a). Additional programs at UNCC provide opportunities for freshmen to participate in peer mentoring programs aimed at helping students transition to college life and prepare them for academics at the university level. Freshmen can participate in tutoring, study hall programs, socials, networking events, peer counseling, and community outreach events while enrolled in the programs and upon the end of their first year, can apply to serve as counselors for the upcoming freshmen class. Tables 4.3 and 4.4 shows freshmen retention rates and 6-year graduation rates (UNCC, 2018a).

TABLE 4.3 Freshmen Retention Rates

	2009	2012	2017
White	76.2	79.0	81.1
Black/African American	81.1	86.3	85.1
Latinx	72.2	82.5	81.1
American Indian	92.9	55.6	64.3
Asian/Pacific Islander	80.9	80.4	84.9
Non-Resident Alien	88.3	90.5	86.8
Women	79.3	82.8	83.3
Men	75.1	78.3	80.7
All Freshmen	77.2	80.4	81.9

TABLE 4.4 Six-Year Graduation Rates

	2007	2012
White	54.1	59.8
Black/African American	53.0	54.8
Latinx	47.2	60.7
American Indian	55.0	50.0
Asian/Pacific Islander	58.5	61.5
Non-Resident Alien	38.1	65.1
Women	54.5	63.7
Men	52.9	54.7
All Freshmen	53.8	58.9

The implementation of a funding program aimed at increasing diversity initiatives on campus, highlighting how to access financial aid on a college campus through outreach programs, and collaborating with community partners and campus organizations to recruit underrepresented student groups provided UNCC the ability to increase overall student enrollment, retention, and graduation rates for underrepresented student groups. Support networks designed for students to thrive at the university contributed to the growth in the graduation rate over a 12-year period.

Faculty Recruitment

The strong focus on increasing student diversity at UNCC led to the need to diversify faculty representation. In 2005, 17.7% of the faculty were persons of color and the progression of faculty through the ranks was slow or nonexistent (UNCC, 2013a). Faculty climate surveys revealed small to moderate disparities between White faculty and faculty of color surrounding responses in the areas of "how well you fit" and "colleagues committed to diversity/inclusion" (The Collaborative on Academic Careers in Higher Education, 2012). Faculty of color noted that the lack of mentorship, diversity within search committees, and opportunities to progress through the faculty ranks were apparent at the university. As faculty of color and senior level administrators called for a more diverse faculty, the faculty affairs and diversity office at the university set out to review recruitment methods and committee searches. All faculty desiring to serve on a search committee were required to attend a two-part recruitment training focused on writing an inclusive job description, developing a recruitment plan, conducting active searches for qualified candidates that align with university and department diversity goals, and so on.

Reviewing faculty representation at the university led to a focus on increasing the number of women professors in science, technology, engineering, and math (STEM). The diversity affairs office formed a database to aid faculty in the hiring of diverse candidates and contributed portions of the database to find women and/or underrepresented minority candidates. Once candidates were selected and hired, they were provided the opportunity to participate in the new faculty learning community. Formed in 2009, the new faculty learning community was created to assist new faculty with the transition into the university's culture. Learning community sessions are held throughout the year and the objectives of the program are to develop a cross-college, cross-discipline collegiality with other new faculty, increase knowledge and awareness of the university's commitment to scholarship, teaching, and service, while also networking with faculty across the campus. Table 4.5 displays the rank, sex, and race of full-time teaching faculty during Fall 2008 and Fall 2017 (UNCC, 2018b).

TABLE 4.5 Full Time Teaching Faculty by Rank, Sex, and Race, Fall 2008 and Fall 2017

	Professor		Associate Professor		Assistant Professor		Lecturer		Total	
	2008	2017	2008	2017	2008	2017	2008	2017	2008	2017
White										
Male	154	165	138	123	100	70	65	74	457	432
Female	38	75	82	105	102	81	116	117	338	378
Total	192	240	220	228	202	151	181	191	795	810
Black or African American										
Male	5	9	9	8	5	8	3	3	22	28
Female	2	0	8	19	12	18	8	13	30	50
Total	7	9	17	27	17	26	11	16	52	78
Latinx										
Male	3	3	6	6	3	4	2	2	14	15
Female	2	4	3	4	6	5	3	7	14	20
Total	5	7	9	10	9	9	5	9	28	35
Asian										
Male	19	39	22	27	37	16	5	4	83	86
Female	1	7	4	14	22	13	4	6	31	40
Total	20	46	26	41	59	29	9	10	114	126

Note: All deans, associate, and associate deans have been excluded; the above data includes phased retirees.

Student Perceptions of Diversity in the Curriculum

Diversity-related issues are incorporated into curriculums contingent upon the student learning outcomes of each college. Within the general education curriculum in which every student partakes in, the liberal arts program included the following diversity learning outcomes (UNCC, 2013a):

- Students are expected to be able to discuss issues of diversity in a historical context.
- Students are expected to be able to discuss issues of diversity in a global context.
- Students are expected to be able to discuss issues of diversity with respect to art.
- Students are expected to be able to discuss issues of diversity as it applies to questions of ethical and cultural critique.

A student learning outcomes assessment reported in 2009 revealed students were not meeting the outlined diversity objectives. One initiative to incorporate diversity into the general curriculum led to a collaboration with a community-based program organized to expand access, inclusion, and equity throughout the Charlotte community. Through this collaboration, UNCC developed the Crossroads student program (UNCC, 2010) aimed at:

- exposing students to themes of access inclusion, equity, and trust within the curriculum;
- connecting UNCC research resources to address issues of access, inclusion, equity, and trust within the city;
- engaging students and faculty in the civic life of the city through service learning opportunities created to reduce the barrier to access, inclusion, equity, and trust; and
- supporting diversity initiatives on campus.

The newly proposed Crossroads curriculum was taught in 11 sections during Spring and Fall of 2011 with over 250 students completing 8,000 hours of service learning with community-based organizations (UNCC, 2012). Over an 8-year span, Crossroads has contributed to embedding diversity within the general education curriculum, but lacked buy-in from every college, thereby hindering its growth and its ability to impact every student on the campus. Although the program has not been adopted university-wide, it is currently housed within the College of Education and is open for other majors to participate.

The 2011 National Survey of Student Engagement highlighted areas of improvement for enriching diverse educational experiences on campus. The results showed 57% of first-year students frequently interacted with students who were different from them in terms of religion, politics, and personal beliefs; 60% of first-year students interacted with students from a different race or ethnic background; and 10% of students by their senior year had studied abroad (UNCC, 2011). The 2013 graduating senior survey results reported 63% of seniors believed they possessed the ability to work with people from diverse backgrounds; 50% of seniors were sensitive to issues associated with racial equity; and 49% of seniors were sensitive to issues related to gender equity (UNCC, 2013b). Each survey or assessment exhibited the potential for growth in the curriculum and classrooms at UNCC.

In 2014, UNCC developed Prospect for Success to be a principal component of the first-year curriculum for undergraduate students. The three goals of the program: intentionality, curiosity, and awareness were created to engage students in professional and personal growth. Awareness promoted students to reflect upon their interactions and experiences with students from diverse backgrounds in an effort to develop an understanding of themselves in a global society. In 2018, the National Survey of Student Engagement reported 84% of first-year students and 79% of seniors at UNCC *very often* or *often* had conversations with people from a different race or ethnicity than their own (UNCC, 2019). In addition, 69% of first-year students and seniors *very often* or *often* had conversations with people with differing political views than their own (UNCC, 2019). Each survey or assessment continues to show the potential for growth in the curriculum and classrooms at UNCC.

THIRD MOVE: REVISE AND MOVE FORWARD

In preparation for the 2016–2021 institutional plan set forth by the university, the diversity plan was revisited in 2015 and the African American and Latino caucuses, as well as the committee on the future of faculty provided feedback, direction, and support of the proposed diversity plan. All parties affirmed the continuing importance of the six objectives outlined in the 2008 diversity plan and added an additional objective to the revised 2015 plan which focused on ensuring the success of the plan through accountability, assessment, and recognition. The diversity committee, led by the provost, selected their first diversity faculty fellow to lead the charge of taking the diversity plan to the next level and implementing sustainable measures to increase access, diversity, and inclusion on UNCC's campus and within the community. In addition to the selection of the first diversity faculty fellow, the diversity committee created a working group to advance the work of the Campus Diversity Plan for Diversity, Access, and Inclusion with a specific focus on the parts of the plan directly linked to the Division of Academic Affairs.

Each member of the working group is appointed by their college dean and associate provost and will serve for 2 years on the committee. In addition, staff caucuses representing Latino, African American, and LGBTQ+ members of the university community elected representatives to serve as members of the working group. Students, appointed by the vice chancellor for student affairs also serve on the committee. Under the direction of the diversity faculty fellow, the working group is separated into subcommittees to address policy reviews, progress, and communication pertaining to their objective of the diversity plan. Each objective serves as a subcommittee and members chose their committees based on their specific interests. The provost works directly with the working group through the diversity faculty fellow and attends working group meetings.

Since its creation in 2018, the diversity working group has submitted 49 recommendations to the provost to improve diversity, equity, and inclusion initiatives across the seven objectives identified in the university's diversity plan. Also, the working group has provided language revisions to the current diversity plan, recommendations to department chairs on the progression and areas of improvement for inclusivity within their college, and an annual report highlighting the accomplishment of the group and areas of improvement for the university. In addition, the working group provided recommendations to the Office of the Chancellor on policies concerning diversity officers within the UNC system. Placing policy revisions and recommendations in writing has proven to be beneficial for the working group as they continue to move towards providing a more equitable and inclusive environment on UNCC's campus.

Celebrating diversity throughout the campus community is necessary to move UNCC's diversity plan to greatness and for the diversity faculty fellow and working group to recognize the importance of such a celebration. In an effort to celebrate diversity year-round, the working group welcomed faculty, staff, and students to submit innovative diversity proposals that will impact the campus community. Precise, inventive, and groundbreaking proposals capture the essence of the university's diversity plan and will be sustainable for years to come. Once proposals are submitted, members of the working group vote upon the acceptance of proposals and provide assistance to proposal leaders.

UNCC continues to strive for greatness through the implementation and sustainability of the university's diversity plan. Under the direction of the diversity faculty fellow and the working group, recommendations are being set forth that calls for diversity and inclusion to be listed as one of the top five criteria for recruiting and hiring new faculty, providing explicit bias training for search committees, incorporating inclusive language and activities in the general curriculum for all students, improving the number of scholarship applicants from low income and underrepresented populations, engaging in public dialogue with surrounding communities concerning how the university can serve them and improve upon diversity efforts, and so much more. Consistent communication between the provost, university diversity committee, and the working group allows for the diversity plan to serve as a living document as innovative possibilities are being proposed to drive each objective. The creation of the diversity plan will ensure that diversity remains the central focus of strategic planning efforts campus-wide.

REFERENCES

Chen, A. (2017). Addressing diversity on college campuses: Changing expectations and practices in instructional leadership. *Higher Education Studies, 7*(2), 17–22. https://doi.org/10.5539/hes.v7n2p17

Harper, S. R., & Simmons, I. (2019). *Black students at public colleges and universities: A 50-state report card.* USC Race and Equity Center. https://www.luminafoundation

.org/wp-content/uploads/2018/09/black-students-at-public-colleges-and-universities.pdf

McFarland, J., Hussar, B., Wang, X., Zhang, J., Wang, K., Rathbun, A., Barmer, A., Forrest Cataldi, E., & Bullock Mann, F. (2018). *The condition of education 2018* (NCES 2018-144). National Center for Education Statistics. https://nces.ed.gov/pubs2018/2018144.pdf

Musu-Gillette, L., de Brey, C., McFarland, J., Hussar, W., Sonnenberg, W., & Wilkinson-Flicker, S. (2017). *Status and trends in the education of racial and ethnic groups 2017* (NCES 2017-051). U.S. Department of Education, National Center for Education Statistics. https://nces.ed.gov/pubs2017/2017051.pdf

National Center for Educational Statistics. (2022). *Characteristics of postsecondary faculty. condition of education*. U.S. Department of Education, Institute of Education Sciences. https://nces.ed.gov/programs/coe/indicator/csc

Smith, D. G., & Schonfeld, N. B. (2000). The benefits of diversity: What the research tells us. *About Campus, 5*(5), 16–23. https://doi.org/10.1177/108648220000500505

The Collaborative on Academic Careers in Higher Education. (2012). *COACHE faculty job satisfaction survey: Provost's report: University of North Carolina at Charlotte*. https://advance.uncc.edu/sites/advance.uncc.edu/files/media/COACHE-2012%20survey%20results.pdf

Turner, C. S. V. (2002). Women of color in academe: Living with multiple marginality. *Journal of Higher Education, 73*, 74–93. https://doi.org/10.1353/jhe.2002.0013

Turner, C. S. V., González, J. C., & Wood, J. L. (2008). Faculty of color in academe: What 20 years of literature tells us. *Journal of Diversity in Higher Education, 1*(3), 139–168. https://doi.org/10.1037/a0012837

UNC Charlotte. (2010). *Crossroads Charlotte: 2010–2015 strategic plan executive summary*. University of North Carolina at Charlotte, Crossroads Charlotte website: https://education.charlotte.edu/sites/education.charlotte.edu/files/media/strategic-plan/REEL%20Strategic%20Plan%202010_2015.pdf

UNC Charlotte. (2011). *The student experience in brief: University of North Carolina at Charlotte*. UNC Charlotte. https://assessment.uncc.edu/sites/assessment.uncc.edu/files/media/NSSE/2011StudentExperienceInBrief.pdf

UNC Charlotte. (2012). *Crossroads Charlotte 2011–2012 annual report*. Retrieved from University of North Carolina at Charlotte, Crossroads Charlotte website: https://advance.charlotte.edu/sites/advance.charlotte.edu/files/media/Annual%20Report%202012%20FINAL_4.pdf

UNC Charlotte. (2013a). *UNC Charlotte campus diversity plan progress report: Executive summary*. https://diversity.charlotte.edu/sites/diversity.charlotte.edu/files/media/Diversity-Plan-Progress-Report-Winter-2012-2013.pdf

UNC Charlotte. (2013b). *Graduating senior survey results*. Retrieved from https://assessment.uncc.edu/sites/assessment.uncc.edu/files/media/Attachment%204_GSS13%20University%20Wide.pdf

UNC Charlotte. (2016). *UNC Charlotte plan for campus diversity, access, and inclusion*. https://diversity.uncc.edu/sites/diversity.uncc.edu/files/media/Campus%20Plan%20for%20Diversity%2C%20Access%2C%20and%20Inclusion%202016.pdf.

UNC Charlotte. (2018a). *UNC Charlott summary dashboard.* https://ir-analytics.uncc.edu/tableau/unc-charlotte-summary-dashboard

UNC Charlotte. (2018b). *Undergraduate level retention and graduation dashboard.* https://ir-analytics.charlotte.edu/tableau/undergraduate-level-retention-and-graduation-dashboard

UNC Charlotte. (2019). *UNC Charlotte campus diversity plan progress report: Executive summary.* https://diversity.charlotte.edu/sites/diversity.charlotte.edu/files/media/2019%20Progress%20Report%20of%20Campus%20Plan%20for%20Diversity-Access-Inclusion%20UNCC.pdf

U.S. Census Bureau. (2010). *2006–2010 American community survey.* https://factfinder.census.gov/faces/tableservices/jsf/pages/productview.xhtml?src=bkmk

U.S. Department of Education, Integrated Postsecondary Education Data System. (2016). *Total full-time faculty by race and ethnicity: Fall 2016.* https://data.aaup.org/ipeds-faculty/

Williams, D. A. (2007). Achieving inclusive excellence: Strategies for creating real and sustainable change in quality and diversity. *About Campus, 12*(1), 8–14. https://onlinelibrary.wiley.com/doi/epdf/10.1002/abc.198

CHAPTER 5

RECOGNIZING AND ADDRESSING IMPLICIT BIAS IN ADJUDICATION AND TITLE IX PROCEDURES

A Case Study Approach

Shawna Patterson-Stephens

*So in the dark we hide the heart that bleeds,
And wait, and tend our agonizing seeds.*
—Countee Cullen

ABSTRACT

This chapter examines some of the ways implicit bias exists, emerges, and develops in conduct hearings and Title IX proceedings on college campuses. Title IX procedures have emerged as a way to correct gender discrimination in higher education, and universities must demonstrate strict accordance with the due process clause of the 14th Amendment. Similarly, investigative procedures and conduct hearings must afford due process as outlined by an institution's respective code of conduct and hearing policy. Still, concealed assumptions continue to influence the manner in which faculty and staff engage with reporting, investigations, hearings, ancillary procedures, and sanctioning. This chapter addresses the ways educators could seek to reduce instances of bias and harm in conduct and Title IX proceedings.

Contemporary discussions on diversity, equity, inclusion, justice, and belonging (DEIJB) feel saturated by an onslaught of disingenuous "allies," overused buzzwords, and ill-informed constituencies (Ekpe & Toutant, 2022). These circumstances are coupled with the manner in which expanded access to education has been met with the incipience of politicization, as status quo traditions throughout the academy have slowly been disrupted by social justice efforts. Proceedings such as Title IX interventions and conduct adjudication have not gone unscathed in this climate, where the Trump administration called into question whether cisgendered men received fair treatment during behavioral investigations and hearings.

In 2017, Betsy DeVos, specifically, inverted federal postsecondary Title IX guidance with new regulations that made it more challenging for survivors and intervention personnel to navigate reporting mechanisms, investigatory processes, and resolution praxis (Grayer & Stracqualursi, 2020). Though the Biden administration rolled back most of DeVos' changes to Title IX procedure, prejudicial attitudes remain ingrained in higher education infrastructure, including conduct hearings and Title IX procedures. It is therefore increasingly important to fortify understandings of DEIJB in order to avoid losing ground on the substantial gains made in postsecondary behavioral interventions over the past 4 decades. Moreover, it is necessary to curtail prejudicial attitudes in conflict management and behavioral interventions to reduce subsequent harm placed upon minoritized communities when instances of bias occur on college campuses.

Concealed assumptions continue to influence the manner in which faculty and staff engage with teaching, policies, and procedures in the postsecondary sector (Easterly & Ricard, 2011). According to Bem (1993), "Hidden assumptions about [identity] remain embedded in cultural discourses, social institutions, and individual psyches that invisibly and systemically reproduce [majority] power in generation after generation" (p. 2). These assumptions—or biases—play a role in vital higher education operations, including campus adjudication and Title IX procedures. This chapter centers the ways implicit bias can undergird conduct hearings and Title IX proceedings, and explores how faculty, staff, and student staff members can work in proactive ways to offset implicit and explicit bias in their daily practice as intervention personnel.

LITERATURE REVIEW

The following review of literature will first contextualize Title IX and conduct proceedings in higher education. These delineations are then further informed by literature inquiring about the confluence of climate, societal interpretations of identity, and the operationalization of bias in the academy. This brief review provides insight into the emergent themes discussed in the case studies proceeding this section.

Campus Adjudication

With variances in understanding and adhering to community standards across intercollegiate constituencies, campus adjudication procedures are commonplace on college campuses (King, 2012). Still, postsecondary responses to conflict and conduct violations are grounded in systemic judicial processes intended to determine guilt or innocence (Himbeault Taylor & Thomas Varner, 2009). While some language has been altered to match the climate faculty and staff hope to espouse on campus—such as implementing the use of the term, *responsible*, rather than *guilty*—U.S.-based approaches to law enforcement are frequently replicated in campus conduct procedures, including the tenets rooted in due process. Due process "stems from federal and state constitutional law... The due process clause of the 14th Amendment of the Constitution encompasses the idea that an individual's liberty and property interests are protected by substantive and procedural due process rights" (Himbeault Taylor & Thomas Varner, 2009, p. 34). Historically, Black, Indigenous, and people of color (BIPOC) folx, particularly Black individuals, have lacked full access to the protections of due process, as they encountered racist enforcement and investigatory procedures, were without adequate legal representation, were met with the presumption of guilt by judges, nor faced a jury truly consisting of their peers. Recent interpretations of "fairness" grounded in Whiteness have been used to further manipulate due process in a manner that reduces protections against vulnerable populations, including BIPOC folx, people with disabilities, women, and LGBTQIA+ communities (Grayer & Stracqualursi, 2020).

Although adjudication is the primary method used to address noncompliance with policy, relying solely upon traditional conduct proceedings to attend to conflict or behavioral issues creates deficiencies in an institution's approach to seeking resolution (Geist Giacomini & Meyer Schrage, 2009). According to Geist Giacomini and Meyer Schrage (2009), adjudication-only models fail to experience alternative solutions to conflict resolution or allow respondents to fully consider their role in the situation. These models also lack intentional opportunities to restore impacted communities, nor do they provide deep consideration for the historical context between intersecting identities and adjudication (Geist Giacomini & Meyer Schrage, 2009). It is therefore imperative for administrative leadership to embed a multivariate approach to conflict resolution infrastructure across the postsecondary sector.

Typically, colleges and universities devise reporting mechanisms for conduct and academic policy violations, which can be implemented by campus safety, full-time staff, faculty, or student–staff members, including resident assistants serving within residence halls (King, 2012). These structures may be centralized and interconnected (e.g., Office of the Dean of Students), or siloed by department and functional area (e.g., School of Dentistry). Documentation and reporting rests upon codes of conduct established by an institution (King, 2012). Intervention personnel, including residence hall directors and deans of students, must review incident reports within a timeframe specified by the institution, and make contact with respondents to schedule a meeting. Some institutions include an information session to review documentation and procedure with respondents prior to a hearing. Other institutions may utilize the hearing as a space to review documentation and procedures with respondents, while also receiving their narrative about the report. Depending upon the nature of the complaint, respondents may simply meet with a residence hall director, dean of students, or case manager to discuss the matter. For those cases requiring escalation, respondents are referred to hearing bodies. Hearing bodies can be composed of faculty and staff, as well as student representatives, and they are often expected to maintain confidentiality in all proceedings. At the conclusion of individualized meetings and hearings, responsibility is determined. Should a respondent be found responsible, they are often sanctioned in accordance with institutional adjudication requirements for code violations (King, 2012).

Title IX Procedures

In keeping with some of the broader ideals espoused by higher education, Title IX legislation and federal guidelines can aid in reinforcing the physical and psychological safety of intercollegiate communities, in addition to cultivating a culture of care and concern on college campuses. Further, application of Title IX can improve gender-based parity in core educational activities and functions, including athletics. According to Posselt and colleagues (2017), the Title IX Amendment:

> Prohibits sex discrimination in all federally funded educational institutions, from preschools through graduate schools. It is a civil rights statute enforced through the Office of Civil Rights, and institutions found in violation of any area covered under Title IX risk loss of their federal funding. (p. 10)

Universities must demonstrate strict compliance with the due process clause of the 14th Amendment (Dutile, 2000; Eckes, 2021). Title IX procedures have emerged as a way to correct gender discrimination in higher education, as observed behaviors associated with Title IX are closely tied to gender discrimination (Johnson, 2017). Title IX is most frequently operationalized within the following higher education domains: (a) gender parity (athletics), (b) sexual harassment and violence, and (c) issues related to the support and service of transgender persons (Harris & Linder, 2017; Johnson, 2017). When legal disputes involving colleges and universities emerge, they are primarily addressed through administrative law. Administrative rules and regulations on college campuses have the force of law, but are not passed by legislature.

Regarding organizational structure, Title IX coordination may be positioned within a singular office reporting directly to the office of the provost or president, or it may serve as a function of institutionalized diversity. Some institutions employ an embedded Title IX officer within specific units, such as human resources and student affairs, while other campuses administer a coordinator to serve for the institution, writ large. Within the anatomy of institutional diversity, the director/vice president may be required to oversee both Title IX investigations and proceedings, as well as responsibilities and objectives associated with DEIJB-related needs. Within well-resourced offices for institutional diversity, the director or vice president supervises a coordinator or assistant/associate vice president who is directly responsible for managing Title IX concerns.

Standards associated with Title IX competency suggest that intervention personnel must be trained and adequately prepared to review, investigate, and adjudicate all cases with subjectivity in order to ensure equal protections (Eckes, 2021). By virtue of the sensitive nature of the themes emerging through these proceedings, it is especially critical for coordinators to comprehend the confluence of sociohistorical context, identity, and their relationship with power, privilege, and oppression within the United States (Harris & Linder, 2017). This standard is relevant, as coordinators are tasked with utilizing impartiality to conduct outreach, support survivors and their advocates, support respondents and their advocates, and in some cases, work alongside hearing bodies to make a determination. Due to the legal aspects of the violations most often associated with campus Title IX procedures, coordinators must also work in concert with campus safety and/or off-campus police, legal council, human resources, student affairs, and athletics staff to identify a resolution.

Implicit Bias, Conduct Hearings, and Title IX Procedures

Opposition to Title IX has relied on several arguments which undermine the efforts of the Office of Civil Rights, including due process, racial bias, freedom of speech, and class bias (Johnson, 2017). These arguments use coded language that center the needs of cisgender men. In other words, opponents of protections for vulnerable populations indicate these provisions violate due process and are prejudiced against cisgender (White) men. However, biases which privilege White men are tightly wound into the mechanics of higher education, impacting everything, from the ways we select students for enrollment, to the procedures we put into place when hiring faculty and staff (Easterly & Ricard, 2011). Those who seek to undermine advances in the field appear to do so in order to maintain systematized modes of oppression (Carter, 2021; Johnson, 2017).

As previously stated, implicit bias is difficult to identify, name, and correct (Turner, 2003; Whittaker et al., 2015). This is coupled with the fact that the climate on college campuses has become increasingly legalistic (King, 2012). The academy and the legal realm have observed increased attention being placed upon the legal nature of discipline proceedings, emphasizing dialogue surrounding students' due process rights—with a priority placed upon protecting cisgender male, White identities (Johnson, 2017). And while these procedures seemingly center a commitment to nurturing college student learning and development (King, 2012), considerations for identity disproportionately infringes upon the right to due process amongst minoritized populations (Carter, 2021).

Promising practices in conflict resolution and behavioral hearings at the collegiate level require hearing officers to demonstrate "basic competency" (Fischer & Maatman, 2008). Hearing officers should engage in formal and informal training that bolsters their understanding of cross-cultural challenges and listening skills, in addition to demonstrating sound judgment, reflection, and professional maturity (Fischer & Maatman, 2008). According to Bach (2003), procedural mechanisms should be established to safeguard the rights of individuals accused of conduct that disregards a campus code. Overall, proceedings should positively guide behavior (Bach, 2003).

During the Obama administration, the Office of Civil Rights determined Black students were being suspended at three times the rate of White students (Sanzi, 2019). These racialized disparities are directly informed by institutionalized environments, which influence Title IX procedure, conflict resolution, and conduct violation management (Smith et al., 2007). In order to assess the impact of bias in adjudication and Title IX proceedings, colleges and universities must examine the ways in which their environments are affected by federal, state, and regional policy; numerical representation; an institutionalized legacy of excluding minoritized communities; and biased behaviors observed in and outside of the classroom (Gurin et al., 2002)

APPLIED PRACTICE: CASE STUDY ANALYSIS

Applied learning provides individuals with opportunities to inculcate new information that allows them to recall and operationalize what was learned. The use of narrative-based scenarios to conceptualize theory is a common apparatus exercised to explicate promising practices within daily operations and functions. Case studies offer rich qualitative information and insightful approaches to exploring future considerations for research and praxis (McLeod, 2019). The following section examines two potential situations involving conduct hearings and Title IX proceedings that provide readers with the opportunity to identify how bias can emerge in procedures, in addition to reflecting on the ways in which identity and institutionalized oppression interact with corrective systems embedded in higher education.

CASE STUDY 1

"I know he did it."

The following case was presented to a hearing panel comprised of faculty and staff.

Emily: Complainant
Jaquan: Respondent

Jaquan and Emily are juniors, live in neighboring suites, and are in the same a cappella group. In the course of the investigative report, they each described the other as a friend, and said that while they had crushes on each other at different points, nothing ever developed. The group had a sing-in party for their new members. The existing group would go to each residence hall and sing-in the new members. The existing members had a pregame before this started, at which both Emily and Jaquan were drinking beer. During the night, both drank from a whiskey bottle that was passed around the group. They then switched back to consuming beer at the after-party, which was in the basement common room of their residence hall. Emily remembers going upstairs with Jaquan, but nothing else until she woke up in her suite common room wearing the dress she had gone out in, though it was in disarray. From how she felt physically (soreness), she could tell she had sex. She woke up on her common room couch with Jaquan beside her. She woke him up and asked if they had sex. Jaquan answered, "No," and left.

After the hearing panel finished reading the investigative report the chair of the hearing panel said, "I know Jaquan wasn't telling the truth." The chair added, "I know he did it."

- Identify the issues raised in the scenario that should be considered. What are the problems/challenges/issues in this case?

- What (or how much) power does each stakeholder have in this case? Why do they have this power (or lack of power)? What kind of power do they possess?
- How might potential responses contribute to, or challenge, stakeholders' privileges and/or feelings of oppression?
- How do your own power, oppression, and privilege shape the way you perceive and potentially respond to this scenario?
- How might this case study relate to current issues you're facing on campus? How does institutional and/or societal context shape how you experienced your case?

CASE STUDY 2

"These two students are basically the same person."

Cynthia, a conduct officer at a large institution, hears two separate, unrelated cases of academic dishonesty on the same day. Case 1 involves a young man, Tony, who identifies as a first-generation Latine student during the proceedings. Tony states that while he admits to cheating, he believes his background should be taken into account. Had he not been ostracized by faculty and peers during the course of the semester, he would not have felt added pressure to cheat on his exam. Case 2 involves Chris, a student who the conduct officer presumes to identify as a first-generation, Latine woman. Chris never explicitly shares their identity. This student admits to an act of academic honesty, but provides no additional context outside of admitting responsibility. The conduct officer decides to suspend Tony, while providing Chris with a warning and supplemental education sanction.

In her notes, Cynthia writes:

> It was clear Chris was remorseful for her behavior and I appreciate that she quickly took responsibility for her actions. Tony was suspended because he refused to acknowledge any wrongdoing; instead, he used his identity as an excuse for cheating on his exam. These two students are basically the same person. They're both Hispanic, first-generation, low-income students with the same opportunities as anyone else at this institution. It is my hope that this process helps Tony to understand his role, how his actions have consequences, and the importance of taking responsibility for his behavior.

- Identify the issues raised in the scenario that should be considered. What are the problems/challenges/issues in this case?
- What (or how much) power does each stakeholder have in this case? Why do they have this power (or lack of power)? What kind of power do they possess?

- How might potential responses contribute to, or challenge, stakeholders' privilege and/or feelings about oppression?
- How do your own power, oppression, and privilege shape the way you perceive and potentially respond to this scenario?
- How might this case study relate to current issues you're facing on campus? How does institutional and/or societal context shape how you experienced your case?

DISCUSSION

For many among you reading this chapter, the incidents described within these case studies ring true to your lived experience as a student and educator. It is an unfortunate circumstance for biases rooted in racism, ableism, patriarchal notions of gender, and heteronormativity to crystallize the tenor of reporting, investigatory, and hearing processes on college campuses. Yet, as illustrated in the aforementioned cases, bias has been systematically institutionalized within the fabric of the academy, leading to identity-based stratifications that inordinately harm BIPOC folx, women, people with diverse abilities, and LGBTQI+ communities. Not only are minoritized populations more inclined to be abused or harassed, they are also more likely to be found responsible for conduct violations in comparison to their White, cisgender counterparts (Harris & Linder, 2017; Johnson, 2017).

Harris and Linder (2017) asserted that strategies aimed towards addressing sexual violence on college campuses lacked identity-specific approaches which take into account the ways identity and sexual violence interact with power, privilege, and systems of oppression. Additionally, situating sexual violence primarily within the context of alcohol use and/or "party culture" negates personal responsibility and often places culpability squarely on the shoulders of survivors (Harris & Linder, 2017). Case Study 1 was authored, not to perpetuate common typifications of rape culture on college campuses, but to call attention to the fact that sexual violence and harassment in the postsecondary is almost always situated as an issue emerging from the party scene—where alcohol is abundant—rather than an issue resulting from the behavior of harassers and rapists. It is within this frame that assumptions on guilt and culpability are displaced on the circumstances of violence and harassment, instead of the act itself. Further still, presumptions surrounding social identity are rooted in a sociohistorical backdrop entrenched in the criminalization of race (Davis, 1998), where accusations of sexual violence were used as vehicles for justifying the lynching of BIPOC folx.

Case Study 1 simultaneously draws upon racialized and gendered biases that often make their way into investigatory and hearing proceedings.

Presumptions about gender and race, coupled with one's lived experience, automatically shaped the way you interpreted the situation. You may have been additionally triggered by the chair's commentary. Suspended in this scenario were the ways in which alcohol and assault are frequently paired together in postsecondary discussions about sexual violence. Take this moment to reflect on the various layers that unfolded in this scenario. Intervention personnel will seldom have access to all of the facts, and must often make a determination based upon firsthand accounts and narratives. These professionals must be willing to face the challenge of withholding their personal interpretations from a situation, while also recognizing when threads of systemic oppression are fashioning the ways a case is being considered.

Equally, Case 2 is steeped in racialized inferences embedded within biased U.S. ideologies on class, meritocracy, trustworthiness, and responsibility. In addition to failing to differentiate both students due to their presumed racialized similarities, there was a leaning towards racialized assumptions that led the conduct officer to believe it was appropriate to make an example out of one student in direct contrast to another student. Brown folx have been stereotyped in the United States in a manner that is sharply tied to deviance and labor (McNamara, 2020). For instance, politicized rhetoric on resource availability and citizenship has uniquely tied Brown folx to immigration, without consideration for the ways in which land was acquired/stolen or how immigration trends are not solely relegated to Brown communities (McNamara, 2020). Such narratives have set the stage for questioning whether Brown folx are trustworthy or deserving of opportunities such as an advanced education.

It is for these reasons that professional development, sustained dialogue, and continued reflexivity are vital to upending discriminatory practices in conduct hearings and Title IX proceedings on college campuses. Gaining insight into contemporary issues, while also learning how to analyze internalized discourses, better prepares intervention personnel to suspend their judgments and contextualize information made available to them, with a layered understanding for how national phenomena and institution-specific data coalesce. Continued reflexivity, practiced within the capacity of a group discussion, during one-on-ones, or in therapeutic settings, allows for individuals to explore how their standpoint is situated in proximity to power and privilege. Those responsible for documenting reports, investigating cases, and delivering hearing proceedings are encouraged to bracket their lived experiences by explicitly naming their positionality in the margins of a case. In moments where a conflict of interest arises as a result of their inability to evaluate material proof outside of themselves, it is promising practice for them to recuse themselves and request an alternate to advance the proceedings.

RECOMMENDATIONS

Awareness and skill-building among intervention personnel is at the core of eliminating bias from conduct hearings and Title IX proceedings. From student-staff who record narratives and offer peer-based support, to the administrative professionals who are charged with leading hearing procedures, building upon one's capacity to extricate bias disproportionately influencing cases involving BIPOC folx will decrease discriminatory proceedings and sanctioning on college campuses.

It is therefore essential for universities to create spaces for faculty, staff, and student-staff to further enhance their intercultural skills and understandings of systematic oppression. First, in collaboration with the executive financial and human resources officers, institutional leadership must finance restorative professional development to units providing oversight for student conduct, academic hearing boards and committees, residence life/residential education, campus safety, Title IX/EEO coordination, counseling, and where applicable, campus intervention teams. Such funding should support intervention personnel in their attempts to access conferences, workshops, courses, certification opportunities, and literature centering de-escalation tactics, restorative justice, and equity-minded approaches to documentation, investigation, and hearing procedures. Institutes and professional development opportunities such as *5 Days for Change* at the University of Illinois, Urbana-Champaign, the *Social Justice Training Institute*, or the *Restorative Justice* certification program can guide faculty and staff in learning how to embed reflexive praxis within intervention infrastructures.

Additionally, campus-based resources should be designed and implemented to further support the learning and development of intervention personnel. In consultation with the vice president for diversity, equity, and inclusion/belonging—as well as the teaching and learning center and intercultural center staff—unit leadership should oversee the creation and utilization of multitiered skill-building workshops. Further, institutions utilizing hearing boards should integrate bias workshops into orientation and training for board representatives. It would be most beneficial if these workshops were developed using different modalities, with self-paced/virtual and face-to-face options, offered throughout the course of the academic year. Connecting workshop completion to a certificate or badge could further incentivize completion in situations where training must remain optional.

Another offering that unit leaders should generate involves policy and procedure development. With regard to interviews/investigations and hearings, it is incumbent upon university leadership to require the implementation of covert and overt bias avoidance protocols. In addition to following an adjudication guide, panelists and conduct officials should be required to follow an accountability protocol. Complainants and respondents must be apprised on a clear delineation of investigatory and hearing proceedings prior to the implementation of follow-up conversations and investigations. Resources for reporting discriminatory behavior, which may occur throughout the process, should be made available prior to the implementation of investigatory proceedings, and again alongside the appeals process. Policies and procedures must explicitly include parity for underserved populations, including trans and gender nonconforming folx, BIPOC folx, and folx with diverse abilities. For instance, accountability procedures should be authorized for individuals and entities demonstrating reporting bias, particularly if data emerges on a particular individual's or entity's discriminatory reporting behaviors. Finally, a system for review and accountability must be created to ensure that units leading investigatory and hearing proceedings do not work independent of the expectation for restorative, equitable, and transparent processes.

It is necessary for unit leadership to also delve into discussions which lead towards a shared understanding of due process—such that the standard is proactive in working against implicit and explicit bias. Participants of these conversations should seek to create shared understandings of due process that are proactive in working against implicit and explicit bias. Moreover, collaborating with regional or conference-level institutions could result in the development of holistic promising practices that adequately suit the needs of the university's diverse constituency.

Assessment, evaluation, and reflexivity close the loop—while also galvanizing the start of a new cord—where consistent follow-up throughout the year allows for intervention personnel and unit leadership to review and respond to findings emergent from reports, investigations, hearing conclusions, and sanctions. Unit leadership should support student conduct, academic hearing boards and committees, residence life/residential education, campus safety, Title IX/EEO coordination, counseling, and campus intervention teams in creating spaces that allow for adequate reflection, with intentionality placed on campus trends, caseload statistics, and caseload outcomes. Such spaces could exist within staff meetings, monthly collaborator meetings, DEIJB campus analysis discussions or committee meetings, and/or senior leadership meetings. Such data should be layered with campus demographic statistics and, when possible, narratives from individuals who report encounters with biased behavior. Units are encouraged to complete annual evaluations of conduct and bias reports, disaggregating demographic data to ensure minoritized communities are not disproportionately represented in conduct cases, or disproportionately impacted by assault and harassment incidents. Units requiring additional support in administering culturally significant evaluation and assessment efforts are encouraged to consult with entities such as the Center for Culturally Responsive Evaluation and Assessment and the National Institute for Learning Outcomes Assessment and Research.

Expansive literature on holistic evaluation and assessment is also available, including *Reframing Assessment to Center Equity* (Henning et al., 2022) and *You are a Data Person* (Parnell, 2021).

In total, it is imperative for intervention personnel to understand the impact and continued influence sociohistorical contexts have on institutional climates. Practitioners, faculty, and student-staff must also apply this understanding in the development of policies that shape conflict management interventions, investigations, adjudication, Title IX hearings, and sanctioning. Knowing that BIPOC and LGBTQI+ constituencies are uniquely vulnerable to bias and discrimination when they encounter conflict management procedures—and failing to reconcile systematic shortcomings—is akin to malpractice. Colleges and universities must move beyond the simple acknowledgement of an increasingly diverse student body. The repercussions and tangential harm biased practice and procedures can cause—particularly as it relates to harassment, violence, and the replication of criminal justice proceedings that criminalize minoritized identities—are antithetical to the cultivation of a safe, inclusive learning environment. Embedding justice for minoritized communities in campus adjudication and Title IX proceedings will contribute towards achieving institutional inclusive excellence goals.

APPENDIX A
Guided Administrative Meeting and Hearing Protocols

ADMINISTRATIVE MEETING

Introduction

1. Welcome respondent and provide them your name and title. Encourage respondent to introduce themselves for ensured validity. Provide respondent with your personal philosophy statement, followed by the purposes for the administrative meeting.

According to Ramsdell (2017), a personal philosophy statement can be situated as follows:

> I believe it is important to understand how one shows up in different environments and spaces they occupy. The FISH! philosophy has been instrumental in my own understanding. This is all about choosing your attitude, playing, being present, and making another person's day. I value and focus on social justice and inclusion immensely due to the ever-changing demographic of today's college student. My experience with social justice training and awareness of privilege, power, and difference has enabled me to better understand myself and others. I hope to create an inclusive environment for all my students and colleagues so that they are able to develop and grow as much as possible. As a whole, my goal is to be able to provide ample resources and support to facilitate personal and professional growth for a student. In practice, it is our job to assist students to meet their needs and see the learning and development that transpires throughout their time at the institution. (Ali Raza)

Guidelines and Notification Protocols

2. Rather than framing the conversation as a punitive manner, utilize a holistic developmental approach to creating a climate of openness and exploration (Schrage, J. M., & Giacomini, 2009). This framing aids in the suspension of judgment and creates opportunities for reciprocal dialogue.
3. Prior to the start of your discussion, provide guidelines for narrative sharing and data collection. Be transparent in how the respondent's narrative will be analyzed and prospectively utilized.
4. In instances where notification has yet to be provided, offer the respondent written documentation of the proposed codes which are

not in compliance; this portion of the process also includes providing the respondent with details citing behavior which was deemed to be noncompliant.

Dialogue

5. Consider context. Utilizing a collaborative data approach (Data Science for Social Impact, 2022), ensure you assess the documentation in alignment with the respondent's recollection of the recorded incident. Be mindful of the source of the report, as well as the institution's tradition in implementing a culturally significant approach to conflict resolution.
6. Engage in reflexivity. Consider the following prompts as you make meaning of the incident report, corresponding interviews, and your discussion with the respondent:
    a. Identify the issues raised in the incident.
        i. Acknowledge gaps in the report and narrative.
        ii. Recognize and assess factors in the learning environment which contribute to shared understanding and meaning making, or a lack thereof.
            1. Is there a reliance on a common vocabulary or experience?
            2. What are the unwritten expectations (hidden curriculum)?
    b. What are the problems/challenges/issues in this incident?
    c. What (or how much) power does each stakeholder have in this incident?
    d. Why do they have this power (or lack of power)? What kind of power do they possess?
    e. How might potential responses contribute to, or challenge, stakeholders' privilege and/or feelings about oppression?
    f. How do your own power, oppression, and privilege shape the way you perceive and are potentially responding to this issue?
        i. In what ways are you bracketing your personal experiences and professional lens (Ahern, 1999)?
    g. How might this incident relate to current issues emerging across campus? How does institutional and/or societal context shape how stakeholders are experiencing this incident?
7. Within the purview of the law and Title IX guidance, points one through six are also applicable to Title IX interviews.

Case Processing

8. Should you find that the case will advance to a hearing*, ensure the respondent has access to the following items:
    a. A full review and understanding of the incident report and supporting documentation;
    b. A full understanding of prospective outcomes in relation to the proposed instances of code noncompliance;
    c. An understanding on the ways they might gather evidence and supporting materials to share during the hearing process;
    d. Access to a professional advocate;
    e. Information to direct emergent questions upon conclusion of the administrative meeting;
    f. Information to direct emergent questions upon conclusion of the conduct meeting;
    g. Institutional appeal protocols.

9. In documenting the conversation and your assessment on next steps, refrain from centering personal judgments on the incident. While all mechanisms for assessment and analysis are embedded with subjectivity, refrain from utilizing language that would lessen opportunities for objectivity in final decision-making processes.

CONDUCT HEARING

Hearing Board Preparation

1. Reiterate the importance of (1) bracketing opinions that are not grounded in the facts of the case, (2) utilizing a holistic developmental approach in creating a space for inquiry, and (3) following the guidance of the accountability protocol to achieve objectivity to the best of their ability.
    a. Examples of bracketing can include knee-jerk reactions to someone's appearance or narrative, assumptions drawn from a person's tone of voice or facial expressions, and/or identifying themes or topics that feel relatable because these themes reflect the lived experiences of a hearing body member.

Introduction

2. Welcome respondent. Each member of the hearing body should provide their name and title. Encourage respondent to introduce

themselves. Provide respondent with the body's philosophy and vision statement, followed by the purposes for the conduct hearing.

An example of such can be found at the University of Nevada-Las Vegas:

> The aim of education is the intellectual, personal, social, and ethical development of the individual. The educational process is ideally conducted in an environment that encourages reasoned discourse, intellectual honesty, openness to constructive change, and respect for the rights of all individuals. Self-discipline and a respect for the rights of others in the university community are necessary for the fulfillment of such goals.
>
> The UNLV Student Conduct Code is designed to promote this environment and sets forth standards of conduct expected of students who choose to join the university community. Students who violate these standards will be subject to conduct sanctions in order to promote their own personal development, to protect the university community, and to maintain order and stability on campus.
>
> As citizens of the larger community in which UNLV is located, students have all the responsibilities and rights that are incumbent upon any citizen. The University is concerned with what happens to students both on and off its campuses and holds students responsible for their own actions. (UNLV, 2023)

Guidelines and Hearing Standards

3. Review the primary targets of the session, emphasizing the expected tone and climate of the space. Reiterate the importance in creating opportunities for respectful dialogue grounded in a pluralistic learning environment.
4. Prior to the start of your discussion, provide guidelines for narrative sharing and data collection. Be transparent in how the respondent's narrative will be analyzed and prospectively utilized.
5. Review documentation of the proposed codes which were deemed noncompliant. Cite specific behaviors.
   a. Citation of behavior must be void of inferences and assumptions. For instance, a board chair may note, "[Respondent] was observed stumbling as they walked down the hall. The odor of alcohol was present and [the respondent] slurred their words when approached." If the reporter documented assumption-based details like, "I thought [respondent] was drunk", they should be omitted from discussion prior to board review, and prior to the hearing process.

Hearing Procedure

6. Consider context. Utilizing a collaborative data approach (Data Science for Social Impact, 2022), ensure board members assess the documentation in alignment with the respondent's recollection of the recorded incident. Maintain the integrity of these discussions with other stakeholders, should their participation apply. Again, the board should be mindful of the institution's tradition in implementing a culturally significant approach to conflict resolution (or lack thereof).
    a. Regarding Title IX hearing procedures, claimants should be offered full autonomy in the ways they are included in proceedings. Their involvement should be framed around their level of comfort and preference. In some instances, for example, a claimant may choose to share their narrative in the same space as the respondent, but while seated behind a screen.

7. Engage in reflexivity. Board members should consider the following prompts as they make meaning of the incident report, corresponding interviews, and their discussion with the respondent (and other stakeholders, as appropriate):
    a. Identify the issues raised in the incident.
        i. Acknowledge gaps in the report and narrative.
        ii. Recognize and assess factors in the learning environment which contribute to shared understanding and meaning making, or a lack thereof.
            1. Is there a reliance on a common vocabulary or experience?
            2. What are the unwritten expectations (hidden curriculum)?
    b. What are the problems/challenges/issues in this incident?
    c. What (or how much) power does each stakeholder have in this incident?
    d. Why do they have this power (or lack of power)? What kind of power do they possess?
    e. How might potential responses contribute to, or challenge, stakeholders' privilege and/or feelings about oppression?
    f. How do your own power, oppression, and privilege shape the way you perceive and are potentially responding to this issue?
        i. In what ways are you bracketing your personal experiences and professional lens (Ahern, 1999)?
    g. How might this incident relate to current issues emerging across campus? How does institutional and/or societal context shape how stakeholders are experiencing this incident?

8. In the manner of all conduct and Title IX hearings within postsecondary contexts, it is essential for board members to understand that their determinations are administrative, not legal. Final outcomes are made based upon a preponderance of data, not reasonable doubt.

Case Processing

9. Should the board find the respondent responsible, ensure the respondent has access to the following items:
    a. A full understanding of the outcome(s) in relation to the determined instances of code noncompliance;
    b. Information to direct emergent questions upon conclusion of the hearing;
    c. Institutional appeal protocols.
10. In documenting the final determination and established outcomes, refrain from centering personal judgments on the incident. While all mechanisms for assessment and analysis are embedded with subjectivity, refrain from utilizing language that embed bias in final reports.

* When possible, mediation or progression through Restorative Justice** conferencing is recommended.
** Refer to Zehr Institute webinar.

Ahern, K. J. (1999). Ten tips for reflexive bracketing. *Qualitative Health Research, 9*(3), 407–411. doi:10.1177/104973239900900309

Estrada, J. & Crane, G. (2021, July 27). *A more compassionate philosophy on student behavior.* Retrieved October 28, 2022 from https://www.ascd.org/blogs/a-more-compassionate-philosophy-on-student-behavior

Data Science for Social Impact (2022, April 6). *Data-informed, equity-driven: Cultivating a collaborative data culture.* Retrieved October 28, 2022 from https://socialpolicyinstitute.wustl.edu/data-informed-equity-driven/

Ramsdell, D. (2017, October 31). Defining your student affairs professional philosophy. *Modern Campus.* Retrieved October 28, 2022 from https://sapro.moderncampus.com/blog/defining-your-student-affairs-professional-philosophy

Schrage, J. M., & Giacomini, N. G. (Eds.). (2009). *Reframing campus conflict: Student conduct practice through a social justice lens.* Stylus.

UNLV. (2023). *Student conduct & hearing board philosophy.* Retrieved May 19, 2023 from https://www.unlv.edu/studentconduct/hearing-board

Zehr Institute for Restorative Justice (2020, November 21). *Liberating restorative justice from co-optation within colleges and universities.* Retrieved October 28, 2022 from https://www.youtube.com/watch?v=vKCei3IwNlU

APPENDIX B
Sample Accountability Protocol

Evaluator Name: _____

Case Number: _____

Date: _____

It is encouraged to utilize the following rubric while engaging in investigatory and hearing-based procedures. This accountability protocol is meant to be a tool implemented by intervention specialists to guide self-assessment and reflection while facilitating administrative discussions and hearings. Employ the "evidence" column to outline rationale for the ranking of each factor.

Note: A listing of reflexivity prompts is available in Appendix A.

Ahern, K. J. (1999). Ten tips for reflexive bracketing. *Qualitative Health Research*, 9(3), 407–411. doi:10.1177/104973239900900309

Factor	1 - Emerging	2 - Developing	3 - Proficient	4 - Exceeding	Evidence
Understanding of Policy and Procedure ☐	Exhibits limited comprehension of policies and procedures guiding the exploration of this specific case.	Has partial understanding of the policies and procedures guiding the exploration of this specific case.	Demonstrates a basic understanding of the policies and procedures guiding the exploration of this specific case.	Full demonstration of ability to comprehend policies and procedures guiding the exploration of this specific case.	
Accountable to Validation Process ☐	Exhibits a latent comprehension of the context situated in participant narratives; is unable to draw connectivity between statements.	Has partial understanding of participant narratives; rarely encourages participants to offer tangible examples to support their narratives.	Has substantial understanding of context situated in participant narratives; inconsistently asks participants to provide supportive examples.	Verifies full understanding of narratives; consistently asks participants to offer tangible examples to support their narratives.	
Use of Reflexivity ☐	Has engaged in a cursory survey of reflexivity prompts; has yet to actively seek ways to circumvent implicit bias.	Has partial engagement with reflexivity prompts; has begun to process ways to circumvent implicit bias.	Has significantly engaged reflexivity prompts with honesty; has begun to outline ways to circumvent implicit bias.	Has fully engaged in reflexivity prompts with honesty; has actively sought ways to circumvent implicit bias (list examples).	
Use of Bracketing ☐	Has limited engagement with bracketing procedures. Has yet to examine the intersection of social location, personal impressions, and the details of the case.	Has partial engagement with bracketing procedures and has begun to connect these data with information emergent from reflexivity prompts.	Has significantly engaged in bracketing procedures; is still reflecting on the ways social location, personal impressions, and assumptions are being applied to this specific case.	In tandem with reflexivity procedures, has thoroughly documented how social location, personal impressions, and assumptions have been applied to this specific case.	

Total:

APPENDIX C
SELF-GUIDED PROFESSIONAL DEVELOPMENT SERIES

In supporting faculty and staff with their comprehension and development within the area of diversity, equity, inclusion, social justice, and belonging, it is necessary to conceptualize the learning process in two tiers: comprehension and application. The following self-guided plan outlines a series of modules situated first, to provide staff with foundational knowledge. The second installment affords faculty and staff with opportunities to apply what they have learned to their practice as postsecondary educators.

TABLE D.1 Self-Guided Plan

Tier 1: Comprehension	
Topic	**Accompanying Material**
Abolitionist Approaches to Citizenship and Sanctuary	• "Administrative Responsibility for Fostering Undocumented Students' Learning" (Barnhardt et al., 2013) • "Critical and Legal Consciousness Formation for Politicized Latinx Undocumented Youth Activists" (Muñoz, 2018) • "How DACA Recipients Navigate Barriers to Higher Education" (Macías, 2018) • "The Liability and Responsibility of Colleges and Universities for the Educational Attainment of DREAMers" (Nguyen, 2018)
Advancing Cultural Competence and Humility	• "An Application of the Cultural Formulation" (Tormala et al., 2018) • "Cultural Humility for People of Color: Critique of Current Theory and Practice" (Moon, 2019) • *Developing Cultural Humility Embracing Race, Privilege, and Power* (Gallardo, 2014). • "Cultural Humility in Education and Work: A Valuable Approach for Teachers, Learners, and Professionals" (Nomikoudis & Starr, 2016)
Considerations for Religious Pluralism in Higher Education Practice	• *Islamophobia in Higher Education: Combating Discrimination and Creating Understanding* (Ahmadi & Cole, 2020) • "Interrogating 'New Anti-Semitism'" (Klug, 2013) • "Spirituality, Religious Pluralism, and Higher Education Leadership Development" (Nash & Scott, 2009) • "Lesbian, Gay, and Bisexual Students Coming Out at the Intersection of Spirituality and Sexual Identity" (Payne Gold & Stewart, 2012) • *Making Meaning: Embracing Spirituality, Faith, Religion, and Life Purpose in Student Affairs* (Small, 2015) • *Remixed and Reimagined: Innovations in Religion, Spirituality, and (Inter)faith in Higher Education* (Snipes & Manson, 2020)
Critical Theory in Higher Education Practice	• "A CRT-Informed Model to Enhance Experiences and Outcomes of Racially Minoritized Students" (Powell et al., 2020) • *Rethinking College Student Development Theory Using Critical Frameworks* (Abes et al., 2019)

Topic	Accompanying Material
Critical Theory in Higher Education Practice (*continued*)	• *Black Feminist Thought: Knowledge, Consciousness, and the Politics of Empowerment* (Collins, 2000) • *Intersectionality* (Collins & Bilge, 2020) • "Critical Race and LatCrit Theory and Method" (Solorzano & Yosso, 2001) • "Critical Race Perspectives on Theory in Student Affairs" (Patton et al., 2007) • *Critical Race Theory in Education: All God's Children Got a Song* (Dixson & Rousseau, 2006) • "Introducing Veteran Critical Theory" (Phillips & Lincoln, 2017) • *Handbook of Critical Race Theory in Education* (Lynn & Dixson, 2013) • "Queer Theory" (Watson, 2005) • "Theorizing Asian America" (Yang, 2002)
Culturally Responsive Assessment and Evaluation	• "A Framework for Teaching Culturally Responsive Approaches to Evaluation" (Boyce & Chouinard, 2017) • "Culturally Responsive Evaluation as a Resource for Helpful-Help" (Symonette, 2014) • *Continuing the Journey to Reposition Culture and Cultural Context in Evaluation Theory and Practice* (Hood et al., 2014) • Jacobson, W. (2015). "Sharing Power and Privilege Through the Scholarly Practice of Assessment" (Jacobson, 2015)
Decolonizing Praxis and Thought in Higher Education	• "Coloniality and Modernity/Rationality" (Quijano, 2007) • *Journal of College Student Development:* Volume 61, Number 6, November–December 2020 • "Mapping Interpretations of Decolonization in the Context of Higher Education" (de Oliveira Andreottti et al., 2015) • *Dismantling Race in Higher Education: Racism, Whiteness and Decolonising the Academy* (Arday & Mirza, 2018) • *The Routledge Companion to Decolonization* (Rothermund, 2006) • "Decolonizing Gender and Education Research: Unsettling and Recasting Feminist Knowledges, Power, and Research Practices" (Manion, 2019) • "Desiring Diversity and Backlash: White Property Rights in Higher Education" (Patel, 2015)
Equity-Focused Leadership in Higher Education	• "A Grounded Theory of Academic Affairs and Student Affairs Partnerships for Diversity and Inclusion Aims" (LePeau, 2015) • "Leadership Practices and Diversity in Higher Education: Transitional and Transformational Frameworks" (Aguirre & Martinez, 2002) • "Privileged Social Identities and Diversity Leadership in Higher Education" (Owen, 2009) • *Culturally Responsive leadership in higher education: Promoting access, equity, and improvement* (Santamaría & Santamaría, 2016) • Burned Out or Burned Through? The Costs of Student Affairs Diversity Work (Anderson, 2021) • *Strategic Diversity Leadership: Activating Change and Transformation in Higher Education* (Williams, 2013)

Topic	Accompanying Material
Examining and Applying Anti-Racist Frameworks to Higher Educational Contexts	<ul><li>"A Framework for Advancing Anti-Racism Strategy on Campus" (NADOHE, 2021)</li><li>*How To Be an Antiracist* (Kendi, 2019)</li><li>*Be Antiracist: A Journal for Awareness, Reflection, and Action* (Kendi, 2020)</li><li>"Encouraging the Development of Racial Justice Allies" (Reason et al., 2005)</li><li>"The Nonperformativity of Antiracism" (Ahmed, 2006)</li><li>*Speaking Treason Fluently: Anti-Racist Reflections From an Angry White Male* (Wise, 2008)</li></ul>
Identity 101	<ul><li>"Navigating Guilt, Shame, and Fear of Appearing Racist: A Conceptual Model of Antiracist White Feminist Identity Development" (Linder, 2015).</li><li>*Why Aren't We There Yet? Taking Personal Responsibility for Creating an Inclusive Campus* (Arminio et al., 2012)</li><li>*Higher Education and First-Generation Students: Cultivating Community, Voice, and Place for the New Majority* (Jehangir, 2010)</li><li>*Trans' in College: Transgender Students' Strategies for Navigating Campus Life and the Institutional Politics of Inclusion* (Nicolazzo, 2017)</li><li>*Beyond the Asterisk: Understanding Native Students in Higher Education* (Shotton et al., 2013)</li><li>*Student Engagement in Higher Education: Theoretical Perspectives and Practical Approaches for Diverse Populations* (Quaye et al., 2019)</li></ul>
Intersections of Identity and Sexual Assault on College Campuses	<ul><li>"Constructing Identity: Campus Sexual Violence Activists' Perspectives on Race, Gender, and Social Justice" (Marine & Trebisacci, 2018)</li><li>"History of Sexual Violence in Higher Education" (Jessup-Anger et al., 2018)</li><li>*Intersections of Identity and Sexual Violence on Campus* (Linder & Harris, 2017)</li><li>"Resisting Erasure: Critical Influences for Men Who Survived Sexual Violence in Higher Education" (Tillapaugh, 2016)</li><li>"Heterosexist Discourses: How Feminist Theory Shaped Campus Sexual Violence Policy" (Wooten, 2016)</li></ul>
Perspectives on Social Justice in Higher Education	<ul><li>*Readings for Diversity and Social Justice*, 4th ed. (Adams et al., 2018)</li><li>"Ending White Innocence in Student Affairs and Higher Education" (Poon, 2018)</li><li>*Disability in Higher Education: A Social Justice Approach* (Evans et al., 2017)</li><li>*Pedagogy of the Oppressed* (Freire, 2000)</li><li>"Introduction to the Emergent Approaches to Diversity and Social Justice in Higher Education" (Patton et al., 2010)</li><li>"The Place of Social Justice in Higher Education and Social Change Discourses" (Singh, 2011)</li></ul>
Queer Perspectives on College Campuses: Identity, Power, and the Lived Experience	<ul><li>"A Retrospective of LGBT Issues on US College Campuses" (Rankin et al., 2019)</li><li>"Campus Microclimates for LGBT Faculty, Staff, and</li><li>"Students: An Exploration of the Intersections of Social Identity and Campus Roles" (Vaccaro, 2012)</li><li>"Exposing the Intersections in LGBQ+ Student of Color Belongingness" (Duran et al., 2022)</li><li>"The State of LGBT and Queer Research in Higher Education Revisited: Current Acadeic Houses and Future Possibilities" (Lange et al., 2019)</li><li>"Toward Intersectional Identity Perspectives on Disability and LGBTQ Identities in Higher Education" (Miller, 2018)</li></ul>

	Tier 2: Application
Topic	**Accompanying Material**
Actualizing Social Justice and Change in Higher Education	• *Teaching for Diversity and Social Justice, 3rd ed.* (Adams & Bell, 2016) • *Promoting Diversity and Social Justice: Educating People From Privileged Groups, 2nd ed.* (Goodman, 2011) • *Reframing Campus Conflict: Student Conduct Practice Through a Social Justice Lens* (Schrage & Giacomini, 2009) • *Multicultural Cmpetence in Student Affairs: Advancing Social Justice and Inclusion* (Pope et al., 2019) • "The Challenges and Triumphs in Addressing Students' Intersectional Identities for Black Culture Centers" (Harris & Patton, 2017) • *Designing Transformative Multicultural Initiatives: Theoretical Foundations, Practical Applications, and Facilitator Considerations* (Watt, 2015)
Facilitating and Navigating Intergroup Dialogue	• *Diversity, Equity, and Inclusion: Strategies for Facilitating Conversations on Race* (Hollins & Govan, 2015) • *The Art of Effective Facilitation: Reflections From Social Justice Educators* (Landreman, 2013) • *Facilitating Intergroup Dialogues: Bridging Differences, Catalyzing Change* (Maxwell et al., 2011) • *So You Want To Talk About Race* (Oluo, 2018) • *Intergroup Dialogue in Higher Education: Meaningful Learning About Social Justice* (Zúñiga et al., 2007)
Identity and Belonging within International Student Contexts	• "A Red Brick Wall: Anti-Immigrant Rhetoric in a Residence Hall Environment" (Duran, 2017) • *International Students and Global Mobility in Higher Education: National Trends and New Directions* (Bhandari & Blumenthal, 2011) • *Intercultural Competence in Higher Education: International Approaches, Assessment, and Application* (Deardorff & Arasaratnam-Smith, 2017) • "Different Is Not Deficient: Contradicting Stereotypes of Chinese International Students in US Higher Education" (Heng, 2018) • "Theoretical Models of Culture Shock and Adaptation in International Students in Higher Education" (Zhou et al., 2008)
Operationalizing Critical Theory in Higher Education Practice	• "A CRT-Informed Model to Enhance Experiences and Outcomes of Racially Minoritized Students" (Powell et al., 2021) • *Rethinking College Student Development Theory Using Critical Frameworks* (Abes et al., 2019) • *Intersectionality, 2nd ed.* (Collins & Bilge, 2020) • *Critical Race Theory in Education: All God's Children Got a Song, 2nd ed.* (Dixson et al., 2016) • *Handbook of Critical Race Theory in Education* (Lynn & Dixson, 2013)
Trauma-Informed Care and Techniques in Higher Education	• "Homelessness and Housing Insecurity in Higher Education: A Trauma-Informed Approach to Research, Policy, and Practice" (Hallett & Crutchfield, 2017) • "A Trauma-Informed Approach to Building College Students' Resilience" (Oehme et al., 2018) • "Recognizing COVID-19 as Trauma: Considerations for Student Affairs Educators and Faculty Developers" (Harder & McGowan, 2020) • "We Wear the Mask": Self-Definition as an Approach to Healing From Racial Battle Fatigue" (Okello et al., 2020)

Topic	Accompanying Material
Trauma-Informed Care and Techniques in Higher Education (*continued*)	• "Student Service Members/Veterans in Higher Education: A Systematic Review" (Barry et al., 2014) • "Practicing What We Teach: Trauma-Informed Educational Practice" (Carello & Butler, 2015) • "Trauma-Informed Practices for Postsecondary Education: A Guide" (Davidson, 2017)
Understanding Social Movements for Justice	• *Contested Issues in Troubled Times: Student Affairs Dialogues on Equity, Civility, and Safety* (Magolda et al., 2019) • "Critical Cultural Student Affairs Praxis and Participatory Action Research" (Poon et al., 2016) • *Campus Uprisings: How Student Activists and Collegiate Leaders Resist Racism and Create Hope* (Douglas et al., 2020) • "Learning From the Experiences of Self-Identified Women of Color Activists" (Linder & Rodriguez, 2012) • *Identity-Based Student Activism: Power and Oppression on College Campuses* (Linder et al., 2019) • *Student Activism, Politics, and Campus Climate in Higher Education* (Morgan & Davis, 2019) • *Identity, Social Activism, and the Pursuit of Higher Education* (Muñoz, 2015) • "Racial Battle Fatigue and Activist Burnout in Racial Justice Activists of Color at Predominately White Colleges and Universities" (Gorski, 2019) • Queer Activist Leadership: An Exploration of Queer Leadership in Higher Education (Pryor, 2021)

Additional Resources: 5 Days for Change (https://oiir.illinois.edu/programs/5-days-for-change); American Indian Higher Education Consortium (https://www.aihec.org); American Revolutionary (YouTube Movies & TV, 2014); American Studies Association, Critical Disability Studies Caucus (https://www.theasa.net/communities/caucuses/critical-disability-studies-caucus); Association for Asian American Studies (https://aaastudies.org); Association for the Study of African American Life & History (https://asalh.org); Critical Race Studies in Education Association (https://www.crsea.org); Hispanic Association of Colleges and Universities (https://www.hacu.net/hacu/default.asp); Latina/o Studies Association (https://latinxstudiesassociation.org); LGBTQ+ Ally Training (https://oiir.illinois.edu/lgbt-resource-center/our-programs/lgbt-ally-network); National Women's Studies Association (https://www.nwsa.org); Paper Tigers (KPJR FILMS LLC, n.d.); Racial Justice Allies and Advocates Training (n.d.); Red Nation Podcast (n.d.); Sisters of the Academy (https://sistersoftheacademy.org); Social Justice Training Institute (https://sjti.org); The Infiltrators (Oscopelabs, 2020); The National Conference on Race and Ethnicity (https://ncore.ou.edu/); Unlikely (https://www.youtube.com/watch?v=B5YASi5J4Kc); Whose Streets? (Magnolia Pictures & Magnet Releasing, 2017); Creating Change (https://www.thetaskforce.org/creatingchange/); Center for Culturally Responsive Evaluation and Assessment (https://crea.education.illinois.edu); National Center for Faculty Development and Diversity (https://www.facultydiversity.org)

REFERENCES

Abes, E. S., Jones, S. R., & Stewart, D.-L. (Eds.). (2019). *Rethinking college student development theory using critical frameworks*. Stylus.

Adams, M., & Bell, L. A. (2016). *Teaching for diversity and social justice* (3rd ed.). Routledge.

Adams, M., Blumenfeld, W. J., Chase, D., Catalano, J., DeJong, K. S., Hackman, H. W., Hopkins, L. E., Love, B. J., Peters, M. L., Shlasko, D., & Zúñiga, X. (2018). *Readings for diversity and social justice*. Routledge.

Aguirre, A., & Martinez, R. (2002). Leadership practices and diversity in higher education: Transitional and transformational frameworks. *Journal of Leadership Studies, 8*(3). https://doi.org/10.1177/107179190200800305

Ahmed, S. (2006). The nonperformativity of antiracism. *Meridians, 7*(1) 104–126. https://www.jstor.org/stable/40338719

Ahmadi, S., & Cole, D. (Ed.). (2020). *Islamophobia in higher education: Combating discrimination and creating understanding*. Stylus.

Anderson, R. K. (2021). Burned out or burned through? The costs of student affairs diversity work. *Journal of Student Affairs Research and Practice, 58*(4), 359–371. https://doi.org/10.1080/19496591.2020.1822853

Arday, J., & Mirza, H. S. (Eds.). (2018). *Dismantling Race in Higher Education: Racism, Whiteness and Decolonising the Academy*. Springer.

Arminio, J., Torres, V., & Pope, R. L. (Ed.). (2012). *Why aren't we there yet? Taking personal responsibility for creating an inclusive campus*. Stylus.

Bach, J. J. (2003). Students have rights, too: The drafting of student conduct codes. *BYU Education & Law Journal*, 1–36. https://digitalcommons.law.byu.edu/elj/vol2003/iss1/2

Barnhardt, C., Ramos, M., & Reyes, K. (2013). Equity and inclusion in practice: Administrative responsibility for fostering undocumented students' learning. *About Campus: Enriching the Student Learning Experience, 18*(2). https://doi.org/10.1002/abc.21112

Barry, A. E., Whiteman, S. D., & Wadsworth, S. M. (2014). Student service members/veterans in higher education: A systematic review. *Journal of Student Affairs Research and Practice, 51*(1), 30–42. https://doi.org/10.1515/jsarp-2014-0003

Bem, S. L. (1993). *The lenses of gender: Transforming the debate on sexual inequality*. Yale University Press.

Bhandari, R., & Blumenthal, P. (Eds.). (2011). *International students and global mobility in higher education: National trends and new directions*. Palgrave Macmillan.

Boyce, A. S., & Chouinard, J. A. (2017). Moving beyond the buzzword: A framework for teaching culturally responsive approaches to evaluation. *Canadian Journal of Program Evaluation, 32*(2). https://doi.org/10.3138/10.3138/cjpe.31132

Carello, J., & Butler, L. D. (2015). Practicing what we teach: Trauma-informed educational practice. *Journal of Teaching in Social Work, 35*(3), 262–278. https://doi.org/10.1080/08841233.2015.1030059

Carter, H. C. (2021). Under the guise of "due process": Sexual harassment and the impact of Trump's title IX regulations on women students of color. *Berkeley Journal of Gender, Law, and Justice, 36*, 180–210. https://doi.org/10.15779/Z38JM23G9Z

Collins, P. H. (2000). *Black feminist thought: Knowledge, consciousness, and the politics of empowerment*. Routledge.

Collins, P. H., & Bilge, S. (2020). *Intersectionality (Key Concepts)* (2nd ed). Polity.

Davidson, S. (2017). *Trauma-informed practices for postsecondary education: A guide*. Education Northwest.

Davis, A. Y. (1998). Race and criminalization: Black Americans and the punishment industry. In W. Lubiano (Ed.), *The house that race built: Original essays by Toni Morrison, Angela Y. Davis, Cornel West, and others on Black Americans and politics in America today* (pp. 264–279). Vintage Books.

Deardorff, D. K., & Arasaratnam-Smith, L. A. (2017). *Intercultural competence in higher education: International approaches, assessment and application*. Routledge.

De Oliveira Andreotti, V., Stein, S., Ahenakew, C., & Hunt, D. (2015). Mapping interpretations of decolonization in the context of higher education. *Decolonization: Indigeneity, Education & Society, 4*(1), 21–40.

Dixson, A. D., Rousseau Anderson, C. K., & Donor, J. K. (Eds.). (2017). *Critical race theory in education: All God's children got a song* (2nd ed.). Routledge.

Douglas, T. M. O., Shockley, K. G., & Toldson, I. (Eds.). (2020). *Campus uprisings: How student activists and collegiate leaders resist racism and create hope*. Teachers College Press.

Dutile, F. N. (2000). Students and due process in higher education: Of interests and procedures. *Florida Coastal Law Journal, 2,* 243–290. https://scholarship.law.nd.edu/law_faculty_scholarship/482

Duran, A. (2017). A red brick wall: Anti-immigrant rhetoric in a residence hall environment. *Journal of Cases in Educational Leadership, 20*(4). https://doi.org/10.1177/1555458917713038

Duran, A., Dahl, L. S., Prieto, K., Hooten, Z., & Mayhew, M. J. (2022). Exposing the intersections in LGBQ+ student of color belongingness: Disrupting hegemonic narratives sustained in college impact work. *Journal of Diversity in Higher Education, 15*(2), 153–166. https://doi.org/10.1037/dhe0000222

Easterly, D. M., & Ricard, C. S. (2011). Conscious efforts to end unconscious bias: Why women leave academic research. *Journal of Research Administration, 42*(1), 61–73. https://eric.ed.gov/?id=EJ955003

Eckes, S. (2021). Sex discrimination in schools: The law and its impact on school policies. *Laws, 10*(34), 1–15. https://doi.org/10.3390/laws10020034

Ekpe, L., & Toutant, S. (2022). Moving beyond performative allyship: A conceptual framework for anti-racist co-conspirators. In K. F. Johnson, N. M. Sparkman-Key, A. Meca, & S. Z. Tarver (Eds.), *Developing anti-racist practices in the helping professions: Inclusive theory, pedagogy, and application* (pp. 67–91). Palgrave Macmillan.

Evans, N. J., Broido, E. M., Brown, K. R., & Wilke, A. K. (2017). *Disability in higher education: A social justice approach*. Jossey-Bass.

Fischer, W., & Maatman, V. (2008). Temperament for practice: The effective student conduct practitioner. In J. M. Lancaster & D. M. Waryold (Eds.), *Student conduct practice: The complete guide for student affairs professionals* (pp. 14–30). Stylus.

Freire, P. (2000). *Pedagogy of the oppressed*. Bloomsbury.

Gallardo, M. E. (Ed.). (2014). *Developing cultural humility: Embracing race, privilege and power*. SAGE.

Geist Giacomini, N., & Meyer Schrage, J. (2009). Building community in the current campus climate. In J. Meyer Schrage & N. Geist Giacomini (Eds.), *Reframing campus conflict: Student conduct practice through a social justice lens* (pp. 7–21). Stylus.

Goodman, D. J. (2011). *Promoting diversity and social justice: Educating people from privileged groups* (2nd ed.). Routledge.

Gorski, P. C. (2019). Racial battle fatigue and activist burnout in racial justice activists of color at predominately White colleges and universities. *Race Ethnicity and Education, 22*(1). https://doi.org/10.1080/13613324.2018.1497966

Grayer, A., & Stracqualursi, V. (2020, May 6). *DeVos finalizes regulations that give more rights to those accused of sexual assault on college campuses.* CNN Politics. https://www.cnn.com/2020/05/06/politics/education-secretary-betsy-devos-title-ix-regulations/index.html

Gurin, P., Dey, E., Hurtado, S., & Gurin, G. (2002). Diversity and higher education: Theory and impact on educational outcomes. *Harvard Educational Review, 72*(3), 330–367. https://doi.org/10.17763/haer.72.3.01151786u134n051

Hallett, R. E., & Crutchfield, R. (2017). Homelessness and housing insecurity in higher education: A trauma-informed approach to research, policy, and practice. *ASHE Higher Education Report, 43*(6), 1–129.

Harder, W. L., & McGowan, B. L. (2020). Recognizing COVID-19 as trauma: Considerations for student affairs educators and faculty developers. *Developments, 17*(3). https://developments.myacpa.org/recognizing-covid-19-as-trauma-considerations-for-student-affairs-educators-and-faculty-developers/

Harris, J., & Linder, C. (2017). *Intersections of identity and sexual violence on campus: Centering minoritized students' experiences.* Stylus.

Harris, J. C., & Patton, L. D. (2017). The challenges and triumphs in addressing students' intersectional identities for Black culture centers. *Journal of Diversity in Higher Education, 10*(4), 334–349. https://doi.org/10.1037/dhe0000047

Heng, T. T. (2018). Different is not deficient: Contradicting stereotypes of Chinese international students in US higher education. *Studies in Higher Education, 43*(1), 22–36. https://doi.org/10.1080/03075079.2016.1152466

Henning, G. W., Baker, G. R., Jankowski, N. A., Lundquist, A. E., & Montenegro, E. (2022). *Reframing assessment to center equity: Theories, models, and practices.* Stylus.

Himbeault Taylor, S., & Thomas Varner, D. (2009). When student learning and law merge to create educational student conflict resolution and effective conduct management programs. In J. Meyer Schrage & N. Geist Giacomini (Eds.), *Reframing campus conflict: Student conduct practice through a social justice lens* (pp. 22–49). Stylus.

Hollins, C., & Govan, I. (2015). *Diversity, equity, and inclusion: Strategies for facilitating conversations on race.* Rowman & Littlefield.

Hood, S., Hopson, R., & Frierson, H. (Eds.). (2015). *Continuing the journey to reposition culture and cultural context in evaluation theory and practice.* Information Age Publishing.

Jacobson, W. (2015). Sharing power and privilege through the scholarly practice of assessment. In S. K. Watt (Ed.), *Designing transformative multicultural initiatives* (pp. 89–102). Stylus.

Jehangir, R. (2010). *Higher education and first-generation students: Cultivating community, voice, and place for the new majority.* Palgrave Macmillan.

Jessup-Anger, J., Lopez, E., & Koss, M. P. (2018). History of sexual violence in higher education. *New Directions for Student Services: Special Issue: Addressing Sexual Violence in Higher Education and Student Affairs, 161*, 9–19. https://doi.org/10.1002/ss.20249

Johnson, A. M. (2017). Title ix narratives, intersectionality, and male-biased conceptions of racism. *Georgetown Journal of Law & Modern Critical Race Perspectives, 9*(1), 57–76. https://www.academia.edu/32570606/Title_IX_Narratives_Intersectionality_and_Male-Biased_Conceptions_of_Racism

Kendi, I. X. (2019). *How to be an antiracist*. One World.

Kendi, I. X. (2020). *Be antiracist: A journal for awareness, reflections, and action*. One World.

King, R. H. (2012). Student conduct administration: How students perceive the educational value and procedural fairness of their disciplinary experiences. *Journal of College Student Development, 53*(4), 563–580. https://eric.ed.gov/?id=EJ984815

Klug, B. (2013). Interrogating 'new anti-semitism.' *Ethnic and Racial Studies, 36*(3), 468–482. https://doi.org/10.1080/01419870.2013.734385

KPJR FILMS LLC. (n.d.). Paper Tigers trailer—KPJR Films [Vimeo video]. https://vimeo.com/110821029

Landreman, L. M. (Ed.). (2013). *The art of effective facilitation: Reflections from social justice educators*. Stylus.

Lange, A. C., Duran, A., & Jackson, R. (2019). The State of LGBT and queer research in higher education revisited: Current academic houses and future possibilities. *Journal of College Student Development, 60*(5), 511–526.

LePeau, L. (2015). A grounded theory of academic affairs and student affairs partnerships for diversity and inclusion aims. *Review of Higher Education: Journal of the Association for the Study of Higher Education, 39*(1), 97–122. https://doi.org/10.1353/rhe.2015.0044

Linder, C. (2015). Navigating guilt, shame, and fear of appearing racist: A conceptual model of antiracist White feminist identity development. *Journal of College Student Development, 56*(6), 535–550. https://doi.org/10.1353/csd.2015.0057

Linder, C., & Harris, J. C. (Eds.). (2017). *Intersections of identity and sexual violence on campus: Centering minoritized students' experiences*. Stylus.

Linder, C., Quaye, S. J., Lange, A. C., Evans, M. E., & Stewart, T. J. (2019). *Identity-based student activism: Power and oppression on college campuses*. Routledge.

Linder, C., & Rodriguez, K. L. (2012). Learning from the experiences of self-identified women of color activists. *Journal of College Student Development, 53*(3), 383–398. https://doi.org/10.1353/csd.2012.0048

Lynn, M., & Dixson, A. D. (2013). *Handbook of critical race theory in education* (1st ed.). Routledge.

Macías, L. F. (2018). The scheme game: How DACA recipients navigate barriers to higher education. *Educational Studies, 54*(6), 609–628. https://doi.org/10.1080/00131946.2018.1530236

Magnolia Pictures & Magnet Releasing. (2017, August 4). *Whose streets? – Official trailer* [YouTube video]. https://www.youtube.com/watch?v=upiJnjJScrw

Magolda, P. M., Baxter Magolda, M. B., & Carducci, R. (Eds.). (2019). *Contested issues in troubled times: Student affairs dialogues on equity, civility, and safety*. Stylus.

Manion, C., & Shah, P. (2019). Decolonizing gender and education research: Unsettling and recasting feminist knowledges, power, and research practices. *Gender and Education, 31*(4), 445–451. https://doi.org/10.1080/09540253.2019.1596392

Marine, S. B., & Trebisacci, A. (2018). Constructing identity: Campus sexual violence activists' perspectives on race, gender, and social justice. *Journal of College Student Development, 59*(6), 649–665. https://doi.org/10.1353/csd.2018.0063

Maxwell, K. E., Nagda, B. A., & Thompson, M. C. (Eds.). (2011). *Facilitating intergroup dialogues: Bridging differences, catalyzing change.* Stylus.

McLeod, S. (2019). Case study method. *Simply Psychology.* Retrieved January 5, 2021 from https://www.simplypsychology.org/case-study.html#:~:text=Strengths%20of%20Case%20Studies&text=Provides%20detailed%20(rich%20qualitative)%20information,impractical%20(or%20unethical)%20situations

McNamara, R. H. (2020). *The criminalization of immigration: Truth, lies, tragedy, and consequences.* ABC-CLIO.

Miller, R. A. (2018). Toward intersectional identity perspectives on disability and LGBTQ identities in higher education. *Journal of College Student Development, 59*(3), 327–346. https://doi.org/10.1353/csd.2018.0030

Moon, S. H., & Sandage, S. J. (2019). Cultural humility for people of color: Critique of current theory and practice. *Journal of Psychology and Theology, 47*(2). https://doi.org/10.1177/0091647119842407

Morgan, D. L., & Davis, C. H. F. (2019). *Student activism, politics, and campus climate in higher education.* Routledge.

Muñoz, S. M. (2015). *Identity, social activism, and the pursuit of higher education.* Peter Lang.

Muñoz, S. M. (2018). Unpacking legality through *la facultad* and cultural citizenship: Critical and legal consciousness formation for politicized Latinx undocumented youth activists. *Equity & Excellence in Education, 51*(1), 78–91. https://doi.org/10.1080/10665684.2018.1441762

NADOHE (2021). *A framework for advancing anti-racism strategy on campus.* https://www.nadohe.org/statements/antiracism-framework

Nash, R. J., & Scott, L. (2009). Spirituality, religious pluralism, and higher education leadership development. In A. Kezar (Ed.), *Rethinking leadership in a complex, multicultural, and global environment: New concepts and models for higher education* (pp. 131–150). Stylus.

Nicolazzo, Z. (2017). *Trans* in college: Transgender students' strategies for navigating campus life and the institutional politics of inclusion.* Stylus.

Nguyen, D. H. K. (2018). #ICEOffOurCampus: The liability and responsibility of colleges and universities for the educational attainment of DREAMers Symposium 2017: Education reform at the intersection of law, politics, and policy. *Belmont Law Review,* 151–182. https://hdl.handle.net/1805/20768

Nomikoudis, M., & Starr, M. (2016). Cultural humility in education and work: A valuable approach for teachers, learners and professionals. In J. Arvanitakis & D. J. Hornsby (Eds.), *Universities, the Citizen Scholar and the Future of Higher Education* (pp. 69–84). Palgrave Macmillan.

Oehme, K., Perko, A., Clark, J., Ray, E. C., Arpan, L., & Bradley, L. (2018). A trauma-informed approach to building college students' resilience. *Journal of*

Evidence-Based Social Work, 16(1), 93–107. https://doi.org/10.1080/23761407.2018.1533503

Okello, W. K., Quaye, S. J., Allen, C., Carter, K. D., & Narikari, S. N. (2020). "We wear the mask": Self-definition as an approach to healing from racial battle fatigue. *Journal of College Student Development, 61*(4), 422–438. https://doi.org/10.1353/csd.2020.0049

Oluo, I. (2018). *So you want to talk about race*. Seal Press.

Oscopelabs. (2020, March 4). *The infiltrators – Official trailer – Oscilloscope laboratories HD* [YouTube video]. https://www.youtube.com/watch?v=jvSuyItYudk

Owen, D. S. (2009). Privileged social identities and diversity leadership in higher education. *Review of Higher Education: Journal of the Association for the Study of Higher Education, 32*(2), 185–207. https://doi.org/10.1353/rhe.0.0048

Parnell, A. (2021). *You are a data person: Strategies for using analytics on campus*. Stylus.

Patel, L. (2015). Desiring diversity and backlash: White property rights in higher education. *The Urban Review, 47*, 657–675. https://doi.org/10.1007/s11256-015-0328-7

Patton, L. D., McEwen, M., Rendón, L., & Howard-Hamilton, M. F. (2007). Critical race perspectives on theory in student affairs. In S. R. Harper & L. D. Patton (Eds.), *New Directions for Student Services* (pp. 39–53). https://doi.org/10.1002/ss.256

Patton, L. D., Shahjahan, R. A., & Osei-Kofi, N. (2010). Introduction to the emergent approaches to diversity and social justice in higher education special issue. *Equity & Excellence in Education, 43*(3), 265–278.

Payne Gold, S., & Stewart, D. L. (2012). Lesbian, gay, and bisexual students coming out at the intersection of spirituality and sexual identity. *Journal of LGBTQ Issues in Counseling, 5*(3–4), 237–258. https://doi.org/10.1080/15538605.2011.633052

Phillips, G. A., & Lincoln, Y. S. (2017). Introducing veteran critical theory. *International Journal of Qualitative Studies in Education, 30*(7), 656–668). https://doi.org/10.1080/09518398.2017.1309586

Poon, O. A. (2018). Ending White innocence in student affairs and higher education. *Journal of Student Affairs, 27*, 13–23. https://sahe.colostate.edu/wpcontent/uploads/sites/10/2018/03/SAHE-Journal-2018.pdf

Poon, O. A., Squire, D. D., Cheung Hom, D., Gin, K., Segoshi, M. S., & Parayno, A. (2016). Critical cultural student affairs praxis and participatory action research. *Journal of Critical Scholarship on Higher Education and Student Affairs, 3*(1), Article 2. https://ecommons.luc.edu/jcshesa/vol3/iss1/2

Pope, R. L., Reynolds, A. L., & Mueller, J. A. (2019). *Multicultural competence in student affairs: Advancing social justice and inclusion*. Jossey-Bass.

Posselt, J., Venegas, K., Ward, J. D., Hernandez, T., & DePaola, T. (2017). *Emerging issues in federal higher education law: A brief guide for administrators and faculty*. Pullias Center for Higher Education, University of Southern California. https://files.eric.ed.gov/fulltext/ED594839.pdf

Powell, C., Demetriou, C., Morton, T. R., & Ellis, J. M. (2021). A CRT-informed model to enhance experiences and outcomes of racially minoritized students. *Journal of Student Affairs Research and Practice, 58*(3), 241–253. https://doi.org/10.1080/19496591.2020.1724546

Pryor, J. T. (2021). Queer activist leadership: An exploration of queer leadership in higher education. *Journal of Diversity in Higher Education, 14*(3), 303–315. https://doi.org/10.1037/dhe0000160

Quaye, S. J., Harper, S. R., & Pendakus, S. L. (Eds.). (2019). *Student engagement in higher education: Theoretical perspectives and practical approaches for diverse populations.* Routledge.

Quijano, A. (2007). Coloniality and modernity/rationality. *Cultural Studies, 21*(2–3), 168–178. https://doi.org/10.1080/09502380601164353

Racial Justice Allies and Advocates Training. (n.d.). *Student affairs at Illinois.* https://oiir.illinois.edu/diversityed/racial-justice-allies-advocates-training

Rankin, S., Garvey, J. C., & Duran, A. (2019). A retrospective of LGBT issues on US college campuses: 1990–2020. *International Sociology, 34*(4). https://doi.org/10.1177/0268580919851429

Reason, R. D., Scales, T. C., & Roosa Millar, E. A. (2005). Encouraging the development of racial justice allies. In R. D. Reason, E. M. Broido, T. L. Davis, & N. J. Evans (Eds.), *Developing social justice allies* (pp. 55–66). Wiley.

Rothermund, D. (2006). *The Routledge companion to decolonization* (1st ed.). Routledge.

Santamaría, L. J., & Santamaría, A. P. (2016). *Culturally responsive leadership in higher education: Promoting access, equity, and improvement.* Routledge.

Sanzi, E. (2019, January 21). *Black Men, title ix, and the disparate impact of discipline policies.* Real Clear Education. https://www.realcleareducation.com/articles/2019/01/21/black_men_title_nine_and_the_disparate_impact_of_discipline_policies_110308.html

Schrage, J. M., & Giacomini, N. G. (Eds.). (2009). *Reframing campus conflict: Student conduct practice through a social justice lens.* Stylus.

Shotton, H. J., Lowe, S. C., & Waterman, S. J. (Eds.). (2013). *Beyond the asterisk: Understanding Native students in higher education.* Stylus.

Singh, M. (2011). The place of social justice in higher education and social change discourses. *Compare: A Journal of Comparative and International Education, 41*(4), 481–494. https://doi.org/10.1080/03057925.2011.581515

Small, J. L. (Ed.). (2015). *Making meaning: Embracing spirituality, faith, religion, and life purpose in student affairs.* Stylus.

Smith, W. A., Allen, W. R., & Danley, L. L. (2007). "Assume the position... You fit the description": Psychosocial experiences and racial battle fatigue among African American male college students. *American Behavioral Scientist, 51*(4), 551–578. https://doi.org/10.1177/0002764207307742

Snipes, J. T., & Manson, S. (2020). *Remixed and reimagined: Innovations in religion, spirituality, and (inter)faith in higher education.* Myers Education Press.

Solorzano, D. G., & Yosso, T. J. (2001). Critical race and LatCrit theory and method: Counter-storytelling. *International Journal of Qualitative Studies in Education, 14*(4), 471–495. https://doi.org/10.1080/09518390110063365

Symonette, H. (2015). Culturally responsive evaluation as a resource for helpful-help. In S. Hood, R. Hopson, & H. Frierson (Eds.), *Continuing the journey to reposition culture and cultural context in evaluation theory and practice* (pp. 109–129). Information Age Publishing.

The Red Nation Podcast. (n.d.). *Land grab universities w/ Bobby Lee & Tristan Ahtone* [audio]. https://soundcloud.com/therednationpod/preview-land-grab-universities-w-bobby-lee-tristan-ahtone

Tillapaugh, D. (2016). Resisting erasure: Critical influences for men who survived sexual violence in higher education. *Social Alternatives, 35*(3), 11–17.

Tormala, T. T., Patel, S. G., Soukup, E. E., & Clarke, A. V. (2018). Developing measurable cultural competence and cultural humility: An application of the cultural formulation. *Training and Education in Professional Psychology, 12*(1), 54–61. https://doi.org/10.1037/tep0000183

Turner, C. S. V. (2003). Incorporation and marginalization in the academy: From border toward center for faculty of color? *Journal of Black Studies, 34*(1), 112–125. https://www.jstor.org/stable/3180861

Vaccaro, A. (2012). Campus microclimates for LGBT faculty, staff, and students: An exploration of the intersections of social identity and campus roles. *Journal of Student Affairs Research and Practice, 49*(4), 429–446. https://doi.org/10.1515/jsarp-2012-6473

Watson, K. (2005). Queer theory. *Group Analysis, 38*(1). https://doi.org/10.1177/0533316405049369

Watt, S. K. (Ed.). (2015). *Designing transformative multicultural initiatives: Theoretical foundations, practical applications, and facilitator considerations.* Stylus.

Whittaker, J. A., Montgomery, B. L., & Acosta, V. G. M. (2015). Retention of underrepresented minority faculty: Strategic initiatives for institutional value proposition based on perspectives from a range of academic institutions. *Journal of Undergraduate Neuroscience Education, 13*(3), A136–A145. https://www.ncbi.nlm.nih.gov/pmc/articles/PMC4521729/

Williams, D. A. (2013). *Strategic diversity leadership: Activating change and transformation in higher education.* Stylus.

Wise, T. (2008). *Speaking treason fluently.* Soft Skull.

Wooten, S. C. (2016). Heterosexist discourses: How feminist theory shaped campus sexual violence policy. In S. C. Wooten & R. W. Mitchell (Eds.), *The crisis of campus sexual violence: Critical perspectives on prevention and response* (pp. 33–52). Routledge.

Yang, L. (2002). Theorizing Asian America: On Asian American and postcolonial Asian diasporic women intellectuals. *Journal of Asian American Studies, 5*(2), 139–178. https://muse.jhu.edu/article/42173/pdf

YouTube Movies & TV. (2014). American revolutionary: The evolution of Grace Lee Boggs [YouTube video]. https://www.youtube.com/watch?v=w2-e8eERg_c

Zhou, Y., Jindal-Snape, D., Topping, K., & Todman, J. (2008). Theoretical models of culture shock and adaptation in international students in higher education. *Studies in Higher Education, 33*(1), 63–75.

Zuniga, X., Nagda, B. A., Chesler, M., & Cytron-Walker, A. (2007). Intergroup dialogue in higher education: Meaningful learning about social justice. *ASHE Higher Education Report, 32*(4), 1–128.

CHAPTER 6

BUILDING A SOCIAL JUSTICE-CENTERED HIGHER EDUCATION AND STUDENT AFFAIRS PROGRAM IN CALIFORNIA'S CENTRAL VALLEY

Varaxy Yi
Susana Hernández
Ignacio Hernández
Jonathan T. Pryor

ABSTRACT

Changing demographics requires higher education and student affairs (HESA) professionals to support diverse students. We discuss the educational contexts that shape a graduate preparation program, our efforts to integrate social justice and equity-oriented values, and the processes of (re)designing curriculum, programs, and services to support diverse students and emerging professionals in the California Central Valley.

Higher education and student affairs (HESA), as a discipline, has grown over the last few decades (Schwartz & Stewart, 2017) with a simultaneous increase in the number of graduate preparation programs across the nation. There are 272 graduate preparation program master's degree options in the United States (NASPA, n.d.). The growing number of programs, paired with changing demographics, indicate a need for HESA professionals well-equipped to support diverse students. As graduate preparation faculty members, we recognize the important roles we play as students' confidantes, mentors, advisors, and coaches (Magolda & Carnaghi, 2017). Additionally, our responsibility is to ensure that HESA professionals have the knowledge, competencies, and dispositions to support students (Carducci & Jaramillo, 2014).

With this in mind, we contextualize our efforts to build a graduate preparation program incorporating social justice frameworks in California's Central Valley. We explore national and local educational contexts that shape the need for a graduate preparation program at California State University, Fresno (Fresno State), detail our efforts to integrate social justice and equity-oriented values into the graduate curriculum, and offer reflections on the process of (re)designing curriculum, programs, and services to support diverse students and emerging professionals. We provide context-specific strategies for building a social justice-oriented HESA graduate preparation program.

HIGHER EDUCATION STUDENT AFFAIRS GRADUATE PREPARATION PROGRAMS

Our understanding of HESA graduate preparation programs has evolved beyond a focus on who enrolls and the faculty in the programs (Underwood & Austin, 2016), how these programs prepare and socialize graduate students into the profession (Benavides & Keyes, 2016; Liddell et al., 2014), and curricular changes (Eaton, 2016; Kuk & Banning, 2009; Renn & Jessup-Anger, 2008). More recently, scholars elucidated the racialized experiences of students of color in these programs (Flowers & Howard-Hamilton, 2002; Harris & Linder, 2018; Hubain et al., 2016; Kelly & Gayles, 2010; Linder et al., 2015). For example, Hubain et al. (2016) found that students of color experience invalidation of their identities and experiences, racial stereotypes, and isolation, while also having to educate their White peers in their graduate programs.

Some scholars identified deficiencies in how programs prepared students to engage in issues of social justice (Bondi, 2012; Kelly & Gayles, 2010; Lovell & Kosten, 2000). For example, Kelly and Gayles (2010) found that students reported resistance to dialogue about race and ethnicity.

Yet, programs are also important sites for developing intercultural maturity (Robbins, 2004). Consequently, there are many recommendations for incorporating social justice and equity-oriented perspectives to better prepare and engage students in such issues (Diggles, 2014; Furman, 2012; Kline & Gardner, 2005; Latz et al., 2017; Linder et al., 2015; Marine & Gilbert, 2022). Furman (2012) argued that programs have a central purpose of developing leaders' capacity for social justice leadership. Recently, Marine and Gilbert (2022) coedited a book highlighting various ways scholars and practitioners incorporate and practice critical praxis in HESA, which combines reflection and action as Freirian concepts to transform systems and structures. As such, we strive to incorporate these areas of critical praxis to support and develop social justice-oriented leaders.

As our student population grows and diversifies, programs must adjust and adapt to their individual and professional needs. We must provide students with the knowledge, abilities, and skills to incorporate social justice, equity, and inclusion values into their professional roles and identities (Carducci & Jaramillo, 2014). Kuk and Banning (2009) recommended programs incorporate a well-designed competency-based program model. Furthermore, the American College Personnel Association (ACPA) and NASPA confirmed social justice and inclusion as core competencies (Harris & Linder, 2018). Similarly, the Council for the Advancement of Standards in Higher Education (CAS), a consortium of over 42 professional associations focused on developing professional standards in student services and student development programs, identified access, equity, diversity, and inclusion as a general professional standard (CAS, n.d.). This shift and focus on social justice education are necessary for equipping HESA professionals to support diverse communities.

GUIDING SOCIAL JUSTICE FRAMEWORKS

Guided by social justice, we employ tenets of critical self-reflection (Ahmed, 2012; Bell et al., 2016; Freire, 1970), social justice-centered pedagogical, and curricular development (Adams, 2016; hooks, 1994). As we began redesigning our master's program, we also intentionally situated the conversation through the values promoted by the ACPA/NASPA social justice and inclusion competency (ACPA/NASPA, 2015). Aligning our graduate program redesign with the theoretical underpinnings of social justice pedagogy and our field's professional guidelines, allowed us to reflect thoughtfully on how we promote social justice across our curricula and in our pedagogical practices.

Equity work is paramount to our practice of preparing future HESA professionals. Ahmed (2012) contends doing diversity work requires an *undoing* of practices that perpetuate systemic oppression. We are then called upon to transform our institutions and enhance diversity and equity (Ahmed, 2012). Thus, leveraging our positions of power and privilege, we redesigned the curriculum rooted in these foundations, to enact our values of equity and inclusion. As social justice education runs the risk of being relegated to one person or one course (Bell et al., 2016), this framing allowed us to interrogate the current structure of our program and consider how we enact these values through the curriculum.

We were also guided by Freire's (1970) notion of deepened *consciousness* and recognized the ongoing nature of our individual educational enlightenment concerning undoing the inequities of our education system. A commitment to socially just education is a commitment to our personal growth and development in advocating for and implementing a social justice curriculum. Bell et al. (2016) challenged educators to develop their critical consciousness of different forms of oppression, including their knowledge of norms that reinforce privilege and marginalization, and our competencies in being able to engage in difficult dialogues to address institutional inequities. A self-examination of an individual's socialization through education and other sociocultural structures necessitates a deeply personal and reflective view of how these conditions may manifest in teaching (hooks, 1994). Adams (2016) argued that as social justice educators, *what* we teach must also be congruent with *how* we teach. This serves as a call for educators to not only be theoretically grounded in a commitment to social justice but also to be firmly committed to social justice pedagogical praxis.

As a collective, we are four of five faculty members in the higher education administration and leadership (HEAL) program. Varaxy Yi is a Khmer American woman, child of refugees, first-generation college graduate and faculty, and from the Central Valley, committed to supporting educational equity for racially minoritized populations. Susana Hernández is a daughter of immigrants, Latinamamischolar, first-generation college graduate and faculty. She is deeply committed to supporting the work of minority-serving institutions (MSIs) and the California State University system. Ignacio Hernández is a Latino man, son of Mexican immigrants, a community college transfer student, and a father. Jonathan Pryor is a white, gay, queer cis man, educated in the Midwest, and served as a practitioner in student affairs for 10 years. Three of us are first-generation college graduates and also from the state of California. We serve and support diverse students, with specific attention to Latinx, Southeast Asian American, and LGBTQ+ communities.

We root ourselves in this work and name our positionalities as an important aspect of engaging in critical self-reflection. Although diverse in background and research trajectories, collectively, we are committed to living our social justice values in the context of the Central Valley. Our work collectively strives to dismantle oppressive systems, policies, and practices that shape the experiences of all minoritized communities. We engage in personal and collective critical self-reflection (Ahmed, 2012; Bell et al., 2016; Freire, 1970). We also recognize that social justice and equity orientations are a process in which we must constantly assess ourselves and readjust accordingly (Bell, 2016).

Lastly, we framed our program-building through the values promoted by the ACPA/NASPA professional competency areas for student affairs educators (ACPA/NASPA, 2015). As leading associations for the HESA field, ACPA/NASPA offers 10 competency areas that speak to the vast nature of the student affairs profession. Student affairs professionals must demonstrate essential "knowledge, skills, and dispositions" across all facets of the profession. Specifically, the social justice and inclusion (SJI) competency asserts that practitioners may infuse the SJI competency "into their practice through seeking to meet the needs of all groups equitably, equitably distributing resources, raising social consciousness, and repairing past and current harms on campus communities" (ACPA/NASPA, 2015, p. 14). This competency reinforces the importance of social justice and inclusion work in all facets of education work. As we prepare future HESA leaders, this commitment must be apparent across the curriculum and in how we approach our work as co-creators of knowledge in the classroom.

CHARACTERISTICS OF THE CENTRAL VALLEY

The Central Valley is unique from other areas in California in that its geography is a blend of urban and rural spaces in one of the largest and wealthiest agricultural regions in the world (Daneneberg et al., 2002). The San Joaquin Valley is typically understood as the region between the Tejon Pass and Bakersfield to the south, Modesto and Stockton to the north, with Fresno in the center. The area makes up 14% of California's total land area—approximately 22,500 square miles—roughly equivalent to the entirety of the state of West Virginia (The Planning Center, 2012). This vast geographic area contrasts with densely populated and more commonly studied population centers like Los Angeles or the San Francisco/Oakland Bay Area.

The agricultural wealth in the Central Valley is contrasted with poor economic development, high poverty rates, and low educational attainment. Although the region continues to endure the effects of long-standing racial and economic inequities through real estate redlining, lower average wages, and high unemployment (Bohn et al., 2019), there is also a long history of resistance to oppression and injustice. For example, Valley labor leaders

Larry Itliong, Dolores Huerta, and Cesar Chavez organized laborers to fight for humane working conditions and improved wages. This long, enduring history of advocacy provides context for us to consider the role of education in supporting social justice work in the region.

Institutions of Higher Education in the Central Valley

California's commitment to postsecondary education was first manifested in the 1960 Master Plan for Higher Education (University of California Office of the President [UCOP], 2009), which established a three-tiered system of the California Community Colleges, the California State University, and the University of California. The confluence of economic instability and rapid demographic change has left the Master Plan's commitment to making higher education accessible to all severely at risk (The Campaign for College Opportunity, 2018). Within the context of California's pioneering public systems of higher education are four California State Universities (Bakersfield, Fresno, Sacramento, and Stanislaus), a University of California in Merced, 13 community colleges, and five community college centers. Many private institutions operate in the area, with others enrolling students through online education programs. These institutions educate the entire geographic region of the San Joaquin Valley.

Educational Attainment in the Central Valley

Fresno State is located in one of the most culturally-diverse regions in the United States. Yet, according to Bohn et al. (2019), trends show Central Valley educational attainment levels have been historically low. In 2000, only 14% of adults (age 25 and older) were college graduates, compared to 28% in the rest of California. The South San Joaquin Valley loses college graduates to the rest of the state while the Sacramento Metro region attracts more college graduates. Fresno State attracts a significant, diverse student population. In Fall 2021, 56.1% Latinx, 17.8% white, 12.4% Asian and Pacific Islander, 2.8% African American, and 0.3% American Indian students enrolled (Fresno State, 2022). More than half of the aggregated Asian population identifies as Southeast Asian American (SEAA; e.g., Cambodian, Lao, Hmong). These enrollment numbers also designate the campus as a Hispanic serving institution (HSI) and an Asian American and Native American Pacific Islander serving institution (AANAPISI). These demographics illuminate the need for diverse HESA professionals who can support various student needs.

BECOMING HEAL

The HEAL program trains most of the HESA professionals in the Central Valley. To ensure we can equip them to support diverse students, we are committed to and in a perpetual state of "becoming" a social justice-centered program. Initially, the program existed in a P–12 context, with courses taught by non-higher education scholars. At the time, the program did not have a strong higher education focus and admitted students who were not necessarily intending to work in a postsecondary education setting but were interested in transitioning into P–12 education contexts. The first higher education scholar was hired in 2009, who began recruiting university and community college staff. In 2013, Susana and Ignacio were hired and spent considerable time and energy thinking about how to build a HESA master's program. A crucial element of this process was identity building. Attention was given to how the program can build a more explicit identity on campus and in the Central Valley. When we thought about the work higher education professionals do in supporting students, we thought about healing. Shortly after that, we developed the acronym HEAL (Higher Education Administration and Leadership), establishing the program to develop HEALers who would transform education in the region. In 2018, two more faculty (Varaxy and Jonathan) were hired, and in 2023 one more faculty (Ángel González) was hired, bringing the total to six HESA faculty As a collective, we continue to rely on our knowledge to grow HEAL. In the following section, we provide historical and current efforts to engage in a program and curricular (re)design process through three phases.

Phase 1: Middle Leaders

Initially, the department of educational leadership offered one education administration master's degree program, which focused on educating P–12 administrators for leading local schools and districts. The program focused on preparing administrators and leaders across various educational contexts. The Middle Leaders degree pathway was conceived as a way to enroll P–12 employees not seeking administrative credentials but who sought leadership positions. Budget analysts, bus drivers, plant operations, and facilities managers were some of the initial areas the Middle Leaders pathway would focus on. Students from a wide range of professional backgrounds and goals took an amalgamation of classes but mostly enrolled in available open course sections. However, as demand for leadership preparation for staff at community colleges and 4-year institutions increased, the college began recognizing the need for higher education leadership preparation and initiated several tenure-track hires over the last decade. This initiated a new era in the department through an overt move away from the Middle

Leaders moniker and a new focus on preparing higher education leaders. The development of a higher education program was carried out by faculty with professional experience in the field and academic training in higher education leadership.

We needed to nurture a mission and vision to establish an identity around its purpose of preparing leaders for HESA. Many of the initial conversations revolved around expertise in the higher education degree and field. Having worked in professional roles in higher education before becoming faculty, we engaged in numerous conversations with the department and school colleagues (e.g., department faculty and chair), staff from the division of student affairs, administrators (e.g., vice president of student affairs, dean, provost, and university president), and the broader campus community about the specialization of the higher education degree. These conversations occurred in a teacher preparation context, with many individuals not understanding that higher education was a field of study. Simultaneously, conversations with off-campus constituents affirmed the need for HEAL to prepare master's graduates. We had to be intentional and strategic about educating the community on the discipline of higher education and the unique contributions that only a HESA graduate program could offer. We worked diligently to educate colleagues about the field and our expertise. It was also important to communicate how we were distinct from a P–12 leadership preparation context.

The Middle Leaders pathway existed with varying descriptions of its role and purpose, without a cohesive identity. Students held disparate perspectives about what the Middle Leaders pathway was and would be. Students began asking for a deeper learning experience focused on social justice. We assigned students readings that helped them make sense of their educational trajectories and lives, which included scholarship focused on those with minoritized backgrounds, including racial and ethnic diversity, first-generation, low-income, LGBTQ+, undocumented status, and other invisibilized identities, to which students could see themselves and their communities represented. Responding to student needs, we began implementing rigorous graduate-level standards and shifting toward a new HEAL pathway.

Phase 2: HEAL Pathway

Once we developed a program vision, we fostered relationships with campus faculty, staff, and administrators to communicate the potential HEAL would have in contributing to the university's mission. We met regularly with administrators to describe the importance of preparing early-career higher education professionals. We participated in university initiatives and committees to highlight our presence and share our expertise on campus. Additionally, we worked considerably to establish autonomy over the program's vision. Part of the initial program building required difficult conversations with colleagues about the field of higher education and developing a respect for the ideas and expertise that the faculty brought to the department and college. We worked diligently to ensure relationships were developed to maintain autonomy over the curriculum and the co-curricular experiences. We made HEAL faculty's expertise and social justice knowledge visible. Early relationship building was crucial for program visibility and communicating our vision. National perspectives and local actions boosted this visibility. We encouraged students to join ACPA, NASPA, or other functional area associations to connect to the student affairs profession. We boosted our visibility by assigning each other's work and inviting each other as guest speakers.

Additionally, we developed a strategic recruitment plan to ensure prospective students had a clearer understanding of how HEAL was unique and geared for individuals interested in careers in higher education. Part of the recruitment plan included building relationships with local and regional partners. As coordinator, Susana set up regular meetings with VPSAs at local community colleges, as well as the comprehensive universities. These meetings resulted in a Careers in Student Affairs month at Fresno State, which had never occurred on campus. This month-long initiative, in partnership with NASPA, created multiple opportunities to highlight the profession, hear from seasoned professionals in the field, and promote and elevate HEAL. Information sessions were held across multiple universities, and the HEAL coordinator met regularly with prospective students. Many initial meetings were meant to build relationships with higher education professionals on the campus and the regional area, who then became partners in promoting the HEAL mission and vision.

We also integrated a cohort model and began providing multiple opportunities for co-curricular engagement. It was important to develop a sense of identity among the students, build rapport and trusting relationships, and provide opportunities for holistic development. Admitted students were required to attend an orientation where they learned the program's expectations and participated in a ropes course to quickly build relationships with their peers. Additionally, alumni played a critical part in this phase of HEAL's development. As they assumed leadership positions on campus and across the region, greater interest was garnered around the program and the higher education profession generally. Alumni were essential in communicating how the program served as professional development, allowed them to develop regional and national networks, and increased their confidence in aligning their work to research.

Phase 3: Elevation from Pathway to Program

After the last two faculty hires in 2018, we began the intentional process of growing HEAL. During the 2018–2019 academic year, we engaged in conversations around redeveloping the HEAL program and curriculum to better support the needs of students and the profession. To elevate from a degree option (pathway) in the education administration (EAD) program into a stand-alone program and degree, we reviewed the current 31-unit curriculum for improvement. In functioning as a pathway under the EAD master's degree, our curriculum was restricted in several ways. First, our class subject headings were limited by the EAD offerings. For example, one of the courses, Site-Based Leadership, while well-suited as a P–12 offering, did not align with other higher education-focused courses.

Additionally, we were restricted from offering HESA-specific topics. To offer these courses, we had to use two special topic designations as course headings to offer Student Affairs in Higher Education and Diversity in U.S. Higher Education. Second, reviewing peer programs, we noted program requirements had shifted, with a noticeable transition from thesis or research projects to portfolios as culminating projects (Kuk & Banning, 2009; Underwood & Austin, 2016). However, due to our course heading restrictions, it was difficult to integrate this as a requirement without impacting the P–12 curriculum. By elevating our pathway to a program, we gained the autonomy to intentionally design an independent graduate program. In doing so, we had to consider our approaches to teaching, our collective understanding of how we can operationalize this program as a faculty, and how to address departmental and institutional policies to support our work.

In response to the above challenges, we (re)envisioned a new 30-unit curriculum better suited to our program goals. To operationalize the new curriculum design, we engaged in deeper reflection of our prior curriculum so we could begin shifting our praxis to a richer social justice curriculum. This work required a shift away from a static curriculum and toward a collectively agreed-upon design that required buy-in from all the faculty in the program. We engaged peer higher education program curricula, ACPA/NASPA competencies, and our graduate school experiences to redevelop new classes. We developed new course headings and course subjects that better reflected the important topics we believed HESA professionals needed to engage with. We also shifted the culminating project to a portfolio option that enabled students to demonstrate the knowledge and skills developed in the program.

Additionally, acknowledging our responsibility for imbuing social justice throughout the coursework, we discussed ways to incorporate these topics holistically throughout the program rather than relegating them to just one class. This new curriculum was then vetted by our program faculty, the department, and various stakeholder groups. As we awaited approval for elevation into a standalone program, we integrated the policies and practices we discussed into the curriculum. Specifically, we focused on how to develop a classroom environment to sustain important conversations around issues of equity and social justice, and policies that address equity issues impacting our students.

Classroom Environment

A major focus of our program and curriculum redesign was considering how to shape our classroom environment to engage students in constructive dialogue around social justice issues. A constructive, inclusive classroom environment is a foundational component for supporting students to engage with difficult conversations and issues of equity. While we included students in setting classroom community guidelines, we recognized that as faculty, we held great influence in shaping these activities. Our goal was to engage all students across various spectrums of background, social identities, and knowledge. Consequently, we intentionally included students in collective community agreement-building.

To achieve this goal, we focused on supporting students to become comfortable with the language we use in the classroom. For example, students are often discomfited when asked to share their pronouns during introductions. It was often the first time they were asked to reflect on their pronouns. We modeled this language repeatedly and asked students to share and become comfortable with these rituals. These were opportunities to engage students in conversations about gender identity focused on inclusivity issues and respect for how others identify. This was one example of highlighting how our program addressed various equity considerations.

We also highlighted the importance of being vulnerable and sharing positionalities in the class. We encourage students to speak from their individual experiences, backgrounds, and knowledge. As educators who are influenced by social constructivist paradigms (Collin, 2013), we recognized knowledge as subjective and socially shaped by interactions. We explicitly share our own experiences and perspectives as shaped by our social identities. We intentionally modeled the challenges we experienced as minoritized and marginalized individuals and when engaging in work from positions of power and privilege. By sharing our vulnerabilities and being open about our challenges, we modeled strength and courage to students. We also encouraged students to practice vulnerability in several assignments throughout the curriculum. As a tool for critical self-reflection (Bell et al., 2016), engaging vulnerability has allowed us to deepen our engagement with social justice concepts in the classroom and strengthen rapport within the cohorts. It is important that students see us not as authority figures but as colleagues engaging in similar challenges. This is collective community building. Creating a space where we can be vulnerable and share our challenges highlights humanity in social justice education.

Program Building

As we grew, we recognized some noticeable gaps in our program policies that did not reflect our social justice orientations. We sought to adopt new policies not already part of the university or department, yet contextualized to our campus community. One of these policies focused on children in the classroom. Given that many of our students are parents, we determined it to be important in our quest to support all students holistically, that we incorporate a policy that reflected our understanding of the responsibilities our students had. The policy specifically includes support for breastfeeding and ill children, as well as guidelines for bringing children into class. We recognized the demands of parenting on our students and the challenges that may arise in any given semester. We felt it was important to openly acknowledge and support parents in this way, and encourage readers to consider what a policy like this may look like for their program.

Additionally, we adopted a "Respect for Diversity" guideline that specifically addressed the use of pronouns in the class and connected to broader nondiscrimination policies. These policies allow us to situate our classrooms as spaces that uphold our values and communicate how we support our students. We recognize policies may shift given contemporary or local challenges our students or community face and seek to adapt our practices accordingly. More recently, we implemented practices that communicate a land acknowledgment of our region, recognizing the rich traditions and representations of Native American peoples and cultures in the greater San Joaquin Valley of California.

Reflecting on how to build a robust program that supports our graduate students, we paid specific attention to how we socialize our students into the HESA profession. This was accomplished partly through establishing a graduate student association (GSA), which allowed students fuller participation in their graduate student experience. We leveraged institutional resources to support student participation in graduate student development (e.g., conference travel funding; professional development). Additionally, students created traditions that established engagement among incoming and current students, alumni, and campus constituents. The GSA facilitated co-curricular programs (e.g., conference preparation, resume/CV workshops, etc.), engaged cohorts through socials, and led end-of-semester celebrations. Engaging students in these ways has fostered a sense of ownership over their graduate experience. We seek to continue this practice as we commit to building a professional network of HESA professionals in the Central Valley.

REFLECTIONS ON BUILDING A SOCIAL JUSTICE-CENTERED PROGRAM IN THE VALLEY

As we continue to engage in efforts to build a social justice-centered graduate preparation program in California's Central Valley, we continually reflect on the challenges and major considerations that inform this work. If we are to heed the call of transforming oppressive systems to ultimately provide transformative learning environments (Ahmed, 2012; Bell et al., 2016), we are left to navigate the opportunities and barriers inherent in a college campus. We recognized the need to consider the context in which we are situated while engaging in the work individually and collectively.

Reframing our graduate program to operate from a social justice curriculum also entailed telling our story and objectives to colleagues, many of whom were operating from different conceptions of social justice praxis. Therefore, we rooted our curricular adjustment in texts foundational to the field of education (e.g., Freire, 1970; hooks, 1994) and also practical, contemporary expectations of our specific field in higher education (ACPA/NASPA, 2015; Adams, 2016; Ahmed, 2012; Bell et al., 2016). We also developed relationships with senior administrators across local institutions who more likely understood the need for robust education and training of HESA professionals, many of whom were their staff. These individuals' support and collaboration ultimately helped build campus awareness of the legitimacy of our program.

Bell et al. (2016) guided our pursuit of program redevelopment. They call on educators to engage their positionality, reflect on the curricular design, and consider our readiness to address and dismantle norms that uphold privilege and bias. As educators, we are challenged to lead the way, not only for our colleagues but also for our students and campus. Thus, the *doing* of the work is a work in progress, where we actively situate ourselves within the context of an institution dedicated to serving a diverse student body. However, barriers continue to exist as we work on telling our story and advancing our program.

Critical reflection necessitates an opportunity to reflect on the biases, assumptions, and practices we bring into the learning environment (Bell et al., 2016; Freire, 1970). Collectively, our graduate training, research agendas, and personal philosophies promoted social justice and inclusion. Still, we also recognized that *doing* the work requires just as much practice and reflective engagement as espousing our values outwardly (Adams, 2016). This tension between *knowing* and *doing* is reflective of the reality that we have been and currently are still experiencing a process. Employing a social justice curriculum required us to reframe how we previously approached our work and begin operating from a newly informed lens. The program's growth requires more work than what can be written down. An individual engagement with perpetual praxis is necessary to implement this work.

Social justice is both a process and a goal (Bell, 2016). As social actors, aware of our agency and social responsibility to our students and communities (Bell, 2016), we continually strive to align our work to social justice values. As we move forward with strengthening HEAL, we acknowledge that this is a continual process shaped by our positionalities and perspectives, which also are constantly evolving as our own understandings of social justice evolve. We know there continue to be gaps in our espoused values, and the lived values we enact; however, we commit to forward movement towards becoming social justice-centered. Our current conversations involve grappling with the gaps in our program, curriculum, and policies, reflection on whether these currently move us toward our goals, and musings on how best to orient our students toward the profession. We consistently (re) analyze our intentions and make adjustments. This process mirrors that of social justice work. Recognition that there may not be a moment of arrival, where we as a program achieve our social justice goals, does not deter us from doing and being better for our students.

APPENDIX A
Higher Education Administration and Leadership (HEAL) Course Curriculum

HEAL 220 Introduction to higher education (3 units)
HEAL 221 Student affairs in higher education (3 units)
HEAL 222 Diversity, inclusion, and equity in higher education (3 units)
HEAL 223 Students in higher education (3 units)
HEAL 225 Higher education leadership and supervision (3 units)
HEAL 224 Foundations of inquiry and applied research in higher education (3 units)
HEAL 226 Assessment in higher education (3 units)
HEAL 227 Law, policy, and ethics in higher education (3 units)
HEAL 228 Current issues in higher education (3 units)
HEAL 298 Project or HEAL 299 Thesis (3 units)

APPENDIX B
INTRODUCTION TO HIGHER EDUCATION

Syllabus for HEAL 220: Introduction to Higher Education	
Semester: Fall	**Higher Education Administration & Leadership** Department of Educational Leadership California State University, Fresno
Course Name: Introduction to Higher Education	**Instructor Name**
Units: 3	**Office Location**
Time: TBD	**E-Mail**
Location: TBD	**Telephone**
Website	**Office Hours**

Catalog Description

Initial course in the Higher Education Administration & Leadership Program. Development of knowledge and skills central to managing educational organizations.

Course Description

In this learning community we will work on the collaborative co-construction of deeper, more nuanced understandings of the ways in which multiple histories and philosophies have influenced higher education and the social construction of higher education leadership in the United States. Being aware of these historical and philosophical foundations will help us develop skills to better understand, critique, and analyze contemporary issues related to leaders (as individuals) and leadership (as a social practice) in higher education.

It is usually expected that students will spend approximately 2 hours of study time outside of class for every one hour in class. Since this is a 3 unit class, you should expect to study an average of 6 hours outside of class each week.

Course Prerequisite(s)

Admission to the Higher Education Administration & Leadership Program.

Required Course Materials

American Psychological Association (2010). *Publication manual of the American Psychological Association.* Washington, D.C.: Author.

Harper, S. R., & Jackson, J. F. L. (Eds.) (2011). *Introduction to American higher education.* New York: Routledge.

Course Specifics

Course Summary

This course is designed to introduce graduate students to the study of higher education, with emphasis on the philosophical and historical contexts of the field. History and philosophy are indispensable foundations for making sense of your subsequent courses as a graduate student and for understanding your day-to-day work life in higher education.

Course Goals

Each individual attends graduate school for many reasons, with career goals being a primary driver. I also believe you are here because you want to shape a new future for higher education. It is hoped you want to be leader who is willing to develop a vision, recreate new futures, and challenge existing norms. The following learning outcomes guide our learning space.

Student Learning Outcomes:

After completing this course, students will be able to:
1. Read higher education research as a field of study from which to develop new perspectives on the social construction of leaders and leadership in U.S. institutions of higher education.
2. Write about how the history, philosophy, and values of higher education connect to their professional practice.
3. Articulate the vision and mission of an institution of higher education.
4. Compare and contrast institutional types in U.S. higher education.
5. Explain the importance of understanding who goes where to college, in light of topics related to college access, persistence, and graduation.

ACPA/NASPA Professional Competencies

1. Personal and ethical foundations
2. Values, philosophy, and history
3. Technology

Assignment and Examination Schedule

Due Date	Assignment	Points/Percent	ACPA/NASPA Competencies
W2	List of experiences	100	PEF
W?	Reading checks	100	PEF/VPH
W3	Short Essay 1	50	PEF/VPH
W8	Short Essay 2	50	PEF/VPH
W13	Short Essay 3	50	PEF/VPH
W4, 7, 11	Institutional Comparison	150	PEF/VPH/TECH
W 12	Film Synthesis	150	PEF/VPH/TECH
W16	Final Paper/Presentation	300	PEF/VPH/TECH
W17	Engaged Participation and Contribution	50	PEF/VPH

Assignments

All assignments are due at 4:00 pm via Canvas on (or before) the date indicated.

Your final grade in this course will be based on the following learning artifacts:

List of experiences (100 points possible; outcome 1)
Due on Canvas Week 2

The purpose of this assignment is for students to begin identifying their personal administrative and leadership experiences in higher education. Students should develop a list of the projects they have worked on or have lead in paraprofessional or professional settings. These may include projects such as student organization leadership, college access outreach programs like Educational Talent Search or Upward Bound, or something related to the student's current job. The list does not need to be exhaustive, but it should be representative of the student's experiences with administration and leadership in higher education.

Reading checks (100 points possible; outcomes 1 and 2) *various dates across the semester*

The purpose of these in class assignments is for students to identify areas of strength and areas for improvement related to their reading comprehension. These reading checks are not "gotcha" opportunities for the instructor, but rather they serve as a method of assessment and ways to stimulate discussions in the learning community.

Three short essays (150 points possible—50 points each; outcomes 1–5) *Due Weeks 3, 8, 13*

The purpose of this assignment is for students to think deeply about their educational journeys and learning goals.

- *Short Essay I: Course and graduate school goals*

    Taking into account their paraprofessional and professional experiences in higher education, students will develop a listing of their learning goals for a) this class and b) the HEAL degree pathway. Students should provide details about how they intend to achieve these goals while also providing a reasonable time frame.

- *Short Essay II: Mid-semester self and course evaluation*

    Students will re-evaluate their goals, making any revisions they deem necessary. Students will write an honest self-assessment of their progress towards meeting their goals from *Short Essay I* and plan(s) of action to do so. When applicable, students will offer rationale for any revised goals along with their plan(s) of action for doing so. This essay meets the Graduate Writing Requirement.

- *Short Essay III: A letter to first-year students*

    Students will write letters to Fresno State students in the First Year Experience (FYE) program. More details will be provided as the semester progresses.

Institutional Comparison (150 points; outcomes 3 & 4); *Due Week 4, 7, and 11*

The purpose of this assignment is for students to interpret, analyze, and compare information about two different institutions of higher education. This assignment has various due dates to allow for ongoing understanding of the two institutions.

Students will select two actual institutions, of different institutional types, to compare and contrast. You should select institutions you are not familiar with or have attended. For example,

- Iowa State University (Public, Land Grant) and Swarthmore College (Private)

Building a Social Justice-Centered Higher Education and Student Affairs Program • 115

- Marquette University (Private, Faith-based) and College of the Muscogee Nation (Tribal College)
- Fresno City College (Public, Community College) and Spelman College (HBCU)
    - *Note:* Institutions may have two or more classification types
- *Part I (Due September 18):* Identify the institutions you have chosen making sure you clearly identify each one's institutional type. Include a short description of each institution and locate an organizational chart for the entire institution (or at least for a major division, *i.e.* Student Affairs). Organizational charts may be found on each institution's website. Provide a brief rationale statement describing why you chose the two institutions.
- *Part II (Due October 9):* Find the following information for both institutions:
    - Carnegie classifications (see: http://carnegieclassifications.iu.edu/index.php)
    - Control (i.e., public or private)
    - Enrollment statistics: Locate meaningful data with disaggregate categories, such as gender, race, first-generation status, etc.
    - Mission and vision statement
    - Basic facts of each institution's location
        ○ Percent of adults with a HS diploma (or equivalent) in the city and state
        ○ Percent of adults with a college degree in the city and state
        ○ Median income in the city and state
        ○ Demographic statistics of the city and state
- *Part III—Final Analysis (Due November 6):* Read through the "About Us" sections of each institution's websites to get an idea of the history and founding of that college or university. Also read about the major divisions (student affairs, academic affairs) and departments to learn more about the institutions.
    - What did you find? Did something stand out? Was there something you could not?
    - Who seems to be the type of student each institution is trying to appeal to?
        ○ Was this expected or were you surprised?
    - What societal and/or cultural markers are being communicated?
        ○ What do you notice about the language being used?
        ○ What icons, shapes, or symbols do you see?

The final analysis should include revisions of Parts I and II.

Film Synthesis: Stolen Education (150 points possible; outcomes 2 & 5) *Due Week 12*

The purpose of this assignment is for students to develop a written synthesis of STOLEN EDUCATION, a 2013 film written and produced by Dr. Enrique Alemán, professor and chair in the department of Educational Leadership and Policy Studies at the University of Texas, San Antonio. Students should avoid writing a report style paper that only reviews the film and place more emphasis on the consequences of what the filmmakers are communicating and how the film relates to the course. Students should follow this general outline for this assignment:

- Describe the subject and purpose of the film
- Outline the major topics and themes discussed in the film
- Analyze the major topics and themes discussed in the film
- Compare and contrast the film to other assigned readings
- How might the film influence your practice in higher education?

Film synthesis assignments should generally be between 1,000 and 1,250 words long.

Group project: Analysis of a higher education system or institutional type (Paper: 200 points possible; Presentation: 100 points possible; outcomes 1–5) *Various due dates*

The purpose of this assignment is for students to learn about the characteristics and functions of various institutional types in higher education. Students should utilize the readings on institutional variety, historical background, campus environments, college access, and how institutional types have evolved over time. A secondary purpose of this assignment is for students to work cooperatively with other members of the learning community.

Projects should describe and analyze one of the following institutional types:

- Career, Technical, or Vocational Colleges
- Community colleges
- Faith-based institutions
- For-profit colleges and universities
- Liberal arts colleges and universities
- Land grant institutions
- Military colleges
- Minority Serving Institutions (*i.e.* Asian American, Native American, Pacific Islander Serving Institutions; Historically Black Colleges & Universities; Hispanic Serving Institutions; Tribal Colleges)
- Private colleges and universities

- State colleges and university systems
- Women's colleges

The choice of the institutional type is up to you and your group, but must be approved by the instructor and should not be changed thereafter. Note: some institutions may be classified as more than one type, for example, Fresno State is a Minority Serving Institution and is also part of a state system.

Note: There are multiple components and due dates associated with this project

Group Project Proposal: As a means of ensuring groups get an early start on this project, each group is required to provide a one-page description of their chosen higher education system or institutional type. In the proposal, groups should briefly identify the higher education system or institutional type while providing references along the way. The proposal should include a timeline that group members will adhere to in order to meet necessary deadlines and avoid procrastination as well as any accountability measures the group agrees to. In addition to the required readings, groups are encouraged to seek additional resources from the research librarians at HML as well as professional associations in higher education. The associations and groups may be national, regional, or local. *The Group Project Proposal is due Week 4.*

The final project should highlight important points on the development of the system or type that justify your arguments. The final paper is comprised of two main sections: *Description* and *Analysis* and is *due Week 17.*

Description of the System or Type: To clarify the scope of your project, groups should begin by writing a detailed description the higher education system or institutional type. Groups should consider addressing the following questions as a means of outlining their paper:

- What is the higher education system or institutional type your group will focus on?
- What are the historical origins of this higher education system or institutional type?
- What is the total number of colleges and universities in the selected higher education system or institutional type?
- What is the geographical distribution across the U.S.?
- Does the higher education system or institutional type have a national professional organization or advocacy group?
- Does there exist a common or shared philosophy, vision, and mission of your selected institutional type?
- What degrees or certificates are (and are not) conferred in the selected institutional type?

- Have workforce needs influenced the curriculum? And, if yes, how?
- Describe in detail the governing structure of the selected institutional type.
- What are the policies that influence the selected institutional type?

Analysis: Groups will demonstrate their comprehension and application of their selected higher education system or institutional type by citing the assigned course reading materials. In their analysis of their selected system or type, groups should consider answering the following questions:

- Develop a profile of the students that attend the institutional type? Provide detailed and current information.
- How has the curriculum influenced the evolution of the system or type? OR How has the system or type influenced the evolution of the curriculum?
  - What can you say about the student demographics and the curriculum of the institutional type?
- What possibilities remain unrealized for the system or type?
- What external forces have influenced the evolution of the system or institutional type?
- What are some of the current leadership issues facing the particular system or type?

Draft Check-in: Groups will submit a draft of their paper and present preliminary information *in class on Week 8.*

Presentation: Groups will develop a presentation on their selected system or type designed for a general audience. Very frequently, as scholar-practitioners in higher education we are called upon to communicate with broad audiences who have varying levels of familiarity about our work. The goal of this presentation is to help students hone their oral communication skills in a public forum. I will provide the rubric used to assess your presentations. *Presentations will be delivered in class on Week 16.*

As members of their group, all students are expected to:

- Contribute equally to the group paper and presentation
- Present findings and distribute a written outline to the class. This outline should provide an overview of the key information presented in your paper and presentation
- Respond to questions from the learning community

Informed contribution and participation (50 points possible; outcomes 1-5) *Due Week 17*

The purpose of this assignment is for students to self-assess their contribution to the learning community, their own learning, the learning of the instructor, and the learning of their peers throughout the semester. Students should use *Short Essays I* and *II* to honestly gauge their own contribution to their learning and participation throughout the course. The hallmarks of a graduate course involve (1) punctual attendance, (2) focused attention and involved participation, and (3) ready preparation (completion of readings, assignments, etc.).

Students will assess their own grade for this assignment and submit a no more than two-page document via Canvas. Students should support their assessment in each area with one brief paragraph. Students should consider the following rubric as a guide when assessing their informed contribution:

- 50–40:
  - The student was present for all class time, arriving on time for all class meetings.
  - The student was *actively* involved in class discussions and activities while utilizing note-taking tactics to support their learning.
  - The student read and critically reflected on all of the course readings and materials and made frequent references to this material while encouraging others to participate.
  - The student submitted all assignments on time.
- 39–30:
  - The student was present for all class time, missing some part of class but arrived late to some class meetings.
  - The student was actively involved in course discussions and activities and occasionally took notes.
  - The student read or skimmed most of the required course reading material but made minimal references to this material in class or in their assignments.
- 29–20:
  - The student missed one or more class meetings and frequently arrived late.
  - The student occasionally involved in course discussion and activities.
  - The student failed to read and/or use a significant portion of the assigned readings.
- ≤ 19:
  - The student missed more than two class meetings and/or made minimal efforts to attend class, to be involved in classroom activities, or to read the assigned readings.

As the instructor, I hold the right to change student assigned grades for this assignment should a student not provide adequate supportive substantiation of their engagement.

Course Evaluation and Grading

You can earn up to 1,000 points in this class. Letter grades will be awarded as follows:

Letter grade	Points earned
A	1,000–900
B	899–800
C	799–700
D	699–600
F	≤ 599

Course Policies and Safety Issues

Attendance and Participation

Attendance and class participation are vital to this course. Please note that missing class (or any part of class) regardless of reason, will result in lower participation points that will affect your grade. As an integral member of the learning space, attendance and participation are central to this course.

Professional courtesy requires that students should notify the instructor prior to class if he/she/they must be absent due to an unforeseen circumstance such as illness or an emergency. These circumstances will require appropriate documentation (i.e. doctor's notice). However, all missed readings must be completed and assignments musts be turned in by the assigned date.

As graduate students, I expect meaningful engagement with the course material and your peers. Relevant participation includes presenting good examples (informed by the readings), raising good questions, recognizing an appropriate level of participation, being sensitive to and responding appropriately to others' comments.

Late Work and Make-Up Work Policy

All assignments must be submitted by the assigned date and time and will only be accepted via Canvas. *Hard copies will not be accepted.* Late assignments will be deducted 10% of a grade and require a written statement explaining the late submission. I will not read any work that is more than one week late, unless there are extenuating circumstances.

If you are absent from class, it is your responsibility to check on announcements made while you are away. If you are absent from class, participation points are unable to be made up given the active learning of the class session being missed.

Plagiarism Detection

The campus subscribes to Turnitin plagiarism prevention service through Canvas, and you will need to submit written assignments to Turnitin. Student work will be used for plagiarism detection and for no other purpose. The student may indicate in writing to the instructor that he/she refuses to participate in the plagiarism detection process, in which case the instructor can use other electronic means to verify the originality of their work. Turnitin Originality Reports will not be available for your viewing.

HEAL Program Policies

Policy on Children in Class

Currently, the university does not have a formal policy on children in the classroom. The policy described here reflects my own beliefs and commitments to student, staff, and faculty parents.

- All exclusively breastfeeding babies are welcome in class as often as is necessary to support the breastfeeding relationship. We never want students to feel like they must choose between feeding their baby and continuing their education. You and your nursing baby are welcome in class anytime.
- For older children and babies, we understand that minor illnesses and unforeseen disruptions in childcare often put parents in the position of having to choose between missing class to stay home with a child and leaving him or her with someone you or the child does not feel comfortable with. While this is not meant to be a long-term childcare solution, occasionally bringing a child to class to cover gaps in care is perfectly acceptable.
- In all cases where babies and children come to class, the instructor asks that you sit close to the door so that if your little one needs

special attention and is disrupting learning for other students, you may step outside until their need has been met.
- If your child needs to attend class, please bring quiet activities appropriate for children to engage with such as crayons and paper, an IPad or video game, etc.

Respect for Diversity

The values of social justice and respect for diversity and diverse thought are central to our work as HEAL faculty. These values also align with the California State University, Fresno Non-Discrimination/Harassment Policies, which emphasize acceptance, fairness, and supporting diversity across difference and experience. (http://www.fresnostate.edu/adminserv/hr/eeo-diversity/discrimination/policies.html)

Additionally, class rosters and University data systems are provided to instructors with students' legal names and gender identifications. However, knowing that not all students use their legal names or sex/gender assigned at birth, we are happy to use the name and/or pronouns you use. We will take time during our first class together to do introductions, at which point you can share with all members of our learning community what name and pronouns you use. If these change at any point during the semester, please let the instructor know and we can develop a way to share this information with others in a way that is comfortable and safe for you.

Course Satisfactory Progress

Earning a "C" grade or below in a master's course in the Higher Education Administration & Leadership Program is not considered to be a satisfactory grade. The first "C" obtained places a student on academic probation and the second "C" acquired will mean dismissal from the program. If a grade of "C" is earned, the course must be retaken without replacement (meaning the original grade received remains on the transcript and is included in GPA calculations).

University Policies and Services

Students With Disabilities

Upon identifying themselves to the instructor and the university, students with disabilities will receive reasonable accommodation for learning and evaluation. For more information, contact Services to Students with Disabilities in the Henry Madden Library, Room 1202 (278-2811).

Honor Code

"Members of the Fresno State academic community adhere to principles of academic integrity and mutual respect while engaged in university work and related activities." You should:
   a. understand or seek clarification about expectations for academic integrity in this course (including no cheating, plagiarism and inappropriate collaboration)
   b. neither give nor receive unauthorized aid on examinations or other course work that is used by the instructor as the basis of grading.
   c. take responsibility to monitor academic dishonesty in any form and to report it to the instructor or other appropriate official for action.

Cheating and Plagiarism

Cheating is the actual or attempted practice of fraudulent or deceptive acts for the purpose of improving one's grade or obtaining course credit; such acts also include assisting another student to do so. Typically, such acts occur in relation to examinations. However, it is the intent of this definition that the term 'cheating' not be limited to examination situations only, but that it include any and all actions by a student that are intended to gain an unearned academic advantage by fraudulent or deceptive means. Plagiarism is a specific form of cheating which consists of the misuse of the published and/or unpublished works of others by misrepresenting the material (i.e., their intellectual property) so used as one's own work. Penalties for cheating and plagiarism range from a 0 or F on a particular assignment, through an F for the course, to expulsion from the university. For more information on the University's policy regarding cheating and plagiarism, refer to the Class Schedule (Legal Notices on Cheating and Plagiarism) or the University Catalog (Policies and Regulations).

Computers

"At California State University, Fresno, computers and communications links to remote resources are recognized as being integral to the education and research experience. Every student is required to have his/her own computer or have other personal access to a workstation (including a modem and a printer) with all the recommended software. In the curriculum and class assignments, students are presumed to have 24-hour access to a computer workstation and the necessary communication links to the University's information resources."

Disruptive Classroom Behavior

"The classroom is a special environment in which students and faculty come together to promote learning and growth. It is essential to this learning environment that respect for the rights of others seeking to learn, respect for the professionalism of the instructor, and the general goals of academic freedom are maintained. Differences of viewpoint or concerns should be expressed in terms which are supportive of the learning process, creating an environment in which students and faculty may learn to reason with clarity and compassion, to share of themselves without losing their identities, and to develop an understanding of the community in which they live. Student conduct which disrupts the learning process shall not be tolerated and may lead to disciplinary action and/or removal from class."

Copyright Policy

Copyright laws and fair use policies protect the rights of those who have produced the material. The copy in this course has been provided for private study, scholarship, or research. Other uses may require permission from the copyright holder. The user of this work is responsible for adhering to copyright law of the U.S. (Title 17, U.S. Code). To help you familiarize yourself with copyright and fair use policies, the University encourages you to visit its Copyright Web Page: http://www.fresnostate.edu/home/about/copyright.html

Canvas course web sites contain material protected by copyrights held by the instructor, other individuals or institutions. Such material is used for educational purposes in accord with copyright law and/or with permission given by the owners of the original material. You may download one copy of the materials on any single computer for non-commercial, personal, or educational purposes only, provided that you (1) do not modify it, (2) use it only for the duration of this course, and (3) include both this notice and any copyright notice originally included with the material. Beyond this use, no material from the course web site may be copied, reproduced, republished, uploaded, posted, transmitted, or distributed in any way without the permission of the original copyright holder. The instructor assumes

Building a Social Justice-Centered Higher Education and Student Affairs Program ▪ 125

no responsibility for individuals who improperly use copyrighted material placed on the web site.

SupportNet

Our campus has developed SupportNet (http://fresnostate.edu/studentaffairs/lrc/supportnet) to connect students with specific campus resources promoting academic success. Students may be referred to it if you believe they need the services provided by SupportNet to succeed in your course.

Subject to Change Statement

This syllabus and schedule are subject to change in the event of extenuating circumstances.

Semester Schedule

Week & Date	Topic	Due Dates
Module 1: Foundations		
Week 1:	Introductions, Syllabus review, Course overview and expectations	
Week 2:	Introduction to the study of higher education	List of Experiences
Week 3:	California's Master Plan for Higher Education	Short Essay I
Week 4:	Institutional missions, institutional types, Minority-serving Institutions	Institutional Comparison I
Week 5:	*Reading Week*	Group Project Proposal
Module 2: Organizational topics in higher education		
Week 6:	Organizational theories	
Week 7:	Organizational effectiveness	Institutional Comparison II
Week 8:	Organizational change	Short Essay II
Week 9:	Organizational leadership	Project Check-in
Module 3: Opportunity in higher education		
Week 10:	Educational opportunity	
Week 11:	*Film: STOLEN EDUCATION*	Institutional Comparison III
Week 12:	*Career Center & Group Work*	Film Synthesis

Week & Date	Topic	Due Dates
Week 13:	Students in higher education	
Week 14:	Legal topics	Short Essay III
Week 15:	College access and the community college transfer function	
Course Conclusion		
Week 16:	Presentations	Group presentations
Finals Week: Week 17	Final Projects	Group project, Informed contribution

Scheduled Readings

Readings may be adjusted (including subtractions and additions) throughout the semester.

Module 1: Foundations

Week 1

Selingo, J. (2015, February 15). What's the purpose of college: A job or an education? *The Washington Post*. [In class]

Week 2

Brint, S., & Karabel, J. (1989). American education, meritocratic ideology, and the legitimation of inequality: The community college and the problem of American exceptionalism. *Higher Education, 18*, 725–735.

Harris, M. (2013). Understanding institutional diversity in American higher education. *ASHE Monograph Series, 39*(3). San Francisco: Jossey-Bass. **[pp. 1–35]**

Harris, M. (2013). Understanding institutional diversity in American higher education. *ASHE Monograph Series, 39*(3). San Francisco: Jossey-Bass. **[pp. 36–68]**

Week 3

Mullin, C.M. (2012, February). *Why access matters: The community college student body (Policy Brief 2012-01PBL)*. Washington, DC: American Association of Community Colleges

Smith, D. G. (1990). Women's colleges and coed colleges: Is there a difference for women? *The Journal of Higher Education, 61*(2), 181–197.

University of California Office of the President. (2009). *Master plan for higher education in California*. University of California Office of the President. Retrieved from: http://www.ucop.edu/acadinit/mastplan/mp.htm

Week 4
Center for Minority Serving Institutions. (2013). *Minority serving institutions: Educating all students*. The University of Pennsylvania, Philadelphia, PA: Author.

Morphew, C. C., & Hartley, M. (2006). Mission statements: A thematic analysis of rhetoric across institutional type. *The Journal of Higher Education, 77*(3), 456–471.

Wilson, R. (2010, February 7). For-profit colleges change higher education's landscape: Nimble companies gain a fast-growing share of enrollments. *The Chronicle of Higher Education*.

Module 2: Organizational Topics in Higher Education

Week 5
Axtell, J. (1971). The death of the liberal arts college. *History of Education Quarterly, 11*(4), 339–352.

Tinto, V. (1975). Dropout from higher education: A theoretical synthesis of recent research. *Review of Educational Research, 45*(1), 89–125.

H&J Ch. 6–10: Curriculum, Teaching, and Learning

Week 6
Boyce, M. E. (2003). Organizational learning is essential to achieving and sustaining change in higher education. *Innovative Higher Education, 28*(2), 119–136.

H&J Ch. 16–18

Tierney, W. G. (1997). Organizational socialization in higher education. *The Journal of Higher Education, 68*(1), 1–16.

Week 7: Reading Week
Bastedo, M. N., Samuels, E., & Kleinman, M. (2014). Do charismatic presidents influence college applications and alumni donations? Organizational identity and performance in U.S. higher education. *Higher Education, 68*(3), 397–415.

Cameron, K. (1978). Measuring organizational effectiveness in institutions of higher education. *Administrative Science Quarterly, 23*(4), 604–632.

Week 8
H&J Ch. 19–20. Organizations, leadership, and governance

Hurtado, S., Milem, J.F., Clayton-Pedersen, A.R., & Allen, W.R. (1998). Enhancing campus climates for racial/ethnic diversity: Educational policy and practice. *The Review of Higher Education, 21*(3), 279–302.

Hurtado, S., Alvarez, C. L., Guillermo-Wann, C., Cuellar, M., & Arellano, L. (2012). A model for diverse learning environments. In J. C. Smart (Ed.). *Higher education: Handbook of theory and research* (pp. 41–122). Springer.

Ospina, S., & Su, C. (2009). Weaving color lines: Race, ethnicity, and the work of leadership in social change organizations. *Leadership, 5*(2), 131–170.

Week 9

Davis, J. R. (2003). *Learning to lead: A handbook for postsecondary administrators.* (ACE/Praeger Series in Higher Education). Lanham, MD: Rowman & Littlefield. [Introduction, Chapter One]

Eddy, P. L. (2010). Leaders as linchpins for framing meaning. *Community College Review, 37*(4), 313–332.

Kezar, A. & Carducci, R. (2009). Revolutionizing leadership development. In A. Kezar (Ed.). *Rethinking leadership in a complex, multicultural, and global environment: New concepts and models for higher education* (pp. 1–38). Sterling, VA: Stylus.

Valverde, L.A. (2003). *Leaders of color in higher education: Unrecognized triumphs in harsh institutions.* New York: Altamira Press.

Module 3: Opportunity in Higher Education

Week 10: Class meets online

Harper, S. R., Patton, L. D., & Wooden, O. S. (2009). Access and equity for African American Students in higher education: A critical race historical analysis of policy efforts. *The Journal of Higher Education, 80*(4), 389–414.

McDonough, P.M., & Gildersleeve, R.E. (2006). All else is never equal: Opportunity lost and found on the P–16 path to college access. In C.F. Conrad and R.C. Serlin (Eds.). *The SAGE handbook for research in education: Engaging ideas and enriching inquiry,* (pp. 59–78)

Museus, S.D., & Kiang, P.N. (2009). Deconstructing the model minority myth and how it contributes to the invisible minority reality in higher education research. In S.D. Museus (Ed.). *Conducting research on Asian Americans in higher education,* New Directions for Institutional Research, 142, (pp. 5–15).

Turner, C.S.V. (2002). Women of color in academe: Living with multiple marginality. *The Journal of Higher Education, 73*(1), 74–93.

Week 11

Watch *Stolen Education*

Luna, R. (Director), & Alemán, E., Jr. (Producer). (2013). *Stolen Education* [Video file]. USA: AlemanLuna Productions.

Tierney, W.G. (1999). Models of minority college-going and retention: Cultural integrity versus cultural suicide. *Journal of Negro Education, 68*(1), 80–91

Week 12

No readings

Week 13

Muñoz, S. M. (2016). Undocumented and Unafraid: Understanding the Disclosure Management Process for Undocumented College Students and Graduates. *Journal of College Student Development, 57*(6), 715–729.

Museus, S., Shiroma, K., & Dizon, J. (2016). Cultural Community Connections and College Success: An Examination of Southeast Asian American College Students. *Journal of College Student Development, 57*(5), 485–502.

Perez, P.A., McDonough, P.M. (2008). Understanding Latina and Latino college choice: A social capital and chain migration analysis. *Journal of Hispanic Higher Education, 7*(3), 249–265.

Renn, K. (2007). LGBT Student Leaders and Queer Activists: Identities of Lesbian, Gay, Bisexual, Transgender, and Queer Identified College Student Leaders and Activists. *Journal of College Student Development, 48*(3), 311–330.

Week 14

Park, J., & Liu, A. (2014). Interest Convergence or Divergence? A Critical Race Analysis of Asian Americans, Meritocracy, and Critical Mass in the Affirmative Action Debate. *The Journal of Higher Education, 85*(1), 36–64.

Teranishi, R., & Briscoe, K. (2008). Contextualizing Race: African American College Choice in an Evolving Affirmative Action Era. *The Journal of Negro Education, 77*(1), 15–26.

Bell, D. (1980). Brown v. Board of Education and the Interest-Convergence Dilemma. *Harvard Law Review, 93*(3), 518–533.

Week 15

Hernández, I., Hernández, S., & de la Teja, M. H. (2017). *Five things student affairs professionals should know about supporting Latinx students in community colleges.* Washington, DC: NASPA.

Hutcheson, P. A. (1999). Reconsidering the community college. *History of Education Quarterly, 39*(3), 307–320.

McDonough, P. M. (1994). Buying and selling higher education: The social construction of the college applicant. *The Journal of Higher Education, 65*(4), 427–446.

Iloh, C., & Tierney, W. G. (2014). Understanding for-profit college and community college choice through rational choice. *Teachers College Record, 116*(8), 1–34.

REFERENCES

ACPA-College Student Educators International & NASPA—Student Affairs Administrators in Higher Education. (2015). *Professional competency areas for student affairs educators.* https://www.naspa.org/images/uploads/main/ACPA_NASPA_Professional_Competencies_FINAL.pdf

Adams, M. (2016). Pedagogical foundations for social justice education. In M. Adams, L. A. Bell, D. J. Goodman, & K.Y. Joshi (Eds.), *Teaching for diversity and social justice* (pp. 45–72). Routledge.

Ahmed, S. (2012). *On being included: Racism and diversity in institutional life.* Duke University Press.

Bell, L. A. (2016). Theoretical foundations for social justice education. In M. Adams, L. A. Bell, P. Griffin (Eds.), *Teaching for diversity and social justice: A sourcebook* (pp. 3–15). Routledge.

Bell, L. A., Goodman, D. J., & Varghese, R. (2016). Critical self-knowledge for social justice educators. In M. Adams, L. A. Bell, D. J. Goodman, & K. Y. Joshi (Eds.), *Teaching for Diversity and Social Justice* (pp. 415–436). Routledge.

Benavides, A. D., & Keyes, L. (2016). New-student orientations: Supporting success and socialization in graduate programs. *Journal of Public Affairs Education, 22*(1), 107–124. https://doi.org/10.1080/15236803.2016.12002231

Bohn, S., Danielson, C., & Thorman, T. (2019, July). *Just the facts: Poverty in California.* Public Policy Institute of California. https://inequality.stanford.edu/sites/default/files/PovertyinCA19.pdf

Bondi, S. (2012). Students and institutions protecting whiteness as property: A critical race theory analysis of student affairs preparation. *Journal of Student Affairs Research and Practice, 49*(4), 397–414. https://doi.org/10.1515/jsarp-2012-6381

Carducci, R., & Jaramillo, D. (2014). Job one: Continuing the journey toward self-authorship. In P. M. Magolda & J. E. Carnaghi (Eds.), *Job One 2.0: Understanding the next generation of student affairs professionals* (pp. 162–191). University Press of America.

Collin, F. (2013). Social constructivism. In B. Kaldis (Ed.), *Encyclopedia of philosophy and social sciences.* SAGE Publications.

Council for the Advancement of Standards in Higher Education. (n.d.). *About CAS.* https://www.cas.edu/about

Daneneberg, A., Jepsen, C., & Cerdán, P. (2002). *Student and school indicators for youth in California's Central Valley.* Public Policy Institute of California.

Diggles, K. (2014). Addressing racial awareness and color-blindness in higher education. *New Directions for Teaching & Learning, 2014*(140), 31–44. https://doi.org/10.1002/tl.20111

Eaton, P. W. (2016). The competency-based movement in student affairs: Implications for curriculum and professional development. *Journal of College Student Development, 57*(5), 573–589. https://doi.org/10.1353/csd.2016.0061

Flowers, L. A., & Howard-Hamilton, M. F. (2002). A qualitative study of graduate students' perceptions of diversity issues in student affairs preparation programs. *Journal of College Student Development, 43*(1), 119–123. https://eric.ed.gov/?id=EJ642672

Freire, P. (1970). *Pedagogy of the oppressed.* Continuum.

Fresno State. (2022). *Office of Institutional Effectiveness: Quick facts.* https://academics.fresnostate.edu/oie/quickfacts/index.html

Furman, G. (2012). Social justice leadership as praxis: Developing capacities through preparation programs. *Educational Administration Quarterly, 48*(2), 191–229. https://doi.org/10.1177/0013161X11427394

Harris, J. C., & Linder, C. (2018). The racialized experiences of students of color in higher education and student affairs graduate preparation programs. *Journal of College Student Development, 59*(2), 141–158. https://doi.org/10.1353/csd.2018.0014

Harris, J. C., & Patton, L. D. (2019). Un/doing intersectionality through higher education research. *The Journal of Higher Education, 90*(3), 347–372. https://eric.ed.gov/?id=EJ1213389

hooks, b. (1994). *Teaching to transgress.* Routledge.

Hubain, B. S., Allen, E. L., Harris, J. C., & Linder, C. (2016). Counter-stories as representations of the racialized experiences of students of color in higher education and student affairs graduate preparation programs. *International Journal of Qualitative Studies in Education, 29*(7), 946–963. https://doi.org/10.1080/09518398.2016.1174894

Kelly, B. T., & Gayles, J. G. (2010). Resistance to racial/ethnic dialog in graduate preparation programs implications for developing multicultural competence. *College Student Affairs Journal, 29*(1), 75–85. https://eric.ed.gov/?id=EJ969827

Kline, K. A., & Gardner, M. M. (2005). Envisioning new forms of praxis: Reflective practice and social justice education in a higher education graduate program. *Advancing Women in Leadership, 19*, 1–8. https://doi.org/10.21423/awlj-v19.a191.

Kuk, L., & Banning, J. (2009, June 1). Student affairs preparation programs: A competency based approach to assessment and outcomes. *College Student Journal, 43*(2), 492–502. https://eric.ed.gov/?id=EJ872263

Latz, A. O., Ozaki, C. C., Royer, D. W., & Hornak, A. M. (2017). Student affairs professionals in the community college: Critically examining preparation programs from a social justice lens. *Community College Journal of Research and Practice, 41*(11), 733–746. https://eric.ed.gov/?id=EJ1153497

Liddell, D. L., Wilson, M. E., Pasquesi, K., Hirschy, A. S., & Boyle, K. M. (2014). Development of professional identity through socialization in graduate school. *Journal of Student Affairs Research and Practice, 51*(1), 69–84. https://doi.org/10.1515/jsarp-2014-0006

Linder, C., Harris, J. C., Allen, E. L., & Hubain, B. (2015). Building inclusive pedagogy: Recommendations from a national study of students of color in higher education and student affairs graduate programs. *Equity & Excellence in Education, 48*(2), 178–194. https://doi.org/10.1080/10665684.2014.959270

Lovell, C. D., & Kosten, L. A. (2000). Skills, knowledge, and personal traits necessary for success as a student affairs administrator: A meta-analysis of thirty years of research. *NASPA Journal, 37*(4), 535–572. https://doi.org/10.2202/0027-6014.1118

Magolda, P., & Carnaghi, J. E. (2017). Evolving roles and competencies: Professional development reconsidered. In J. H. Schuh, S. R. Jones, & V. Torres

(Eds.), *Student Services: A Handbook for the Profession* (pp. 532–540). John Wiley & Sons.

Marine, S. B., & Gilbert, C. (2022). *Critical praxis in student affairs: Social justice in action.* Stylus.

NASPA—Student Affairs Administrators in Higher Education. (n.d.). *Graduate program directory.* https://www.naspa.org/careers/graduate/graduate-program-directory

Pérez Huber, L. (2010). Using Latina/o critical race theory and racist nativism to explore intersectionality in the educational experiences of undocumented Chicana college students. *Educational Foundations, 24,* 77–96. https://files.eric.ed.gov/fulltext/EJ885982.pdf

Renn, K. A., & Jessup-Anger, E. R. (2008). Preparing new professionals: Lessons for graduate preparation programs from the national study of new professionals in student affairs. *Journal of College Student Development, 49*(4), 319–335. https://doi.org/10.1353/csd.0.0022

Robbins, K. (2004). Struggling for equality/struggling for hierarchy: Gender dynamics in an English as an additional language classroom for adolescent Vietnamese refugees. *Feminist Teacher, 15*(1), 66–79. https://www.jstor.org/stable/40545907

Schwartz, R., & Stewart, D.-L. (2017). The history of student affairs. In J. H. Schuh, S. R. Jones, & V. Torres (Eds.), *Student services: A handbook for the profession* (pp. 20–38). John Wiley & Sons.

The Campaign for College Opportunity. (2018). *A call to action and blueprint to increase college graduates and keep our economy strong.* https://collegecampaign.org/portfolio/california-higher-ed-blueprint/

The Planning Center. (2012, March 27). *San Joaquin Valley demographic forecasts 2010 to 2050.* Fresno Council of Governments. https://agendas.fresnocog.org/itemAttachments/60/ITEM_V_D_San_Joaquin_Valley_Demographic_Forecasts_-_Final_28_Mar_2012.pdf

Underwood, S. J., & Austin, C. E. (2016). Higher education graduate preparation programs: Characteristics and trends. *Journal of College Student Development, 57*(3), 326–332. https://www.learntechlib.org/p/192952/

University of California Office of the President. (2009). *Master plan for higher education in California.* University of California Office of the President. http://www.ucop.edu/acadinit/mastplan/mp.htm

CHAPTER 7

THE BLACK MALE RESEARCH BOOTCAMP

Intentionally Shaping Black Men's Doctoral Student Socialization

Jesse Ford
Tamara Bertrand Jones

ABSTRACT

Historically, socialization activities have focused on discipline-based knowledge and skills required for professional success. Still, these socialization activities do not address the nuances of identity, particularly race and gender for Black men that are essential for success in academia. Moreover, there are nuances to academia for those aspiring to become tenure-track faculty, and the tenure and promotion processes for Black men are not often articulated in traditional socialization processes. Thus, socialization issues are especially acute for Black men faculty given their limited representation in academia, notwithstanding efforts to diversify higher education and the professoriate specifically. The Black Male Research BootCamp (BMRBC) represents a socialization intervention for Black men doctoral students. Black men doctoral student participants identified the importance of Black male spaces in which

Advancing Inclusive Excellence in Higher Education, pages 133–150
Copyright © 2023 by Information Age Publishing
www.infoagepub.com
All rights of reproduction in any form reserved.

to learn, grow, and engage with other Black men scholars. We offer suggestions for Black men doctoral students and faculty, and institutions interested in supporting Black men doctoral students.

> It is the first day of the spring semester at Leaf University, a prominent, predominantly White, research-intensive institution in the Pacific Northwest. Matt, a Black cisgender man from southwest Orlando, is an information sciences doctoral candidate in his third year. Matt received his bachelor's and master's degrees in information sciences from a historically White college, Tree University in the southeast. Throughout his tenure at Tree University, Matt was instructed by Black professors and surrounded by Black classmates. As a member of a community devoted to his achievement, he viewed these relationships as highly influential during his time at Tree.
>
> Matt's journey at Leaf University was vastly different from his experience at Tree University. He was the only student of color in his courses and there were no faculty members of color in his graduate program. In addition, only 7% of the student body identified as students of color, and less than 1% as Black men. Consequently, the number of graduate student organizations was minimal, very few students of color participated in these spaces, and Matt had no connections to other doctoral students in his program or at the institution.
>
> As a result, Matt suffered with feelings of isolation, alienation from family, peers, and mentors, and encountered several obstacles based on his race and gender. Due to the requirements and structure of his academic degree, he had not had the opportunity to build any local community. In addition, Matt encountered numerous racial microaggressions as he attempted to navigate doctoral education. Matt asked the faculty in his program and his peers for advice on how to respond to remarks such as, "You are only here because you are Black" and "You must play football, that's the only reason Black men are admitted to this institution." They did not have advice for him, and would offer contritely, "I'm so sorry that happened to you." Matt starts to change his mind about his future as a doctoral candidate, even though he only has one year left before he completes his degree.

UNDERSTANDING THE LANDSCAPE: BLACK DOCTORAL STUDENTS IN HIGHER EDUCATION

The number of Black and Brown students on college campuses has grown by 20% in the past 30 years (Gasman et al., 2008). Despite more students, especially students of color, pursuing graduate and professional education, evidence of racialized experiences, like Matt's, continues to grow. In fact, research on higher education shows that issues arising from race and racism are common in doctoral education for Black students (Briscoe, 2022; Burt et al., 2017; Burt et al., 2019; Griffin & Ford, 2022; Ingram, 2013; Jett, 2019; Minnett et al., 2019; Wallace, 2022; Wallace & Ford, 2021).

Within the context of doctoral education, Black students navigating academic environments often describe feelings of being undervalued, instances of microaggressions (Burt et al., 2017; Ingram, 2013), and isolation due to a lack of community (Ballard & Cintrón, 2010; Felder & Baker, 2013). These psychosocial factors align to produce negative outcomes for Black men's educational experiences, such as low degree attainment (Harper, 2012), greater isolation in academic environments (Ingram, 2013), and race-related stress (Burt et al., 2017). Additionally, for Black men in graduate education, navigating academic spaces and developing a racial identity can be challenging (Felder et al., 2014). As a result, many Black doctoral students are constantly exploring ways to establish an identity within historically White spaces and learning skills to navigate the "hidden curriculum." Platt (2015) explained Black men doctoral students must "play the game," further explaining that playing the game is doing what is expected to advance or understand the "hidden curriculum" of academic spaces. The political nature of the doctoral environment adds an additional layer of context to their experience (Rasheem et al., 2017). Due to the bias against minoritized people of color that is common in academia, playing the game also means that many students must hide, and in many cases overperform to prove they belong.

One area where Black students often hide, or camouflage, themselves is in pursuing race-related research. Blacks in academia with a race-focused research agenda have been accused of "navel-gazing" (Bertrand Jones, 2015). In a system where students have been traditionally marginalized, race-related research could hinder Black men's degree completion (Platt & Hilton, 2017) and future career trajectory. Taken together, these threats to Black men's success in academia call for a deeper examination of their socialization into doctoral education.

In this chapter, we will examine current literature on socialization and the experiences of Black men doctoral students. We describe the genesis of the Black Male Research BootCamp (BMRBC) as a socialization intervention designed to disrupt traditional socialization processes and empower Black men doctoral students as they progress toward dissertation completion. We provide suggestions for practitioners, faculty, researchers, and institutions looking to better understand the challenges and opportunities of holistically supporting and graduating Black men in doctoral programs.

SOCIALIZATION: THE PROCESS FOR SUPPORTING CURRENT AND FUTURE TRAJECTORIES

Socialization has historically been considered an essential factor in the academic and professional success of new faculty and administrators (Clark & Corcoran, 1986; Johnson, 2001; Lucas & Murry, 2002). While many definitions of socialization exist, the process is typically described as a process where the values, norms, knowledge, and beliefs of a group are imparted to a new member (Clark & Corcoran, 1986; Johnson, 2001; LaRocco & Bruns, 2006; Reynolds, 1992; Tierney & Bensimon, 1996). Effective socialization starts in graduate school (McCray, 2011) and happens before a new faculty member or administrator starts their first job.

More specifically, graduate student socialization is defined as the two-way "developmental process through which a doctoral student acquires a disciplinary identity and understanding of disciplinary practices and norms through knowledge acquisition, investment [or commitment], and involvement" (Weidman et al., 2001). Unfortunately, new scholars often have not received adequate socialization to become productive or advance professionally in faculty and administrative roles (Griffith & Ford, 2022; LaRocco & Bruns, 2006; Ortlieb et al., 2010; Reynolds, 1992). Historically, socialization activities have focused on discipline-based knowledge and skills required for professional success. Still, these socialization activities do not address the many unstated and undocumented parts of academic culture that new faculty feel important to their professional success (Bertrand Jones & Osborne-Lampkin, 2013; Johnson, 2001; LaRocco & Bruns, 2006; Reynolds, 1992). Moreover, there are nuances to academia for those aspiring to become tenure-track faculty, and the tenure and promotion process for Black men are not often articulated in traditional socialization processes (Ford, 2022).

BLACK MEN'S RACED AND GENDERED EXPERIENCES IN HIGHER EDUCATION

Socialization issues are especially acute for Black men faculty given their limited representation in academia (Platt & Hilton, 2017), notwithstanding efforts to diversify higher education and the professoriate specifically (Smith, 2020). Increasing the number and percentage of Black faculty can lead to more holistic support for students of color in doctoral programs. For example, traditionally the presence of more minoritized faculty role models broadly influences the recruitment and graduation of minoritized doctoral students as well as socializes these students to life in the academy (Ayers, 1983; Blackwell, 1983; Brown, 1991; Ford, 2022; Platt & Hilton, 2017). Diverse faculty also provide knowledge of diverse student populations and offer nontraditional views about teaching and professional goals (Ellis, 2001; Turner & Thompson, 1993). Ultimately, having a more diverse faculty can lead to broader and deeper use of existing and new research paradigms, not only for the faculty themselves but also for other members of the university community (Antonio, 2002; Garrison-Wade et al., 2012).

Despite documented benefits of having diverse faculty in higher education institutions, consistent historical evidence has shown that faculty of color have different experiences in academia as compared to their White counterparts (Cole et al., 2017; Johnson-Bailey & Cervero, 2004; Ponjuan, Martin et al., 2011; Stanley, 2006, 2007; Thompson & Dey, 1998; Thompson & Louque, 2005; Tillman, 2001). Additionally, faculty of color receive less social support than their White colleagues (Ponjuan et al., 2011). The lack of support often results from conflicting values of individual faculty members and the academy at large (Stanley, 2007). As a result, Black faculty often miss professional opportunities because of limited access to the formal and informal networks that exist in many professions and disciplines, ultimately compromising their professional success (Frierson, 1990; Modica & Mamiseishvili, 2010; Patitu & Hinton, 2003; Turner & Thompson, 1993). Building upon the already challenging transition from graduate student to professor, Black faculty also experience isolation and alienation in departments where they may be the only face of color (Cole et al., 2017; Ford 2022; McCray, 2011). The intersectionality of race and gender add additional layers to the already complex environment for Black faculty (Collins, 1990; Ford, 2022; Gregory, 2001; Griffin & Reddick, 2011; Johnson-Bailey & Cervero, 2004; Tillman, 2011). Taken further, due to marginalization and lack of mentoring, Black men faculty are often not familiar with the tenure process (Ford, 2022; Griffin et al., 2013).

These challenges, coupled with the fact that new faculty often have not received adequate socialization to become productive faculty members, further confound Black faculty experiences in academia. Given the challenges identified in the literature for faculty of color generally and Black faculty specifically, graduate student socialization activities do not adequately address many of the challenges facing Black men in the professoriate, which is often seen as the training ground for Black men who wish to become faculty members. In other words, "How can higher education faculty and institutions better support and develop Black men who seek to become scholars and faculty in higher education?"

CONCEPTUAL FRAMEWORK AND QUESTIONS GUIDING THE INQUIRY

The research in this chapter builds on the socialization framework created by Bertrand Jones and Osborne-Lampkin (2013), which centers mentoring, professional development, and academic preparation as critical components of this key process in graduate education. Bertrand Jones and Osborne-Lamkin (2013) findings highlight each of these concepts as vital parts of the doctoral and early career faculty journey. More specifically, Bertrand Jones and Osborne-Lampkin (2013) suggest that academic preparation is defined as "formal school experiences—undergraduate, graduate, or postgraduate academic study," while mentoring involves "relationships—peer, informal, and formal; within and outside of the professional context," and professional development is "formal and informal experiences—professional or paraprofessional daily work, additional training and development in the professional context" (p. 61).

Understanding these concepts provided a framework for doctoral and early career faculty socialization that helped to contextualize the activities in the Research BootCamp (RBC), an early career professional development intervention, originally designed for Black women. Using this framework, we sought to describe the kind of environment that would support Black men's socialization and ultimate doctoral degree attainment and reimagine how professional development could be used to cultivate that type of environment.

THE RESEARCH BOOT CAMP PROGRAM STRUCTURE

Since 2005, the Sisters of the Academy Institute (SOTA) RBC has assisted over 500 women and women of color doctoral students with dissertation completion and helped junior scholars develop sustainable research agendas. Using a culturally responsive approach to socialization, the RBC model centers the intersectionality of Black women throughout the program and has helped Black women by providing a counterspace for their development, improving their formal networks, developing mentoring relationships, and highlighting the benefits of early career professional development (Bertrand Jones & Osborne-Lampkin, 2013; Bertrand Jones et al., 2015; West & Bertrand Jones, 2021). The signature RBC model focuses on Black women's experiences in society and the academy, while recent SOTA partnerships with other higher education institutions and organizations have expanded the model by offering RBCs focused on women of all races and ethnicities, women of color in STEM, and the RBC for Black men doctoral students that is the focus of this chapter. SOTA's Signature RBC maintains its focus on interdisciplinary Black women doctoral students and junior scholars.

Typically, the RBC is an intensive, biannual 4-day professional development program designed to assist in the development of advanced doctoral students' dissertation research preparation and junior scholars' preparation for tenure and promotion and increased research productivity. Through individual and small group mentoring, with a focus on knowledge and skill development and values clarification, the RBC helps mitigate socialization issues for early career scholars (doctoral students and junior scholars) and provides access to a network of Black and other scholars of color. Building on the model of the signature RBC for Black women, we sought to create a space where Black men doctoral students were centered, and the issues identified by Black men themselves (Ballard & Cintrón, 2010; Burt et al., 2017; Burt et al., 2019; Felder & Baker 2013; Ingram, 2013) and others in the literature that receive little attention could be intentionally addressed.

For the BMRBC, we piloted a 5-day program where participants were organized into two levels of advanced doctoral students—the first group consisted of doctoral students having completed coursework and preparing dissertation research proposals (designated as Level 1 participants), the second group had successfully defended their research proposals and were collecting or had collected data (designated as Level 2 participants). At the beginning of the week participants presented their research ideas and goals for the week and summarize their progress at the end of the RBC in another research presentation. A panel of senior scholar mentors offered their critique and suggestions for future direction at both presentations. Daily seminars and workshops on research methodology, writing for scholarly publication, and life management within academia, among other topics specific to the participant level were presented. Participants also had time for individual writing and received feedback during mentoring sessions with an assigned senior scholar, targeting the areas identified by Tillman (2001) and Bertrand Jones and Osborne-Lampkin (2013). RBC personnel, from the senior scholar mentors to workshop presenters, are predominantly Black women; during the BMRBC, Black men scholars served in these roles. Collectively the BMRBC works to provide a culturally responsive method for supporting and developing Black men scholars.

Previous research on the RBC has highlighted three critical ways that participants' socialization was positively influenced—first, by creating a community of Black women scholars the women felt supported and understood (Bertrand Jones & Osborne-Lampkin, 2013). Second, by being surrounded by Black women who were experts who had successfully completed dissertations and attained tenure and promotion phases, the Black women senior scholars helped build participants' confidence through providing critique and insight into their research development. Lastly senior scholars helped participants develop action steps for success during the nebulous dissertation and tenure and promotion processes in the academy (Bertrand Jones & Osborne-Lampkin, 2013).

To identify Black men's unique areas of concern, we conducted focus groups with Black men in doctoral programs during the planning phase of the RBC. Their feedback affirmed that the existing RBC structure designed for Black women, remained aligned with their core experiences in graduate education. This notion is not entirely surprising as the commonality in Black men's and Black women's experiences of racism remind us of this truth (Collins, 2004). Their feedback helped us modify some aspects of the RBC to provide a focused space for Black men. After the program, we spoke with participants about their experience and perspectives on what made the RBC experience most meaningful for them.

COLLECTING BLACK MEN'S EXPERIENCES: DATA COLLECTION AND ANALYSIS

We collected participants' experiences in a group interview following their participation at the BMRBC (Patton, 2015; Rossman & Rallis, 2012). We felt that a qualitative case study design would support our goal of understanding how the men experienced the BMRBC. Immediately following the program, the men participated in a 60-minute focus group to provide additional insights on their overall experiences in graduate school and the BMRBC. In addition to the focus group, participants completed three surveys to evaluate their experiences—(a) a daily survey to track their learning from daily sessions; (b) an overall evaluation to provide feedback on their experience; and (c) a retrospective pretest to assess growth in their RBC-specific knowledge, skills, and values over the week-long process.

In this chapter we share the experiences of seven Black men doctoral students who participated in the week-long BMRBC program designed to increase their productivity and contribute to their scholarly development. Six of the seven participants were students at State University and one student studied at University One. The participants represented various academic disciplines, including curriculum and instruction, educational leadership and policy studies, business management, and political science. The men were in various stages of their doctoral school journey, but all had completed their comprehensive exams prior to attending the BMRBC and represented a mix of Level 1 and Level 2 scholars.

DESIGNING CULTURALLY RESPONSIVE SUPPORTIVE ENVIRONMENTS

The need for supportive environments is well documented in the literature for contributing to the academic experiences of Black men in education. Brunsma et al. (2017) posit that a supportive community is important for all graduate students, but more vital for graduate students of color. As we noted earlier, for many Black doctoral students, higher education systems manifest feelings of alienation, stress, racial microaggressions, and isolation (Brunsma et al., 2017; Burt et al., 2017; Ingram, 2013). To combat these feelings, both students and institutions attempt to provide solutions to these well-documented experiences. Unfortunately, these efforts often fall short of what Black men need to feel supported. During our discussions with the Black men doctoral students who participated in the BMRBC, they identified core components of the environment that supported their socialization and progress toward graduation.

Safe Space to Acknowledge and Discuss Race

In the BMRBC, participants spoke about the "cultural Blackness" that anchored the program, in the space they could reflect on shared racial experiences and understanding and where their Blackness faded into the background—it was something they did not have to think about for the week. This was particularly salient for participants who were the lone—or one of a few—Black men in their respective programs, such as Osman. He admitted:

> Getting to actually see African American males, who have been through this process, and for them sharing with us their experiences being African American males, and, you know, all of that—that has been different. You know, there may have been one at this presentation, or two at another presentation out of a panel of however many different people. But to have this to be exclusively for us and by us.

This quote confirms the continuing argument that representation matters for people of color in the academy. Among these men, having others validate their experiences with racism while simultaneously seeing role models of success in the academy was especially meaningful.

Participants also acknowledged a focus on race throughout the program as a distinguishing feature from other professional development. This feature could be described as FUBU (For Us By Us), the name of a '90s Black-owned clothing line targeted to Black consumers. Osman explained:

> I always felt there was a great need to step up focus and attention for African American males, and that is what stood out as a difference in this particular bootcamp. Many of the presenters, getting to actually see African American males, who have been through this process, and for them sharing with us their experiences being African American males, and, you know, all of that—that has been different. You know, there may have been one at this presentation, or two at another presentation out of a panel of however many different people. But to have this to be exclusively for us and by us.

Access to Same Race, Same Gender Mentors

Many students establish mentoring relationships with faculty members (Rasheem et al., 2017). In addition to establishing connections, the purpose of these relationships is to foster learning and growth for the graduate students. The connections needed extend to peers in doctoral programs, as research has also highlighted the role that peers, and near-peers have in providing support during doctoral education (Griffin et al., 2020). However, mentoring within historically White environments often lacks culturally responsive techniques to engage students in the academy properly. For the Black men who attended the BMRBC, they told us that same race, same gender mentoring relationships, supportive environmental networks, mentorship from Black women, and peer to peer mentor–protégé connections were influential aspects of mentoring for them.

In our discussions with the men, they expressed the desire for same race, same gender mentoring relationships. Due to the lack of Black men faculty members and mentors across college campuses, during the BMRBC we intentionally provided participants with a Black man senior-scholar mentor. The senior-scholar mentor had been a member of the academy in administrative and teaching roles while successfully navigating diverse and even hostile academic and professional environments. Osman, a Level 2 participant, described his senior scholar mentor as "a resource... that you could use." He stated that through connecting and working with his senior scholar mentor, he better understood:

> First, that this can be done. You can actually not just get out and get a doctorate, but actually thrive and do well. Two, you have a lot of experience, so when he spoke and he was giving information, all of it, to me... was very useful. Three, you can have a kind of down-to-earth personality, someone you would want to get to know.

Participants in the BMRBC built connections with peers of the same racial and gender backgrounds. Justin stated, "And so coming here with this kind of opportunity, I felt, oh, this is a good connection, you know, to build that base, and keeping in touch with people that I think are like me."

"Culturally Black" Communication

In reflecting on the shared race of the workshop presenters, senior scholar mentor, and participants, the men described a shared communication style that was grounded in Blackness. Young (2007) refers to this as code meshing. Code meshing is defined as the ways in which standard English is blended with other dialects and language to reflect how African Americans actually speak. Taken further, BMRBC participants acknowledged that being surrounded with Black scholars set the tone for receiving and interpreting feedback provided throughout the week. For example, Osman explained:

> Sometimes when you hear the same information from a different angle, or from a different person, you receive it differently. And so even though many of the things were covered—like I've been to a qualitative [workshop], so therefore, I've heard a lot of stuff that was in the qualitative presentation. I've been to, you know, a mentoring program, so I heard a lot of the stuff that was provided about mentoring. But what made it different was having the qualitative presentation, the mentoring presentation, this presentation, that presentation, all with the focus being on African American males. That's what made it different to me.

Marcus described this communication style as "more genuine." He explained:

> When we were given advice, it seemed more genuine. It wasn't just this [is] good advice. You should do it because it's good. It seemed like, it's good advice, we want you to succeed because we're all in this together... It's this is a good idea because I think it's a good idea for you because I care about you.

CONNECTING OUR FINDINGS TO THE BROADER DISCUSSION

Given the experiences of the Black men in our study, it is important to acknowledge the importance of race in the challenges these men face in academia and the ultimate responsibility that institutions must provide counters for those challenges. During the BMRBC, those remedies came from a community of scholars with whom they shared many common experiences. The understanding generated by a shared lived experience based on race not only allowed for the commonalities to be explored, but also provided a framework for the importance of the diversity in the collective differences in Black men's experiences. At the BMRBC, Black male doctoral students were able to develop and expand their professional networks of Black male scholars. The expansion of their networks provides opportunities that support their professional success (i.e., Modica & Mamiseishvili, 2010; Patitu & Hinton, 2003; Turner & Thompson, 1993). These networks—senior, peer, and other—established at the RBC provide social support, create outlets for professional development, build research capacity, and influence success in the academy (Jean-Marie & Brooks, 2011; Stanley & Watson, 2007). This type of support increases the likelihood of exposure to collaborative research opportunities (Bagada et al., 2015) and the development of social relationships with men who share a common profession and can relate to challenges these men face (Brooms & Davis, 2017).

Moreover, the importance of race and racism in higher education must be acknowledged. Literature has frequently positioned race and racism at the center of the issues faced by Black males in educational institutions (Burt et al., 2017; Ingram, 2013). However, this research identifies race, racism, and racialized experiences as factors that must be considered when designing new interventions and programs to ensure their success. Similarly to the RBC for Black women, this space offered an environment for participants to address issues related to racism and racialized experiences, emphasizing that both were crucial to their understanding of their place in the academy. While the BMRBC does not remove the barriers of race or racism for Black men, it does provide a professional enclave for sharing strategies for navigating racialized experiences and environments as Black men seek to move beyond merely surviving doctoral education and develop techniques to thrive in the academy.

Lastly, the BMRBC is a professional development intervention that may lead to the professoriate. There are racialized issues at all stages of education, including K–12 experiences (Jackson et al., 2021), undergraduate education (Harper, 2012), and doctoral education (Burt, 2017), and faculty positions (Ford, 2022). Despite these racial obstacles, Black men navigate educational environments. The notion that Black men can succeed in academic environments and become faculty members was a significant conclusion of this research, in the midst of racialized experiences and racism. In addition to providing a supportive environment, the BMRBC presented participants with real-life examples of Black men who earned doctorates and became faculty. This chapter demonstrates that Black men continue to need to see Black men who resemble them in academic spaces.

RECOMMENDATIONS AND REFLECTIONS FROM THE BLACK MALE RESEARCH BOOTCAMP

The BMRBC intervention has implications that will fill a void in the literature as it relates to the experiences of Black men doctoral students. Its significance centers on the reformation of professional development as socialization. As students look for opportunities to expand their knowledge and network, experiences like the BMRBC offer a counterspace to traditional professional development that may not center their needs, or address race, racism, or the racialized experiences of Black men.

1. Take agency for your experience. If there are no, or limited, faculty of color in your program, department, or even college, search for these scholars outside of your program/department/college. Scholars outside of your area can provide unique perspectives and thus valuable insight on issues you experience.
2. Seek mentors beyond your academic institutions. Same race and same gender mentors are not always an option for each institution. Sometimes students must move beyond their academic homes to find other scholars to serve as mentors and supporters. Conferences and other professional development spaces can serve as venues to seek out mentors.
3. Network with your doctoral peers. The relationships with peers—fellow students of color, and others are paramount to your success as a doctoral student. Students often possess a wealth of knowledge, pass on unwritten rules, norms, and customs, and represent future leaders in your field. Developing relationships with your peers not only benefits you during your studies, but can lay the foundation for needed connections and opportunities postgraduation.

For faculty, staff, departments, and institutions committed to supporting Black men doctoral students, we offer the following recommendations:

1. When you do not understand, ask. Black men are the narrators of their stories and lived experiences. If you do not understand how to support them, ask them. Consider taking the time to establish relationships with these students and explore ways to understand and improve their experiences.
2. Cultivate safe and supportive environments. Education is filled with racial and gender disparities. Nonetheless, these inequalities are rarely thought about when creating or cultivating environments. When these spaces are designed with intentionality that takes into account race, gender, and other demographic characteristics, the identities of Black men and other minoritized populations, it allows these students to feel supported within the environment. This support is essential to validating their feelings and contributions in the academy.

3. Provide faculty possibility models. Every institution should work to ensure the success of Black men enrolled in doctoral programs. In addition, this support should involve providing examples of what it means to be a faculty member and what this career path can encompass for this population. If necessary, go outside of your department, college, or even institution to locate and connect Black men students with Black men role models and mentors.
4. Create formal structures for socialization, support, mentoring, and professional development. These formal mechanisms offer an opportunity to enact espoused institutional commitment to student success. By allocating resources, both financial and human, dedicated to creating and sustaining programming targeted toward minoritized population's needs and success, institutions can ensure that students need not seek outside of "home" for support. If institutions lack faculty of color to support these initiatives, partnering with organizations like Sisters of the Academy Institute, or the National Center for Faculty Development and Diversity, can offer solutions for role models, mentors, and culturally responsive programming for doctoral students and other scholars.

This list, while not comprehensive, asks both Blcak men and institutions to play an active role in supporting Black men in doctoral programs.

CONCLUSION

The BMRBC represents a viable model for supporting Black men and creating an environment that is sensitive to their marginalized identities. We strongly encourage institutions, faculty, and staff, along with other stakeholders, to explore best practices to support the academic and professional success of Black men on your campuses. Even though these strategies can differ from person to person, providing opportunity for Black men to discuss their needs, this discussion often begins with a purposeful attention on empowering Black men. When individuals are unsure about how to proceed, the question "What do you need?" can often go a long way!

REFERENCES

Alfred, M. V. (2001). Success in the ivory tower: Lessons from Black tenured female faculty at a major research university. In R. O. Mabokela & A. L. Green (Eds.), *Sisters of the academy: Emergent Black women scholars in higher education* (pp. 57–80). Stylus.

Antonio, A. L. (2002). Faculty of color reconsidered: Reassessing contributions to scholarship. *The Journal of Higher Education, 73*(5), 582–602.

Ayers, G.E. (1983). Critical issues: The illusion of equal access. *Planning and Changing, 14,* 49–55.

Ballard, H. E., & Cintrón, R. (2010). Critical race theory as an analytical tool: African American male success in doctoral education. *Journal of College Teaching and Learning, 7*(10), 11–23. https://doi.org/10.19030/tlc.v7i10.152

Bertrand Jones, T. (2015). Me-search IS research: My socialization as an academic. In D. J. Davis, R. J. Brunn, & K. Venegas (Eds.), *Intersectionality of research and education* (pp. 252–260). Stylus.

Bertrand Jones, T., & Osborne-Lampkin, L. (2013). Black female faculty success and early career professional development. *Negro Educational Review, 64*(1–4), 59–75. https://eric.ed.gov/?id=EJ1014334

Bertrand Jones, T., Osborne-Lampkin, L., Patterson, S., & Davis, D. J. (2015). Creating a "safe and supportive environment": Mentoring and professional development for recent Black women doctoral graduates. *International Journal of Doctoral Studies, 10,* 483–499. http://ijds.org/Volume10/IJDSv10p483-499Jones1748.pdf

Blackwell, J. E. (1983). *Networking and mentoring: A study of cross-generational experiences of Blacks in graduate and professional schools.* Southern Education Foundation.

Brown, C. (1991). Increasing minority access to college: Seven efforts for success. *NASPA Journal, 28*(3), 224–230.

Brunsma, D. L., Embrink, D., & Shin, J. H. (2017). Graduate students of color: Race, racism, and mentoring in the White waters of academia. *Sociology of Race and Ethnicity, 3*(1). https://doi.org/10.1177/2332649216681565

Burt, B. A., Knight, A., & Roberson, J. (2017). Racializing experiences of foreign-born and ethnically diverse Black male engineering graduate students: Implications for student affairs practice, policy, and research. *Journal of International Students, 7*(4), 925–943. https://doi.org/10.32674/jis.v7i4.182

Burt, B. A., McKen, A., Burkhart, J., Hormell, J., & Knight, A. (2019). Black men in engineering graduate education: Experiencing racial microaggressions within the advisor–advisee relationship. *The Journal of Negro Education, 88*(4), 493–508. muse.jhu.edu/article/802583

Clark, S. M., & Corcoran, M. (1986). Perspectives of the professional socialization of female faculty: A case of accumulative disadvantage? *The Journal of Higher Education, 57*(1), 20–43.

Cole, E., McGowan, B., & Zerquera B. (2017). First-year faculty of color: Narratives about entering the academy, *Equity & Excellence in Education, 50*(1), 1–12. https://doi.org/10.1080/10665684.2016.1262300

Collins, P. H. (2004). *Black sexual politics: African Americans, gender, and the new racism.* Routledge.

Ellis, E. M. (2001). The impact of race and gender on graduate school socialization, satisfaction with doctoral study, and commitment to degree completion. *Western Journal of Black Studies, 25*(1) 30–46.

Felder, P., & Baker, M. (2013). Extending Bell's concept of interest convergence: A framework for understanding the African American doctoral student experience. *International Journal of Doctoral Studies, 8,* 1–20. https://doi.org/10.28945/1754

Felder, P. P., Stevenson, H. C., & Gasman, M. (2014). Understanding race in doctoral student socialization. *International Journal of Doctoral Studies, 9,* 21–42. http://ijds.org/Volume9/IJDSv9p021-042Felder0323.pdf

Ford, J. R. (2022) In the trenches: Just trying to make it as black men in early career faculty roles. *International Journal of Qualitative Studies in Education, 36*(3), 341–355. https://doi.org/10.1080/09518398.2022.2127014

Garrison-Wade, D. F., Diggs, G. A., Estrada, D., & Galindo, R. (2012). Lift every voice and sing: Faculty of color face the challenges of the tenure track. *Urban Review, 44,* 90–112.

Gasman, M., Hirschfeld, A., & Vultaggio, J. (2008). "Difficult yet rewarding": The experiences of African American graduate students in education at an Ivy League institution. *Journal of Diversity in Higher Education, 1*(2), 126–138. https://doi.org/10.1037/1938-8926.1.2.126

Griffin, K. A., Baker, V. L., & O'Meara, K. (2020). Doing, caring, and being: "Good" mentoring and its role in the socialization of graduate students of color in STEM. *Socialization in Higher Education and the Early Career* (pp. 223–239). Springer.

Griffith, T. O., & Ford, J. R. (2022). Say her name: The socialization of Black women in graduate school. *Journal of Student Affairs Research and Practice.* https://doi.org/10.1080/19496591.2022.2042006

Harper, S. R. (2012). *Black male student success in higher education: A report from the National Black Male College Achievement Study.* Center for the Study of Race and Equity in Education. https://rossierapps.usc.edu/facultydirectory/publications/231/Harper%20(2012)%20Black%20Male%20Success.pdf

Ingram, T. N. (2013). Fighting F.A.I.R. (feelings of alienation, isolation, and racism): Using critical race theory to deconstruct the experiences of African American male doctoral students. *Journal of Progressive Policy & Practice, 1*(1) 1–18. http://caarpweb.org/wp-content/uploads/2013/09/INGRAM11.pdf

Jackson, L., Ford, J., Randolph, C., Schleiden, C., Harris-McKoy, D., & McWey, L. (2021). School climate as a link between high school Black males' math identity and outcomes. *Education and Urban Society, 53*(4), 469–487. https://doi.org/10.1177/0013124520931453

Jean-Marie, G., & Brooks, J. S. (2011). Mentoring and supportive networks for women of color in academe. In G. Jean-Marie & B. Lloyd Jones (Eds.), *Women of color in higher education: Contemporary perspectives and new directions* (pp. 91–108). Emerald Group Publishing Limited.

Jett, C. C. (2011). "I once was lost, but now am found" the mathematics journey of an African American male mathematics doctoral student. *Journal of Black Studies, 42*(7), 1125–1147.

Johnson, B. J. (2001). Faculty socialization: Lessons learned from urban Black colleges. *Urban Education, 36*(5), 630–647. https://doi.org/10.1177/0042085901365007

Johnson-Bailey, J., & Cervero, R. M. (2004). Mentoring in Black and White: The intricacies of cross-cultural mentoring. *Mentoring and Tutoring, 12*(1), 7–21.

LaRocco, D. J., & Bruns, D. A. (2006). Practitioner to professor: An examination of second career academics' entry into academia. *Education, 126*(4), 626–639.

Lucas, C. J., & Murry, J. W. (2007). *New faculty: A practical guide for academic beginners*, 2nd ed. Palgrave Macmillan.

McCray, E. D. (2011). Woman(ist)s' work: The experiences of Black women scholars in education at predominantly White institutions. In G. Jean-Marie & B. Lloyd-Jones (Eds.) *Women of color in higher education: Turbulent past, promising future* (Vol. 9, Diversity in Higher Education Series; pp. 99–125). Emerald Group Publishing.

Minnett, J. L., James-Gallaway, A. D., & Owens, D. R. (2019). Help a sista out: Black women doctoral students' use of peer mentorship as an act of resistance. *Mid-Western Educational Researcher, 31*(2) 210–238. https://mwera.org/MWER/volumes/v31/issue2/V31n2-Minnett-FEATURE-ARTICLE.pdf

Modica, J. L, & Mamiseishvili, K. (2010). Black faculty at research universities: Has significant progress occurred? *The Negro Educational Review, 61*(1–4), 107–122. https://eric.ed.gov/?id=EJ908045

Ortlieb, E. T., Biddix, J. P., & Doepker, G. M. (2010). A collaborative approach to higher education induction. *Active Learning in Higher Education, 11*(2), 109–118. https://doi.org/10.1177/1469787410365655

Patitu C. L., & Hinton, K. G. (2003). The experiences of African American female faculty and administrators in higher education: Has anything changed? In M. F. Howard-Hamilton (Ed.), *New directions for student services: Meeting the needs of African American females* (pp. 79–93). Wiley.

Patton, M. Q. (2015). *Qualitative research & evaluation methods: Integrating theory and practice*. Sage.

Platt C. S. (2015). Everyday struggle: Critical race theory and Black male doctoral student experience. In C. Spencer Platt, D. B. Holloman, & L. W. Watson (Eds.), *Boyhood to manhood: Deconstructing Black masculinity through a life span continuum* (pp. 107–130). Peter Lang Publishing.

Platt, C. S., & Hilton, A. (2017). Why so much blackness? Race in the dissertation topics and research of Black male doctoral students. *Spectrum: A Journal on Black Men, 5*(2), 23–44. https://doi.org/10.2979/spectrum.5.2.02

Ponjuan, L., Conley, V. M., & Trower, C. (2011). Career stage differences in pre-tenure track faculty perceptions of professional and personal relationships with colleagues. *The Journal of Higher Education, 82*(3), 319–346.

Rasheem, S., Alleman, A. S., Mushonga, D., Anderson, D., & Ofahengaue Vakalahi, H. F. (2018). Mentor-shape: Exploring the mentoring relationships of Black women in doctoral programs. *Mentoring & Tutoring: Partnership in Learning, 26*(1), 50–69. https://doi.org/10.1080/13611267.2018.1445443

Reynolds, A. (1992). Charting changes in junior faculty: Relationships among socialization, acculturation, and gender. *The Journal of Higher Education, 63*(6), 637–652.

Rossman, G. B., & Rallis, S. F. (2012). *An introduction to qualitative research: Learning in the field*. Sage.

Stanley, C.A. (2006). Coloring the academic landscape: Faculty of color breaking the silence in predominantly White colleges and universities. *American Educational Research Journal, 43*(4), 701–736.

Stanley, C. A. (2007). When counter narratives meet master narratives in the journal editorial-review process. *Educational Researcher, 36*(1), 14–24.

Stanley, C. A., & Watson, K. L. (2007). Meeting the professional development needs of new faculty: A three-year evaluation study of a new faculty orientation program. *Journal of Faculty Development, 21*(3), 149–160. https://www.ingentaconnect.com/content/magna/jfd/2007/00000021/00000003/art00002?crawler=true&mimetype=application/pdf&casa_token=9E5S4DizrvQAAAAA:EdJfOYTYEEnD-uc8DrSAy0i1ewU96D2rJb_Zjk12GZRIfoalT_iJbKi1bX01QtEYQxsYaO13PK9yhjWT-sUHfA

Thompson, C. J., & Dey, E. L. (1998). Pushed to the margins: Sources of stress for African American college and university faculty. *The Journal of Higher Education, 69*(3), 324–345.

Thompson, G. L., & Louque, A. C. (2005). *Exposing the "culture of arrogance" in the academy: A blueprint for increasing Black faculty satisfaction in higher education.* Stylus.

Tierney, W. G., & Bensimon, E. M. (1996). *Promotion and tenure: Community and socialization in academe.* Suny Press.

Tillman, L. C. (2001). Mentoring African American faculty in predominantly White institutions. *Research in Higher Education, 42*(3), 295–325. https://doi.org/10.1023/A:1018822006485

Turner, C. S. V., & Thompson, J. R. (1993). Socializing women doctoral students: Minority and majority experiences. *Review of Higher Education, 16*(3), 355–370. https://doi.org/10.1353/rhe.1993.0017

Wallace, J. K. (2022). Nevertheless, we persist: Exploring the cultural capital of Black first-generation doctoral students at non-Black serving institutions. *The Review of Higher Education, 45*(4), 515–548. https://doi.org/10.1353/rhe.2022.0005

Wallace, J. K., & Ford, J. R. (2021). "They don't value my knowledge": Interrogating the racialized experiences of Black first-generation doctoral students in HESA programs at HWIs. *Journal of First-Generation Student Success, 1*(2), 127–144.

Weidman, J. C., Twale, D. J., & Stein, E. L. (2001). Socialization of graduate and professional students in higher education: A perilous passage? *ASHE-ERIC Higher Education Report, 28*(3). Jossey-Bass Higher and Adult Education Series. Jossey-Bass.

Young, V. A. (2007). *Your average nigga: Performing race, literacy, and masculinity.* Wayne State University Press.

CHAPTER 8

MEET THEM IN THE CENTER

A Model for Embedded Sexual Misconduct Survivor Advocacy and Support Services

Sarah Colomé

ABSTRACT

Grounded in Black and Latine feminist thought, this chapter explores how one campus worked to pivot from a cultural competence paradigm to one of community-driven innovation and service. The chapter begins by examining the current state of sexual misconduct on college campuses, the need for culturally specific and driven programs and services to meet marginalized student needs, and the framework used to create and implement an Embedded Confidential Advisory Model in support of campus survivors. The chapter then provides practical examples of how to engage campus and community partners to enact an intersectional framework in the procurement, recruitment, hiring, onboarding, operationalization, and daily practice of an embedded confidential advisor (campus survivor advocate).

> *At its most visionary [feminist theory] will emerge from individuals who have knowledge of both margin and center.*
> —hooks, 1984, "Preface"

Achieving a world without sexual misconduct requires an approach grounded in collective liberation. As university and college campuses advance their understanding of sexual violence as a public health issue, comprehensive approaches rooted in social justice frameworks are often subsequent considerations. Frequently purported in speech, the operationalization of collective liberation can be challenging for those working to prevent and respond to sexual misconduct on our campuses. This chapter will discuss the process of crafting collaboration across logical, yet commonly underutilized alliances in a higher education context through an embedded confidential advisor (CA) partnership with campus cultural centers.

In 2020, the Women's Resources Center (WRC) at the University of Illinois Urbana-Champaign (UIUC) activated a new initiative to strategically steward resources that more collectively addressed sexual misconduct and other forms of oppression through the creation and implementation of the embedded confidential advisor model (embedded model). Founded in 2009, the WRC grew to become composed of three key divisions: gender equity, sexual misconduct prevention, and sexual misconduct advocacy and support. The latter involved staff serving as designated CAs, which, in the state of Illinois, is equivalent to a survivor advocate. At UIUC, a CA's primary responsibility is to provide emergency and ongoing holistic advocacy and support to survivors of sexual misconduct, both students and employees. At the time of this publication, UIUC defined *sexual misconduct* as "Title IX Sexual Harassment, sexual harassment, sexual assault, dating violence, domestic violence, stalking, unwelcome sexual, sex or gender-based conduct, sexual violence, or sexual exploitation" (University of Illinois Board of Trustees, n.d., "Sexual Misonduct"). Through a survivor-centered, trauma-informed lens, CAs provide crisis and case management, referral services, and support in navigating survivor rights and options. Care can include but is not limited to addressing physical and mental health needs, academic, housing, and employment needs, offering healing strategies, and exploring campus reporting options, disciplinary options, and criminal legal options.

The WRC utilized an intersectional framework for its sexual misconduct prevention and response efforts, working across the three tiers of prevention as defined by the Centers for Disease Control (Dills et al., 2016). Grounded in intersectional praxis, the staff approached their work with the understanding that survivors carry a multitude of interconnected identities that require attention when providing advocacy and support services. Harper and Kezar (2021) define *collective liberation* as a "[recognition] that all of our struggles are intimately connected and that the work of liberating the oppressed and the oppressor falls on everyone" (p. 1). In his foundational book *Pedagogy of the Oppressed*, Paulo Freire (1970) describes *praxis* as "reflection and action upon the world in order to transform it" (p. 36), emphasizing the necessary marriage of theory and practice to achieve true social change. The WRC engaged these cyclical concepts as informed action through community accountability that prioritized the needs and insights of our key stakeholders: students of color.

Until the hiring of UIUC's first advocacy and wellness coordinator in late 2019, the institution did not have employees whose primary job duty was the provision of CA services for survivors of sexual misconduct. Prior, CA duties had been assigned to the director and assistant directors of the WRC, leaving staff overstretched between their primary job duties, and their roles as CAs. Due to a vast amount of work and limited staffing, student trust and comfort often lay with individual staff members rather than the entity of the WRC or its scope of focus. Challenges in cultivating belonging for marginalized students within a campus unit's physical space(s) or philosophical approach, is a documented obstacle (Esposito, 2011; Harper & Hurtado, 2007; Harwood et al., 2018). Recognizing the multitude of barriers for students of color in accessing essential advocacy services, the WRC decided to explore how culturally significant and community specific prevention and response strategies could better meet the needs of survivors from these student populations.

Similar to Ladson-Billings' (1995) culturally relevant teaching, a culturally significant approach to campus sexual misconduct is "committed to collective, not merely individual, empowerment" (p. 160). As communal hubs, campus cultural centers provided an opportunity to employ sexual misconduct prevention and response practices that were grounded in, and accountable to, the specific needs of students within marginalized communities through a nonhomogenous approach. Linder (2018) calls attention to the need for a power-conscious lens for campus sexual assault efforts. With attention to the role of power in relation to identity, Linder outlines the imperative nature of recognizing and addressing the role that power plays in these harms, and the systems that purport to prevent and address them (Linder, 2018). Utilizing this lens often calls for a disruption of the status quo, coupled with a willingness to be vulnerable and recognize both individual and institutional limitations that are often rooted in Whiteness. Acknowledging the interrelation of causality resulting in all forms of identity-based oppression required the WRC to pivot, and in this instance, that pivot was critically dependent on partnership.

The embedded model was created in partnership with two of UIUC's cultural centers: La Casa Cultural Latina (La Casa) and the Bruce D. Nesbitt African American Cultural Center (BNAACC), as a means to more strategically meet students of color where they were. This pivot positioned the WRC to meet survivor needs in multiple locations, while engaging community strengths to better address the barriers marginalized students face when seeking support.

HISTORICAL AND CONTEMPORARY SEXUAL MISCONDUCT ISSUES

Since the nonprofit industrialization of the movement to end sexual violence, many national organizations, and crisis agencies and campuses have fallen into "errors of omission" (Washington, 2001, p. 1279). This absence of attention to the diverse needs of marginalized survivors results in the use of "monocultural White feminist approaches" that Washington (2001) describes as often "alienating and noneffective" for Black women who are sexual assault survivors (Washington, 2001, p. 1280). Monocultural approaches, lack of diverse staff, race-neutral programming, and lacking staff capacity are noted barriers to meeting the interrelated and yet distinct needs of Black, Indigenous, and people of color (BIPOC) survivors (Harris, 2020; Washington, 2001; Wooten, 2017). To effectively eradicate sexual misconduct from our communities with attention to social identities, campus researchers, administrators, and practitioners must be conscious of, and address the role of power in their work.

The Deference to Power and Privilege

According to the Association of American Universities (AAU), 13% of college students are harmed through nonconsensual sexual contact, however prevalence rates vary drastically when accounting for the many facets that compose our identities (Cantor et al., 2020). For instance, a commonly cited statistic asserts that 1 in 4 undergraduate women will experience sexual violence at some point while enrolled in college, which is supported by the AAU's 2020 findings. Complicating this statistic, two systematic reviews of campus sexual assault studies within the last 10 years discovered most campus sexual misconduct prevalence study samples were predominantly composed of White, heterosexual, cisgender female students (Fedina et al., 2016; Linder et al., 2020). Unpacking this predominantly used campus statistic reaffirms longstanding knowledge within marginalized communities; students of color, LGBTQIA+ students, and students living with disabilities are harmed by sexual violence at a significantly higher rate than those in dominant identity groups (Cantor et al., 2020; Coulter et al., 2017). Furthermore, despite decades of research, few studies use methodologies that employ substantive multivariate depth. Coulter et al.'s 2017 national study of more than 71,000 students highlights the importance of disaggregated data in their analysis of victimization through the lenses of gender, sexuality, and race and ethnicity. Using multilevel logistic regression models, the authors expound on commonly homogenized data groupings such as "people of color" and "LGBTQ[IA]+." For example, compared to their White transgender peers, Black and Latine transgender students were 3 and 1.5 times more likely to experience some form of unwanted sexual contact (Coulter et al., 2017). Without acknowledging the multitudes that exist within student identity, efforts will inevitably fall into what Harris (2020) refers to as "race-evasiveness," leading to policies, practices, and procedures deferring to White students' experiences (p. 3).

Decentering Whiteness Through Praxis

The interrogation of race within campus sexual assault research is an essential factor in understanding the experiences of survivors of color, and to best craft approaches that disrupt rather than reinforce institutional and interpersonal oppression. Compounding experiences of racialized trauma, anti-Blackness, misogynoir, ableism, transphobia, homophobia, colonization, and other interrelated forms of oppression complicate and deepen the trauma experienced by survivors of sexual misconduct with marginalized identities seeking services (Bach et al., 2021). Theories and concepts commonly used to trouble traditional approaches to sexual assault research include Collins' (2008) Black feminist thought, and Crenshaw's intersectionality, critical race feminism and critical race theory (Crenshaw 1989; Howard 2018; Long 2021; Quiros et al., 2019; Washington, 2001; Wooten, 2017). Born out of the 1970s critical race theory emergence in legal academia, Wooten's (2017) work described critical race feminism as a framework to "address the gendered aspects of structural injustices, particularly within the law" (p. 407). Crenshaw's (1989) intersectionality called us then, to attend to the intersecting realities of race and gender, particularly as it relates to the power-conscious realities of Black women, similar to Collins' Black feminist thought which she later describes as "self-defined oppositional knowledge" (Collins et al., 2021, p. 690). These lenses are critical for practitioners and scholars, as mainstream approaches neglect the realities of survivors with marginalized identities, consciously and unconsciously normalizing frameworks rooted in the needs of White, cisgender, heterosexual women. In the context of higher education, Linder et al.'s (2020) power-conscious framework alongside Hong and Marine's (2018) deconstruction of traditional prevention approaches through a social justice paradigm, speak to the need for campus practitioners to better navigate what critical race scholars describe as the multiple locations of identity (Bell, 1992; Crenshaw, 2011; Wieskamp & Smith, 2020). As each person possesses a multitude of social identities (e.g., race, gender, and ability), individualized care must attend to each aspect of identity, how they interact with one another, and how they are navigated in society.

FRAMING THE EMBEDDED CONFIDENTIAL ADVISOR MODEL

One could argue that a fundamental hurdle to reducing sexual misconduct on college campuses is that traditional approaches are based on research that for the past decade, defers to the needs and experiences of White, heterosexual, cisgender women, as noted by Linder et al. (2020). Throughout the literature, scholars who engage a racial analysis call for culturally specific and significant outreach, prevention programming, response protocols, advocacy, support services, and research in relation to campuses and other locales (Crenshaw 1989, 2008; Fedina et al., 2016; Harris, 2020; hooks, 1984; McMahon & Seabrook, 2020; Patton & Ward, 2016; Quiros et al., 2019; Wooten 2017). UIUC's embedded model echoes Linder's (2018) power-conscious framework, which addresses the role of power in operational and interpersonal practices, in addition to "nam[ing] and call[ing] attention to systems of domination as a strategy for interrupting oppression" (Linder et al., 2020). The embedded model is also an attempt to activate what Moraga and Anzaldúa (2015) call "theory in the flesh":

> A theory in the flesh means one where the physical realities of our lives—our skin color, the land or concrete we grew up on, our sexual longings—all fuse to create a politic born out of necessity. Here, we attempt to bridge the contradictions in our experience. (p. 23)

The embedded model is an adaptable strategy that unapologetically pivots from higher educations' deference to identity- and power-neutral policies, practices, and analysis mechanisms (Linder et al., 2020). Instead, it aims to address the interlocked nature of survivors' social positions by attending to the totality of identity while centering students of colors' experiences and ways of knowing. By co-locating a CA within a partnered campus cultural center, the embedded model creates opportunity for emergent, community-specific sexual misconduct prevention and response services.

CREATING AN EMBEDDED CONFIDENTIAL ADVISOR PARTNERSHIP

The embedded model was inspired by the embedded efforts of other health service entities that partner with campus spaces (such as medical providers), deepened through intentional partnership that rethinks space sharing, and grounded in a shared mission. The aim of the model was to explore a new approach to community-centered prevention, advocacy, and support that equitably valued the knowledge, lived experiences, and skills of all parties involved.

At UIUC, 40% of undergraduate women report an unwanted sexual experience, however this definition varies from other surveys in that it includes attempted sexual assault, fondling, completed coercive sexual assault, and completed rape (Bystrynski & Allen, 2019). Within the same scope of harm, 16.7% of undergraduate men, 21.3% of graduate women, and 7.8% of graduate men reported an unwanted sexual experience since enrolling at the institution. The biannual Sexual Misconduct and Perceived Campus Response Survey findings are shared in the institution's Campus Climate Report, which at the time of publication did not disaggregate rates by race or ethnicity. Within the existing data, students involved in a Greek letter organization, LGBTQIA+ students, and women with disabilities were more at risk of experiencing sexual assault than their peers (Bystrynski & Allen, 2019).

Of UIUC's Fall 2019 incoming class, 74.92% were charged in-state tuition (University of Illinois Urbana-Champaign, n.d.), which is notable as Illinois high schoolers experience physically forced sexual intercourse more frequently than the national U.S. average (Centers for Disease Control and Prevention, n.d.). Disaggregating available data, Black (15.2% compared to 7.2%) and Asian (8.6% compared to 4.1%) students were more than twice as likely to be victimized compared to their paralleled national average (Centers for Disease Control and Prevention, n.d.). These findings underscore the importance of attending to the diverse survivor needs of current, and incoming students of color.

Cultivating a Coalition

The WRC began hosting formal and informal spaces in 2017 for transparent conversations with students about what aspects of their lives were, and were not, represented in programs and services. Feedback opportunities were not limited to students; WRC staff sought out colleagues on and off campus to better understand the perceptions of the WRC's space, services, and accessibility, among marginalized students, and the employees who predominantly serve them. Among the feedback received was a lack of awareness of the WRC's location, and a perceived lack of accessibility. For students who did not already have a direct connection to the WRC, the perception of an all-White staff created a barrier, regardless of the values in which the office's work was being done. Thus, a willingness to receive honest feedback without defensiveness or retaliation, paired with clear, actionable follow up that addressed shared concerns, was an essential component of cultivating trust, and buy-in for new approaches. Grounded in Crenshaw's (1989) initial intention for the intersectionality framework, the embedded model became part of a larger effort that served to both center the experiences of those most marginalized by campus sexual assault, and create space to imagine new and innovative approaches to deconstructing the prevention and response paradigms that were crafted by, and sustained through White-centered approaches.

Partner Identification for Collaborative Design

The shared grouping of the BNAACC, the WRC, and La Casa within the Office of Inclusion and Intercultural Relations (OIIR) at UIUC was a key factor in the ability to conceptualize and establish the embedded model, as proximity provided space for regular conversation and collaboration to meet the various, intersecting needs of students. Within formal and informal meeting spaces, OIIR staff were able to discuss pressing and emerging issues, and how each unit's work merged to meet the needs of marginalized students. From these conversations, intensive partnerships were cultivated with several OIIR centers eager to discuss how to craft community-driven approaches to end sexual misconduct.

Proximity was important to building trust, as peers had the opportunity to observe WRC staff in practice, noting the extent to which staff's actions matched their stated values. Conversations about the root cause of sexual misconduct were framed through the desire for power and control, and were unpacked to outline how sexual misconduct is inherently connected to students' experiences with racism, transphobia, and other forms of oppression. Building these trusted relationships took time, honest conversation, and care-driven accountability.

A strong relationship between La Casa and the WRC existed well before the embedded model was established, and collaborations with aligned colleagues, including La Casa's assistant director, served as an important foundation to the model's success. Due to her active partnership, embrace of intersectionality as a pedagogical praxis, and commitment to student-driven change, La Casa's director was identified as a potential partner in testing the embedded model. Shortly after La Casa's director began at UIUC in 2019, informal conversations broached the concept of the embedded model. After initial discussions about the proposal, La Casa's director sought feedback from staff and students about the feasibility of such a partnership, and that summer, both directors sat down to outline what a location-based collaboration could look like. The WRC director took the lead in coordinating communication, designing the model, and hiring, with critical insights from La Casa's director throughout the process. La Casa's director also led the internal communication within La Casa, modeling the potential and importance of what would become the embedded model.

To ensure the relationship remained collaborative and positive for both partner centers, the directors explicitly stated their concerns about potential limitations, inviting honesty from one another, with the agreement that a partnership of this format could not be successful without that commitment. The acceptance of honest feedback was measured by validation, openness to holding space for each other's experiences, and a willingness to work together to solve any issues that arose. This approach to collaboration was a commitment for both the creation of the embedded model, and for the ongoing implementation of the partnership. For those interested in a similar approach but without a previous relationship, consider how one might:

- Cultivate an authentic and power-conscious relationship between staff through formal and informal relationship building. What education, and self-reflection do you and your team need to seek out independently? What knowledge might your partners need, and how can that education occur with attention to power?
- Model your understanding of this interconnection in your daily practices. How are you reflecting a power-conscious framework in policy, practice, supervision (if applicable), and community accountability? Pay attention to differences in your behaviors that may show up when your intended partner(s) are, or are not, in the room.
- Establish a foundation of shared work. How might you identify how the mission of each center is interconnected and interdependent?

The embedded model required a joint effort with the La Casa professional staff, as well as student staff. Each director committed to ongoing conversation to address issues as they arose, and to review the successes and challenges of the embedded model at the end of the academic year. Key to the planning discussions were the following conversation drivers:

- What structures need to be in place for staff to understand and support this initiative?
- How do we create an intentional partnership, without falling into traditional visitation modes of embedded positions?
- How do we navigate power, privilege, and space? Particularly if the CA doesn't share the identity of the hosting cultural center?
- How do we courageously step into a partnership of growth, rather than perfectionism?

From the onset, the directors agreed that the first year of the program was intended to serve as a beta-test for the embedded model. The directors recognized that gaps or problems would likely arise and agreed that failure is an opportunity to reassess and pivot.

Hiring Embedded Confidential Advisors

Well-intentioned staffing often misses the mark when target stakeholders are not involved in the promotion of open positions, or the selection and onboarding of new hires. With this in mind, WRC staff made a practice of interrogating places and spaces where they may not be actualizing their values. Throughout the construction of the model, and the hiring of both CAs, the directors discussed the importance of involving staff and students within the communities where the embedded CA would be working. Partnership in action requires ongoing feedback, not solely during the inception of an initiative, but throughout the actualization and evaluation of collaborative work. To ensure implementation centered the needs, insights, and strengths of target communities, the directors of La Casa, WRC, and later, BNAACC, discussed the following:

- How can we center student feedback in the recruitment, interview, and hiring process?
- Who are the stakeholders who may not traditionally have an opportunity to weigh in on staff positions that directly affect their communities?
- What considerations need to be incorporated in the interview process for this unique role?
- What might candidates need to know to make an informed decision about joining the campus community, OIIR, and the WRC?

Search Committee Development and Onboarding. The first search committee was composed of representatives from the Title IX & Disability Office, BNAACC, Illini Union, Office of the Dean of Students—Student Assistance Center, and a highly involved WRC student and member of a historically Latina Greek letter organization. The broad range of stakeholders, and the committee's onboarding meeting were essential to successfully filling the open positions. In addition to introducing committee members at the meeting, the WRC director portal to ensure accessibility, outlined the embedded model, and stressed the importance of selecting finalists who possessed the self-awareness, adaptability, and knowledge to be cross-placed with campus partners. Coupled with the job requirements, the committee was encouraged to prioritize:

- Candidates' ability to serve students of color, and work in partnership with those whose jobs were predominantly focused on serving these students;

- Candidates' practical understanding of intersectionality, and the barriers often experienced by survivors of color; and
- Candidates' approach to navigating spaces and groups they do not share an identity with.

Finalist Interviews. After preliminary interviews, the first coordinator (CA) search culminated with final interviews on campus, beginning with (a) a warm welcome from a member of the search committee picking candidates up from their airport or hotel, (b) asking candidates if they had any preliminary questions before their day started, and (c) walking or driving candidates to their first meeting. Throughout the day, students or campus partners would walk candidates between meetings to establish relationships with potential new hires from the onset of their time on campus. Finalist interviews for the second coordinator position (to be embedded in BNAACC) were conducted virtually due to COVID-19 and began with a similar informal conversation with the search chair to start the day. A sample finalist itinerary can be found in Appendix A.

A key component of finalist interviews were the Campus and Community Partner Meeting, and the meeting with students, both of which served multiple purposes: (a) ensuring the candidate hired was a person stakeholders would feel comfortable collaborating with, (b) verifying stakeholder comfort in referring people to the candidate for advocacy and support services, and (c) providing space for the candidate to ask for insights about the WRC, campus, and community to assess if Illinois was a place they could feel welcome, connected, and celebrated. Guiding the selection of who would be invited were the following questions:

- Which stakeholders can best weigh in on the ability of the candidate to meet the unique, intersectional needs of our Black and Latine students?
- Which stakeholders can best speak to the strengths of the WRC and OIIR, as well as their opportunities for growth?

To provide space for transparency, both partner meetings occurred without the director (hiring authority), WRC staff, or the search chair in the room. Prior to each meeting, the director encouraged stakeholders to (a) be as transparent as comfortable about their experiences with and perceptions of the WRC, (b) discuss the strengths and needs of the campus, and (c) remember their opinions of the candidates' suitability for the role were pivotal to the hiring decision. The director also informed students what questions may not be legally asked of a candidate.

Collaborative and Student-Centered Onboarding

Illinois' first full-time Advocacy and Wellness Coordinator (a CA) was hired in December of 2019 and embedded within La Casa, and a second CA was hired in Spring 2020 to be embedded in the BNAACC. Past BNAACC directors, along with the previous assistant director, were key partners in adapting the embedded model for BNAACC. Rather than simply assigning CAs to show up to a respective partner center, the directors, professional- and student-staff worked together to select available and feasible space for the CA to be based that could be seamlessly woven into the happenings of the partner center, while still ensuring the protection of survivor confidentiality. These parameters called for rooms that had a door, and did not disrupt day-to-day activities of La Casa or the BNAACC.

Preparation discussions focused on what forms of education cultural center staff would need about the context and operations of the embedded model, and appropriate timing to ensure all staff felt confident and comfortable in explaining the partnership to others. By embracing the unique set up of each center, a combination of staff meeting presentations, presentations and meet-and-greets with student leadership councils, and one-one-ones with student-staff were used to introduce the embedded model to center stakeholders. Within each respective presentation, the WRC staff included information on the (often unrecognized) history of anti-sexual misconduct activism within Latine and Black communities, relevant risk statistics, an introduction to the CA, the embedded model's structure, the partner center's role in the model's operation, confidentiality considerations, time for questions, and time to begin imagining potential collaborations between the CA, and the student staff of each center (Appendix C). To avoid role confusion, staff from both centers were made aware that the CA was to be considered a center partner, and not an additional staff member of the BNAACC or La Casa. Staff and students were also provided a clear distinction between privacy and confidentiality to avoid confusion and to reduce well-intended but unrequired and nonconsensual reporting reporting. While all parties were able to commit to keeping information private, non-CA center staff members' status as responsible employees coupled with students' lack of confidential status (including an occasional overlap between the two) meant that only CAs were able to ensure information would not be shared with anyone else. The only exception would be if information shared with a CA fell under the scope of mandated reporting such as the risk of harm to self or others.

How each CA interacted as a vested part of the partner center's community varied according to the host center and student needs. For example, in one center the CA attended full staff meetings while in the other, the CA attended student-staff meetings. CAs were expected to regularly invest in relationships with students and staff, actively seek out organic opportunities for collaboration, amplify students as critical thought leaders, and support the needs of the host center's programs as time allowed, while keeping identity, and spatial awareness in mind. An ever-present responsibility, these trusted relationships further heightened the WRC staff's ability to amplify student and staff leaders, their stories and needs, and reframe campus conversations to better outline and address the interwoven nature of power, privilege, and oppression.

Community-Driven Supervision Structures

Remaining conscious of perceived and actual acts of taking up space was a priority of the directors. Balancing adaptability with clear goals and expectations required ongoing dialogue such as:

- Do CAs and partner staff have a clear understanding of their supervision structure and how to engage in problem solving?
- How might we cultivate a sense of belonging among CAs while shared between spaces?
- How are CAs navigating positionality, space taking, and power, in the host center?
- How are the CAs engaging with students and staff in an authentic, relationship-driven manner that decenters a clinical approach to prevention and response?
- How are the CAs engaging with host centers to grow as individuals and care providers?

Essential to the embedded model's success was the ongoing awareness and navigation of CA positionality, and how power and privilege were at play within the placement. These discussions were pivotal to the model's creation and implementation, as well as the ongoing supervision of the CAs. Supervision required transparency among all persons involved. Prior to implementing the model, directors and CAs discussed how varying issues and concerns would be navigated, should they arise. Due to vacancies, the WRC director served as the direct supervisor of the CAs, including hiring, onboarding, and coaching. Addressing concerns that may arise during cross-placement was at the discretion "of the host center's director. For example, La Casa's director could address concerns directly with the CA, which the CA and WRC director would then debrief about later, or she could relay her concern to the WRC director to address with the CA. No issues arose that required the latter approach during the first year of implementation, however, proactive discussions about how issues would be handled provided clarity for each team in terms of supervision and problem solving.

RESULTS AND ROADBLOCKS

Partnership of this kind requires an ongoing commitment to rethinking what wellness, safety, and belonging might mean for students of color at a predominantly White institution. The shared learning and collaboration resulting from the embedded model helped to de-homogenize education and the assumptions that influence service provision to better embrace intersectional realities that include race, gender, sexuality, culture, language, size, and skin tone, among others. In addition to students and partners noting improved awareness and understanding of resources and services, CAs and other WRC staff were also better able to demystify survivor options, highlight community-specific needs, and promote current prevention and advocacy efforts within Black and Latine spaces. And yet, none of these outcomes would be possible without the trust, patience, and thoughtful partnership of our collaborators in La Casa and the BNAACC.

Increased proximity to students and opportunities to present or informally engage through the lens of partnered anti-oppression work expedited relationship building between new CAs and student groups. After introductory presentations, student-staff anecdotally reported an improved understanding of the role, services, and confidentiality offered through the embedded model. A significant aid in cultivating overall student trust was the overt embrace of the embedded model by partner center staff, and later, student-staff. Cross-placement also created a pathway for more authentic and informal conversations spanning the three tiers of prevention that addressed desire, love, dating, hooking up, consent, boundaries, conflict resolution, and abuse, supporting students in building healthy relationship dynamics, as well as leading to more culturally relevant marketing, trainings, and service provision.

UIUC's cultural centers are a 15-minute walk from the WRC, so physical placement in partner centers provided a consistent presence that bridged the WRC with all four cultural centers. As such, the embedded model led to increased engagement with new and less commonly engaged student groups. While the impact of COVID-19 limited the WRC's ability to assess if the model led to increased service provision specifically among Black and Latine survivors, the WRC did see increased presentation and partner requests from historically Black, Latine and multicultural Greek letter organizations; heightened crossover student engagement; and more substantive partnerships with the BNAACC and La Casa including community-specific sexual misconduct programming, cultural programming, and search committee invitations. CAs were also able to offer staff support to La Casa and the BNAACC if one were understaffed for a period of time. Leveraging WRC resources in support of partners when they were not appropriately staffed was one of many ways the embedded model provided a redistribution could also work of resources that prioritized the holistic needs of UIUC's Black and Latine community members. As such, the partnership provided space to identify opportunities for new collaborations that emphasize the importance of shared knowledge, capacity, resources, and responsibility across partners, spaces, and communities.

Concurrent to these positive results however, remains the reality that institutions of higher education were not established for or with students of color in mind. The ramifications of this truth are extrapolated through value posturing, the lack of accountability for individual or system-based harm, and the frequently insufficient staffing, funding, and support for spaces and initiatives aimed at supporting and celebrating students of color. This continued institutional abandonment contributes to and perpetuates the challenges that advocates have in preventing sexual misconduct, and supporting students of color, whether they are survivors or not. As such, it is imperative that initiatives are grounded in the understanding that the work of preventing and responding to sexual misconduct is inherently the work of racial justice and liberation.

The strength of partnership between the centers made it possible to adapt as necessary, however frequent burnout and turnover within campus cultural and resource centers resulted in disruptions to the cultivation of new approaches for collaborative prevention and advocacy initiatives. These roadblocks were further fortified by COVID-19, forcing the second CA search, and the embedded model, to shift virtually. While limiting the potential of the model, these barriers did not prevent the successes noted above, nor the continuance of the model once Illinois returned to in-person classes.

CONSIDERATIONS FOR FUTURE INITIATIVES

The embedded model was an effort to explore how one campus might better work to end sexual misconduct by centering the needs, strengths, and experiences of marginalized student populations. UIUC's approach began with La Casa and the BNAACC's partnership, with the ultimate aim of expanding to other partner locations, if the initial model was successful and UIUC agreed to increase staffing capacity. A multitude of considerations resulted from the first iterations of the model. Building upon the learnings outlined throughout this chapter, some additional considerations for future initiatives would include capacity, record retention, outreach, data collection, and evaluation.

An ongoing commitment within the WRC was to attempt to include a *minimum* of one student, and OIIR staff member for all searches. Search committees, while time consuming, are an opportunity for professional advancement. The WRC intentionally used invitations for these service appointments to create avenues for experience, résumés, and applications among communities that often encounter institutional barriers to professional advancement. This intention was complicated by the lack of sufficient staffing and capacity for UIUC's campus cultural centers, however initial outreach always included these stakeholders. To ensure partner insights were garnered, final interviews included meetings at La Casa and the BNAACC, in addition to cultural center staff participating in the Campus and Community Partner Meeting. The inequitable resourcing of campus cultural centers further calls upon potential partners like the WRC to engage collaboration from the onset of partnership, remain adaptive, advocate on behalf of partner needs, and create processes that prioritize the communities we purport to center.

Record retention and historical context is key to sustaining an interdisciplinary collaboration in a field with such high turnover. By incorporating the purpose and functionality of these initiatives in staff recruitment, hiring, and onboarding, the sustainability of a partnership like that of the embedded model can help withstand staff and leadership departures. Similarly, establishing a standard incorporation of the embedded model into new staff onboarding at the start of semesters would be useful in reducing the stress that comes with competing schedules at busy times of the school year, and ensuring the totality of essential training content is maintained from semester to semester.

Searches for the CA positions were promoted broadly, within the financial limitations of the WRC's budget; however, recruiting a diverse pool of applicants to central Illinois for such specialized roles remained a challenge. For the second CA search, the WRC utilized a new recruiting tool to reach broader pools of candidates. Inspired by La Casa's director, the WRC director designed an information session (Appendix C) to be offered twice and co-led by the hiring authority, search committee chair, and Human Resources. Session content included an overview of the WRC, OIIR, partner centers, job responsibilities, benefits, and the local area. Time was left for questions, which provided space for those unsure their experience would meet the position's minimum qualifications. In addition to garnering excitement about the campus and local community, sessions were meant to proactively assist candidates in determining if UIUC and the type of accountability and collaboration within the embedded model's structure, aligned with their hopes for their next professional chapter.

As previously noted, UIUC's Campus Climate Survey Report did not disaggregate data according to racial and ethnic differences. Spurred by programmatic partnership with a multicultural fraternity, WRC staff reached out to the survey's primary investigators to access a multivariate analysis. From this request, a more detailed conversation led to agreement surrounding the need to advocate for disaggregation in future reports, intentionally distributing findings to key stakeholders, and leverage findings as a means for campus response. These conversations also reinforced the need for dedicated funding to substantively evaluate and assess the broader implications of the embedded model through culturally informed qualitative and quantitative methodologies.

Just as the embedded model has not been used as a template approach at the University of Illinois, this chapter is not a step-by-step guide to implementing the model at other institutions. The unique strengths and needs across institutions require thoughtful, collaborative, and most importantly, community-driven approaches to ending abuse and reducing the barriers to sexual misconduct support services. This examination of one campus's attempt at better serving Black and Latine students and creating a world without abuse will hopefully serve as an invitation to others to step into innovation that can build more intentional, and ultimately more effective services and programs.

APPENDIX A

Sample Itinerary for Finalist Interview (On-Campus)

8:45 a.m. **Welcome and Hotel Pick Up**
Led by search committee member (student)
Women's Resources Center (WRC) student walks candidate to La Casa Cultural Latina

9:00–9:50 a.m. **Meeting With Search Committee** (50 minutes)
Includes a student, and representatives from Title IX and Disability Office, Bruce D. Nesbitt African American Cultural Center, Illini Union, and the Office of the Dean of Students-Student Assistance Center
Location: La Casa Cultural Latina
WRC student walks candidate to next location

10:00–10:50 a.m. **Meeting With Campus and Community Partners** (50 minutes)
Includes representatives from La Casa Cultural Latina, Residence Life, and YWCA University of Illinois
Location: Bruce D. Nesbitt African American Cultural Center
WRC staff or intern walks candidate to next location

11:00–11:50 a.m. **Meeting With Women's Resources Center Staff** (50 minutes)
Includes Women's Resources Center Associate Director, Assistant Director, and Office Support Specialist
Location: Women's Resources Center
Students meet candidate at WRC and walk to lunch together

12:00–12:50 p.m. **Lunch With Students** (50 minutes)
Includes representatives from the Women's Resources Center (Interns and Peer Facilitators), and the Native American House/Native American & Indigenous Student Organization (NAISO)

12:50–1:15 p.m. **Break**

1:15–2:15 p.m. **Meeting With Women's Resources Center Director** (60 minutes)
Location: Women's Resources Center
Search committee member walks candidate back to hotel

Meet Them in the Center • **169**

APPENDIX B

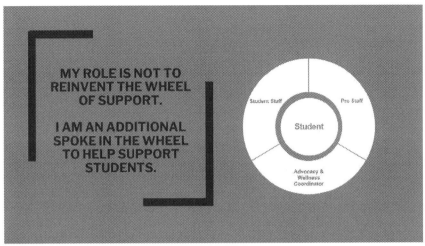

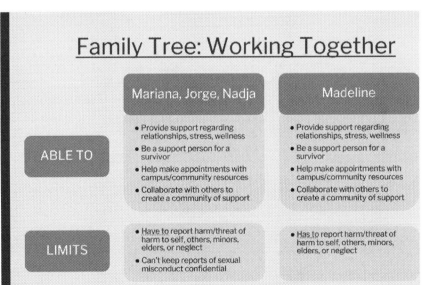

Figure 8.B Sample slides from partner onboarding.

APPENDIX C

Figure 8.C Sample promotion for information sessions.

REFERENCES

Bach, M. H., Beck Hansen, N., Ahrens, C., Nielsen, C. R., Walshe, C., & Hansen, M. (2021). Underserved survivors of sexual assault: A systematic scoping review. *European Journal of Psychotraumatology, 12*(1), 1895516. https://dx.doi.org/10.1080%2F20008198.2021.1895516

Bell, D. (1992). *Faces at the bottom of the well: The permanence of racism.* Basic Books.

Bystrynski, J., & Allen, N. E. (2019). *Campus climate report.* University of Illinois Urbana-Champaign. https://wecare.illinois.edu/docs/Campus-Climate-Survey-2019.pdf

Cantor, D., Fisher, B., Chibnall, S. H., Harps, S., Townsend, R., Thomas, G., Lee, H., Kranz, V., Herbison, R., & Madden, K. (2020). *Report on the AAU campus climate survey on sexual assault and misconduct.* Association of American Universities. https://www.aau.edu/sites/default/files/AAU-Files/Key-Issues/Campus-Safety/Revised%20Aggregate%20report%20%20and%20appendices%201-7_(01-16-2020_FINAL).pdf

Centers for Disease Control and Prevention. (n.d.). *Illinois, high school youth risk behavior survey, 2019.* https://nccd.cdc.gov/youthonline/app/Results.aspx?LID=IL

Collins, P. H., da Silva, E., Ergun, E., Furseth, I., Bond, K. D., & Martínez-Palacios, J. (2021). Intersectionality as critical social theory: Intersectionality as critical social theory, Patricia Hill Collins, Duke University Press, 2019. *Contemporary Political Theory, 20*(3), 690–725. https://doi.org/10.1057/s41296-021-00490-0

Coulter, R. W., Mair, C., Miller, E., Blosnich, J. R., Matthews, D. D., & McCauley, H. L. (2017). Prevalence of past-year sexual assault victimization among undergraduate students: Exploring differences by and intersections of gender identity, sexual identity, and race/ethnicity. *Prevention Science, 18*(6), 726–736. https://doi.org/10.1007/s11121-017-0762-8

Crenshaw, K. (1989). Demarginalizing the intersection of race and sex: A Black feminist critique of antidiscrimination doctrine, feminist theory, and antiracist politics. *University of Chicago Legal Forum, 1*(8), 139–168. https://chicagounbound.uchicago.edu/uclf/vol1989/iss1/8

Crenshaw, K. (2008). *On gendered violence and racialized prisons* [Video]. University of California Television (UCTV). https://youtu.be/d1v9E83yTNA

Crenshaw, K. (2011). Twenty years of critical race theory: Looking back to move forward commentary: Critical race theory: A commemoration: Lead Article. *Connecticut Law Review, 43*(5), 1253–1352. https://opencommons.uconn.edu/cgi/viewcontent.cgi?article=1116&context=law_review

Dills, J., Fowler, D., & Payne, G. (2016). *Sexual violence on campus: Strategies for prevention.* National Center for Injury Prevention and Control, Centers for Disease Control and Prevention. https://www.cdc.gov/violenceprevention/pdf/campussvprevention.pdf

Esposito, J. (2011). Negotiating the gaze and learning the hidden curriculum: A critical race analysis of the embodiment of female students of color at a predominantly White institution. *Journal for Critical Education Policy Studies, 9*(2). http://www.jceps.com/archives/679

Fedina, L., Holmes, J. L., & Backes, B. L. (2016). Campus sexual assault: A systematic review of prevalence research from 2000 to 2015. *Trauma, Violence, & Abuse, 19*(1), 76–93. https://doi.org/10.1177/1524838016631129

Freire, P. (1970). *Pedagogy of the oppressed.* Seabury.

Harper, S. R., & Hurtado, S. (2007). Nine themes in campus racial climates and implications for institutional transformation. *New directions for student services, 2007*(120), 7–24. https://doi.org/10.1002/ss.254

Harper, J., & Kezar, A. (2021). *Leadership for liberation: A leadership framework & guide for student affairs professionals.* Pullias Center for Higher Education.

Harris, J. C. (2020). Women of color undergraduate students' experiences with campus sexual assault: An intersectional analysis. *The Review of Higher Education, 44*(1), 1–30. http://dx.doi.org/10.1353/rhe.2020.0033

Harwood, S. A., Mendenhall, R., Lee, S. S., Riopelle, C., & Huntt, M. B. (2018). Everyday racism in integrated spaces: Mapping the experiences of students of color at a diversifying predominantly White institution. *Annals of the American Association of Geographers, 108*(5), 1245–1259. https://doi.org/10.1080/24694452.2017.1419122

Hong, L., & Marine, S. B. (2018). Sexual violence through a social justice paradigm: Framing and applications. *New Directions for Student Services, 2018*(161), 21–33. https://doi.org/10.1002/ss.20250

hooks, B. (1984). *Feminist theory: From margin to center.* Pluto Press.

Howard Jr., J. L. (2018). *Building a model of Black women's confidence in campus sexual assault resources: A critical race feminist quantitative study* (Publication No. 2252) [Doctoral dissertation, Clemson University]. https://tigerprints.clemson.edu/all_dissertations/2252

Ladson-Billings, G. (1995). But that's just good teaching! The case for culturally relevant pedagogy. *Theory Into Practice, 34*(3), 159–165. https://www.jstor.org/stable/1476635

Linder, C. (2018). *Sexual violence on campus: Power-conscious approaches to awareness, prevention, and response.* Emerald Group Publishing.

Linder, C., Grimes, N., Williams, B. M., & Lacy, M. C. (2020). What do we know about campus sexual violence? A content analysis of 10 years of research. *The Review of Higher Education, 43*(4), 1017–1040. https://doi.org/10.1353/rhe.2020.0029

Long, L. (2021). The ideal victim: A critical race theory (CRT) approach. *International Review of Victimology, 27*(3). https://doi.org/10.1177/0269758021993339

McMahon, S., & Seabrook, R. C (2020). Reasons for nondisclosure of campus sexual violence by sexual and racial/ethnic minority women. *Journal of Student Affairs Research and Practice, 57*(4), 417–431. https://doi.org/10.1080/19496591.2019.1662798

Moraga, C., & Anzaldúa, G. (Eds.). (2015). *This bridge called my back: Writings by radical women of color.* SUNY Press.

Quiros, L., Varghese, R., & Vanidestine, T. (2019). Disrupting the single story: Challenging dominant trauma narratives through a critical race lens. *Traumatology, 26*(2), 160–168. https://doi.org/10.1037/trm0000223

University of Illinois Board of Trustees. (n.d.). *Policy definitions & key terms.* https://wecare.illinois.edu/policies/terms/#misconduct

University of Illinois Urbana-Champaign. (n.d.). *Fall 2021 New Beginning Freshmen 10-Day Profile* [Table of enrollment class demographics from September 4, 2021]. https://www.dmi.illinois.edu/stuenr/abstracts/FA21freshman_ten.htm

Washington, P. A. (2001). Disclosure patterns of Black female sexual assault survivors. *Violence Against Women, 7*(11), 1254–1283. https://doi.org/10.1177/10778010122183856

Wieskamp, V. N., & Smith, C. (2020). "What to do when you're raped": Indigenous women critiquing and coping through a rhetoric of survivance. *Quarterly Journal of Speech, 106*(1), 72–94. https://doi.org/10.1080/00335630.2019.1706189

Wooten, S. C. (2017). Revealing a hidden curriculum of Black women's erasure in sexual violence prevention policy. *Gender and Education, 29*(3), 405–417. https://doi.org/10.1080/09540253.2016.1225012

CHAPTER 9

CHALLENGING INTERSECTIONAL MARGINALIZATION IN IDENTITY BASED CENTERS

Jonathan A. McElderry
Stephanie Hernandez Rivera
Shannon Ashford

ABSTRACT

Identity centers have served to facilitate diversity, equity, and inclusion (DEI) work in higher education. These centers emerged after the 1960s soon after the integration of schools, student activism and protests for increased services, and more supportive campus environments primarily for people of color and women. Identity-focused centers continue to emerge at institutions across the country and are often referred to as "safe spaces." Some centers are tasked with serving multiple communities such as multicultural centers or diversity centers, while others focus on a "single" identity or community such as Black culture centers (BCC), Latino centers, or women's centers.

Identity centers have continued to emerge at institutions across the country and have often been referred to as "safe spaces." Mitchell and Sawyer (2014) state that "identity has shaped the creation of centers to bring together students with a shared identity (e.g., race, gender, and sexuality)" (p. 201). In this chapter, we understand identity centers as spaces on campus intended to support historically marginalized students of a particular identity group (Renn & Patton, 2011). These spaces typically provide social, academic, and cultural support, facilitate programs and initiatives, and aid students in their identity development (Parker & Freedman, 1999; Patton, 2006; Saia, 2022). They are centers focused on race, ethnicity, sexual identity, gender, disability, religion, and so on (Renn & Patton, 2011). We recognize from our own experiences as scholar-practitioners working in higher education that identity centers provide a space of self-preservation for marginalized students. They also, however, can recreate oppressive conditions and experiences for students with multiple marginalized identities.

There are instances when students who possess multiple marginalized identities experience intersectional-marginalization; marginalization based on experiencing more than one oppressive system simultaneously. This chapter provides an understanding of the emergence of identity centers, how students may experience intersectional-marginalization, and how practitioners can create spaces, programs, and efforts that are multidimensional as opposed to singularly-focused. It is necessary for identity centers to approach advocacy and identity exploration in a way that embraces the various dimensions of student experience. Our hope is that this chapter will provide practitioners an opportunity to raise their awareness and efforts towards thinking *and* acting with an intersectional lens.

LITERATURE REVIEW

Identity centers such as Black culture centers (BCC), multicultural centers, women's centers, and LGBTQIA+ centers have worked to advocate for and support students with marginalized identities. This literature review provides a deeper understanding of how identity centers emerged, the ways in which they have supported marginalized students, and institutional practices in relation to these centers. Additionally, we present literature that demonstrates how students with multiple marginalized identities can often experience an intersectional marginalization where they can "fall through the cracks" (Crenshaw, 2016) of the work identity centers attempt to accomplish.

The Emergence of Identity Focused Support

The social unrest related to civil rights, feminism, third world women's movement and other movements of the sixties and seventies were major contributing factors to the development of Black studies, ethnic studies, Chicano studies, and women's studies programs (Christian, 1989; López, 1997). For some students, academic programs such as these, might have been the first spaces in which students could explore their identities and experiences, critique oppressive systems, and engage in consciousness-raising activities, particularly from culturally salient ways of doing (Beltrán, 2010; Berger & Radeloff, 2014; Chu, 1986).

Although it would be difficult to identify all of the factors that led to the emergence of varying identity centers, the social unrest of the sixties and seventies, demands from student organizations and changing demographics on college campuses can be identified as contributing factors. BCCs have been used as places of support for Black students at PWIs and as "safe havens in an alien environment" (Patton, 2006, p. 628). BCCs emerged during the Black Student Movement in the 1960s/1970s (Patton, 2010) at a time when campuses were being integrated. Unfortunately, PWIs were not prepared for the "social, cultural, and academic needs" of Black students (Patton, 2006, p. 628). Women's centers grew in part of the social unrest of the 1960s and 1970s and also as a result of the "hostility" they experienced on college campuses when their presence continued to rise (Bengiveno, 2000, p. 2). This however was not always the case, as Guy-Sheftall and Wallace-Sanders (2002) highlight the founding of the Women's Research and Resource Center established at Spelman College, a historically Black college, in 1981. Women's centers have experienced challenges in support; at times not receiving structural support from institutions, while simultaneously being called upon when issues around gender emerge (Parker & Freedman, 1999). Support has also wavered for BCCs, which at times, have been pressured to merge into a broader umbrella of support for multiculturalism (Patton, 2006). LGBTQIA+ centers emerged in part as a response to heterosexist attacks and heterosexist campus climates (Sanlo et al., 2002). Identity centers have also served as spaces of advocacy for marginalized students (Harris & Patton, 2017).

Although perceptions might exist that a need to engage in intersectional praxis is a contemporary problem, women of color have emphasized the need to engage in spaces that recognize the interconnectedness of oppression. In the emergence of Black studies and women's studies, Black women articulated the pressure they felt to choose between disciplines and how both disciplines did not always honor their contributions (Christian, 1989; Lorde, 1984). Asian women also described the need to engage in consciousness-raising activities that challenged both sexism and racism, in part as a result of the exclusion and invisibility they experienced in race-focused and gender based movements, respectively (Chu, 1986). Similar consciousness groups were created by Chicanas during the student movements of the 1960s, as they often were invisible in leadership roles in student organizations and Chicano studies departments, although they widely participated (López, 1997, p. 103).

The Negotiation of Identity Centers

Identity centers in higher education have done important work around supporting identity development, providing counterspaces for marginalized students, as well as educating the campus community. In our experience as practitioners, we have observed the impact that services, programs, and identity centers have on supporting students' needs. In the same breath, we have also witnessed how these spaces can perpetuate the systems they set out to disrupt.

Kevin Kumashiro (2001) articulates this sentiment in his work on thinking about the intersections of race and sexuality: "Ironically, our efforts to challenge one form of oppression often unintentionally contribute to other forms of oppression, and our efforts to embrace one form of difference often exclude and silence others" (p. 1). At times efforts to uplift and serve specific identities, ignore other identities that shape how a student experiences the campus community.

Although the literature is scant on this concept in relation to identity centers in higher education, the minimal literature that exists demonstrates how students with intersectional-marginalized identities experience challenges navigating institutions of higher learning and identity spaces (Linder & Rodriguez, 2012; Negrete & Purcell, 2011; Vaccaro & Mena, 2011). Negrete and Purcell (2011) underscore the importance of multicultural student services offices engaging intersecting identities such as sexual and gender identities. They provide tangible recommendations and recognize the challenges multicultural centers face in being tasked to serve large, diverse populations. Kumashiro (2001) also addresses the "troubling intersections" of race and sexuality and provides recommendations for conducting anti-oppressive education. Jennrich and Kowlaski-Braun (2014) also posit that engaging in intersectional praxis in identity centers requires that students also grapple with privileged identities and experiences. This complicates engagement in identity centers if students come to see these spaces are those where they are validated in their oppressed identity, but not challenged in their privilege. We hope to expand some of this work in this chapter by providing our own experiences and knowledge as scholar-practitioners.

Goode-Cross and Tager (2011) identified how Black gay and bisexual men might "minimize" one identity in order to be accepted by peers with whom they share a different identity. The article underscores the challenge the participants experienced engaging as their full selves on college campuses, which is similar to a study on queer student activists of color at a PWI (Vaccaro & Mena, 2011). The study focused on students' experiences navigating two marginalized social identities and the challenges of balancing their responsibilities and commitments to support their peers with similar identities. These challenges ultimately led to exhaustion which manifested through suicidal ideation and attempts. The participants expressed the need for social support and networks on their respective campuses, but acknowledged that student organizations based solely on race or sexual orientation did not always meet the needs of their intersecting identities. The final result was the creation of a support group for queer students of color.

At times women of color describe being ostracized in communities specific to race and gender based on multi-ethnic identities, phenotype, queer identity, and gender identity (Hernandez Rivera, 2020; Linder & Rodriguez, 2012; Revilla, 2010). Literature about women of color also recognizes the ways they work to find and create spaces to engage their intersecting identities. An example is manifested through ethnic and race-based sororities (Delgado-Guerrero et al., 2014; Delgado-Guerrero & Gloria, 2013; Greyerbiehl & Mitchell, 2014) or through the development of friendships with one another (Linder & Rodriguez, 2012; Martinez Alemán, 2000). Women of color have also developed support groups and spaces (Croom et al., 2017; DeFreece, 1987; Revilla, 2005) and in recent years, women of color retreats have occurred at campuses across the country (Hernandez Rivera, 2020).

Much of the literature referenced above has demonstrated, for both queer students of color and women of color, the onus has largely been placed on them to address their experiences and issues they find important. This then begs the question of how identity centers are serving students with multiple marginalized identities? Are these students "falling through the cracks" of services, programs, representation, and advocacy? Based on our own experiences, we argue this indeed has been the case. We provide a summary of these experiences and our argument to those working in identity-focused centers to think and act in an intersectional manner in order to better serve students at the margins of the margins.

THINKING AND ACTING THROUGH AN INTERSECTIONAL LENS

This section of the chapter provides readers with the experiences and identities that shape and inform how we understand this work. Our experiences working in higher education with marginalized populations in different capacities provides a breadth of experiences from large to small, public to private institutions. We will provide a brief understanding of our positionality, relationship to this work, and why we believe it is necessary to think and act more intersectionality when serving marginalized students.

Jonathan

I am a Black, cisgender, queer, man born and raised in central Virginia. Through my professional and personal work, I have grown to understand ways in which I am privileged and marginalized by the identities I hold and how they intersect to create a unique lived experience. I believe it is important for us to work towards intersectional inclusion and equity because as Audre Lorde stated "we do not live single issue lives" and the intersection of our identities, both privileged and marginalized, shape our world views and how we navigate the world. As a first generation college student who now holds a terminal degree, I have grown to understand the ways in which access and class is directly correlated with who succeeds in our society. My career in higher education has been primarily focused on diversity, equity, and inclusion (DEI) work, specifically in the context of identity-based centers. I have worked in multicultural, Black culture, and intercultural at both public and private institutions and now supervise centers focused on race, ethnicity, and diversity education, as well as gender and sexual identities. Working in such areas, I have seen the need for an intersectional approach when working with students to assist in better understanding themselves along with supporting and articulating their lived experiences. Additionally, my service with higher education associations and organizations has expanded my understanding of how to support students through intersectional marginalization, and how I can take that knowledge back to my college campuses.

Further, I have seen through my own personal navigation how the intersection of my marginalized and privileged identities has impacted my life experiences and trajectory. Therefore, my purpose is to work towards creating more equitable experiences for marginalized students through their daily lived experiences and co-curricular involvement at PWIs.

Stephanie

I'm a Boricua, woman of color, queer woman born and raised in New Jersey. Although I have a variety of other identities, both privileged and marginalized, the identities above are ones that are most salient to me and that I constantly reflect on. As an undergraduate student, my consciousness around social issues and *isms* significantly increased by taking classes in women's and gender studies, which soon became one of my majors, and later what I obtained my Master of Arts degree in. I worked in higher education for 5 years before pursuing a full-time doctoral degree in higher education. During this time, I worked in equity and diversity work, serving marginalized communities, predominantly students of color. In all of the institutions where I have worked, I attempted to more specifically serve a population that was often ignored and invisible, women of color. I witnessed the ways women of color endured additional mental and emotional labors and spaces that centered women and people of color respectively, didn't always acknowledge or address issues specific to women of color. During this time, I collaborated with others to develop initiatives to support the experiences of women of color and in my doctoral work, I continue to do research that prompts practitioners and institutions of higher education to consider and support the well-being of women of color.

Shannon

I am a Black, cisgender, heterosexual, woman born and raised in Ohio. While there are other identities that are important to me, those listed are most salient in my day-to-day lived experience. As I reflect on my intersecting identities and how they came into my consciousness, the process began during my undergraduate career where I earned a specialization in African-American studies. During that time and through my first full-time job working in college access, I saw the world through the single lens of my Black identity. It wasn't until graduate school that I began to understand intersectionality, specifically the intersections of my race, gender, and sexuality. Through my studies, interactions with colleagues and students, professional development opportunities and personal reflections, I have come to understand that I am both privileged and marginalized in these identities. My career in higher education has primarily focused on DEI work along with student engagement and leadership. I have worked in a multicultural center at a public institution and as a DEI practitioner at two private institutions. Working in these specific areas has exposed me to the importance of approaching my work through an intersectional lens when creating and facilitating workshops and programming. This intersectional approach has also proven to be impactful to model for students and colleagues the ways in which they can reflect on their intersecting identities.

THEORY

Within this chapter, intersectionality is central to the understanding of the issue of intersectional-marginalization experienced by students who hold multiple marginalized identities. Although a variety of scholars, activists, and theorists had been writing about the concept of multiple marginalized identities, intersectionality wasn't coined until 1989 by Kimberlé Crenshaw, a legal scholar. Crenshaw used intersectionality to describe how a Black woman, Emma DeGraffenreid, was experiencing hiring discrimination at General Motors because of both her race and gender identities. Crenshaw articulates in her 1989 paper, how Black women are "theoretically erased" in feminist theory and antiracist politics. Through underscoring different legal cases, Crenshaw demonstrates how a single-axis framework with a single-issue analysis, does not capture the ways Black women are discriminated against and how they can "fall through the cracks" of addressing issues of equity that are specific to them in an intersectional way. In this, Crenshaw challenges anti-racist movements and feminist theory to acknowledge and address the intersection which is necessary to include Black women. Similarly, Crenshaw addresses this in her piece on how Black women and other women of color experience interpersonal violence (1991). She provides three different forms of intersectionality to underscore the differences in experience for women of color who experience violence. These forms of intersectionality are:

- Structural intersectionality—Structures create and organize services, practices, laws, that produce unique effects/experiences for those at the intersections.
- Political intersectionality—When political movements working towards justice for different groups (feminism, anti-racism, LGBTQIA+, etc.) interact to exclude or marginalize those at the intersection, or reinforce injustice.
- Representational intersectionality—When images or tropes are taken to be representative of the group, ignore or distort the complexity of the group.

In recent years, intersectionality has become more popularized; however, it isn't always used appropriately. It's important to acknowledge that intersectionality is not synonymous with multiple marginalized identities, but rather how power collides to shape the experiences of those at the intersections of multiple dominating forces. Crenshaw has used intersectionality and encouraged others to use intersectionality as a frame to not throw away cases such as DeGraffenreid, which had originally used a single-issue analysis. Our use of intersectionality seeks to assist practitioners in understanding how students experience intersectional-marginality in institutions of higher learning in various contexts and can fall through the cracks. We seek to do this by applying the different forms intersectionality can take to shape the lives of those who experience intersectional-marginality, particularly as it relates to work within identity centers. In some instances, the examples are focused on race and gender, and in others, sexual identity may also be included. We recognize intersectionality's origins in the plight of Black women and other women of color, and seek not to co-opt, but demonstrate its appropriate transferability to others who experience intersectional-marginality in systems of education.

HOW TO SERVE STUDENTS BY THINKING AND ACTING INTERSECTIONALLY

Jonathan

In my current role, I serve as the dean of student inclusive excellence and an assistant professor at Elon University in North Carolina. In my role I am responsible for: leading student-centered initiatives to achieve the Boldly Elon goals to advance a more diverse, equitable, and inclusive community; serving as a member of both the student life and inclusive excellence leadership teams, sharing responsibility for leading long-range plans and annual priorities of the divisions and the university; providing guidance and support for two student life departments—the Center for Race, Ethnicity, and Diversity Education (CREDE) and the Gender and LGBTQIA Center (GLC), as well as leading the implementation of equity audits across the Division of Student Life, coordinating the establishment of a process for staff to create individualized intercultural learning plans, working collaboratively to coordinate dialogue experiences for staff and students, and advising or leading other key initiatives.

Having worked in a multitude of identity-based centers at large and mid-sized public institutions, as well as a small, private liberal arts institution, I identify three areas for serving students through an intersectional approach: design, programming, and campus partnerships. When thinking about working within identity-based centers with an intersectional approach, the aesthetics are important in appealing to a broad audience of students. Students should be able to walk in and see themselves reflected in the pictures, quotes, cultural artifacts, and design of the center. Practitioners need to pay close attention that there is a balance of identities presented throughout the center. Additionally, including a variety of spaces throughout the center for students to engage in different capacities is important. Having a general space where students can commune, a meeting room for student organizations to hold executive board meetings, as well as a quiet study area for those looking to complete schoolwork while remaining in community within the space.

The next area to focus on when thinking of serving students is to examine the programming offered. Although the center may be based on race, gender, (dis)ability, sexual orientation, it is important for staff to understand the ways in which intersectional approaches are important. Staff within each of the centers should ensure that the programming offered reaches multiple aspects and identities of the students intended to be served. Incorporating cultural heritage months and weeks into the programming of the center is important to bring institutional recognition to each of the student populations served. Additionally, offering programming that looks at the intersection of various identities can increase a sense of belonging amongst students by feeling as though there is a place for them.

Lastly, collaborations between academic departments, campus offices, other identity based centers, and student organizations can positively impact how students experience campus. Collaborating to bring diverse keynote speakers is important when thinking of the representation of invited guests. Faculty have a role where they can help educate the entire campus through offering extra credit or requiring attendance to support a keynote speaker as an assignment for students. Establishing positive working relationships with faculty across campus can help engage students that may not typically attend a program offered by the center. Creating opportunities for student organizations and identity centers to work collaboratively is beneficial in developing cross cultural relationships and building community on campus. Finally, working with campus offices—whether it be the Counseling Center or Student Activities and Campus Recreation—can debunk myths and raise awareness about the services each of the offices offers to campus and instill DEI as a part of everyone's work.

Stephanie

I am currently a professor of instruction, and previously worked as a practitioner in student affairs doing equity and inclusion work. It is important for practitioners of varying identities to think about how they work with women of color to create initiatives and programs that support our experience. Before doing this, they should self-educate by reading and viewing work by women of color about our experiences (Hill Collins, 2002; Lorde, 1984; Moraga & Anzaldúa, 1983; Noriega, 2015; Wing, 1997).

Representational intersectionality recognizes how White women can become representative of all women, and men of color for people of color. Therefore, practitioners should be conscious of executing events, programs, and initiatives that "represent" women and "people of color," but don't engage the interconnectedness of the two. Working alongside women of color students can challenge the representational intersectionality that women of color experience; it can ensure they are part of the conversation, but that they also have agency and voice in efforts that are developed to support their experience. It can also work to ensure particular tropes and images are not upheld about women of color in these respective communities. As Jennrich and Kowalski-Braun (2014) highlight, "All participants have to be committed to confronting the ways in which they benefit from privilege and suffer from oppression" (p. 207). Thus it is imperative that when practitioners seek to support students through consciousness-raising activities or identity development efforts, they also ask students to be conscious of the fullness of their experience.

Additionally practitioners can take the initiative to bring women of color together to collaborate on these programs, as well as ensuring that when coordinating any other efforts they are taking into consideration intersectional-analysis and experience (Museus & Griffin, 2011). The experiences I provide below demonstrate the ways I have worked to support the experiences of women of color students.

At the first institution, I worked in a women's center doing equity and diversity programs. Although women's centers provide opportunities to engage critically and intentionally about gender, patriarchy, and sexism, there are a variety of other identities and forms of oppression that women are affected by. Women's centers can perpetuate structural intersectionality (Crenshaw, 1991) when they are not conscious of the services they provide or the practices they employ that exclude women of color. When I first arrived at this space, there was a student staff of nine student employees, all of which were White, except for one student. The perception from women of color on campus was that the space was a White woman's space and, with that, White women ended up "representing" who the space was actually for (Crenshaw, 1991). The scope of my work meant that I largely worked with students of color; therefore, I made it my mission to recruit students of color and more specifically women of color to work on staff. I recall participating in a meeting where I was advocating for the hire of an AfroLatina student who had experience and was qualified for a position within the center. I recall being questioned in this meeting on if this woman would be a "good fit." I ended up pushing back on the coded nature of this language. It was clear to me that the center typically hired White people who had what could be understood as a "hipster" or "edgy" vibe. Fit became code for a specific kind of person, one that did not include women of color with a different disposition. Although the hiring practice was not an institutionalized-policy, it was ideological and resulted in structural intersectionality. Informal standards created by ideology are particularly challenging to navigate as they exist beneath the surface. Practitioners need to be astute to these kinds of dynamics in the areas where they work in order to avoid recreating oppressive conditions and expectations.

In my next position, I oversaw a multicultural center. In this role, I would continue to support women of color undergraduate students. I recall a Black undergraduate woman who approached me with the idea of coordinating a women of color retreat on campus. In this instance, I used my connections with women of color to provide names of individuals who would be beneficial in developing this space. Within that first meeting, consisting of about 10 women of color, if not more, women described feeling as though they did not have a space to engage the interconnectedness of their identities and that all of the centers: women's center, BCC, LGBTQIA+ resource center, and the multicultural center (where I worked), were not always conscious or developed programs and events for their intersectional-experience. This meant, supporting students in executing this initiative, but also discussing these realities and perceptions with colleagues. It meant identifying pathways for collaboration and having open dialogue about the thoughts and perspectives of our students impacted by more than one oppressive system and increasing our programming and efforts in this regard.

Alongside the coordinating student for the women of color retreat, we worked to ensure that queer women of color were represented on the committee, recognizing that this initiative could easily default to heterosexual women of color being representative of the community (Crenshaw, 1991). This is also connected to political intersectionality as communities of color can also perpetuate heterosexism and cissexism (Alimahomed, 2010) when doing this form of coalition-building, we did not want the issues queer women of color experience to go unexamined. We reached out directly to individuals and connected with the queer and trans students of color groups on campus. We also ensured that our initial invitation was extended to students who held diversity of identity outside of being racially minoritized women.

The initiative still remained student-led. They were responsible for planning the content they wanted to see and I attended all of the meetings to answer logistical questions and ensure that students had everything they needed. Every now and again I would provide critique and expand students' thinking around content they wanted to deliver at the retreat. However, I largely served in a supportive role answering questions, ensuring students could secure funding from across campus, and that they had full agency over the experience they desired for themselves. I sent emails to colleagues in different departments and would make sure that financial restraints were not a barrier to the success of this experience. Structural intersectionality can result in individuals assuming that programs for women or people of color meet the needs of women of color; therefore, it is necessary to advocate for initiatives that speak to and engage the complexity of identity.

What students were able to accomplish in those years was incredible. They coordinated applications and selected retreat attendees, developed content on their own, delivered workshops, created activities, constantly thought of innovative ways for attendees to be validated and engage in dialogue, and would do their best to ensure that all attendees were welcomed and included. Inevitably however, it was a student who had the idea to meet the needs of her community; the reality that women of color are creating efforts and spaces for themselves is also demonstrated in scholarship (Croom et al., 2017; Hernandez Rivera, 2020; Lenzy, 2019; Revilla, 2005, 2010). When working with student populations in the future, I will assess and engage students with multiple and intersectional-marginalized identities in a conversation about how I can best serve their needs.

Shannon

I currently serve as the director for DEI at Duke University in the Office for Institutional Equity. Through my current experience and past roles working at both a private liberal arts institution and a large public institution in cultural centers and student engagement offices, I focus on personal identity development and reflection, cultivating strategic campus partnerships and creating inclusive programming to achieve structural and representational intersectional approaches.

As a DEI practitioner who aims to provide programming and educational opportunities to all students at various points in their identity development, it is important for me to understand how my lived experiences impact how I view the world and how the world views me. Cultural competence and identity development is lifelong work, so while I may serve as an expert in this subject for students, I must be aware that there is always more to learn about myself. Second, the more comfortable I am in understanding my intersecting identities and how they shape my experience, the better I can teach others. A few examples of my personal and professional development activities include reflective journaling about transformative experiences, taking assessments to learn about my identities and how I relate to others and participating in intensive identity development institutes and seminars with colleagues across the country.

Engaging thoughtfully and strategically with campus partners and student organizations yields structural and representational intersectionality in my daily work. Through the aforementioned personal development activities and reflection, I am increasingly more aware of my blindspots as it relates to intersectionality. Due to these blindspots, I consult with colleagues in the LGBTQ Center, Women's Center, Religious Life, Disability Services, and others to assist in the curriculum development of training and workshops with an intersectional approach. In addition to consulting with colleagues, I also collaborate with diverse student organizations to develop student-centered programming that is relevant to their lived experience, specifically at the intersections of age, class, and other marginalized identities.

Lastly, in order to challenge structural intersectionality in my workshops and programs, I utilize concepts of universal design to ensure I meet the needs of various identities. Universal design was first coined by architect, Ronald Mace, to describe the creation of environments that can be utilized by all, regardless of their ability. Though universal design began as a concept in regards to structural accessibility, student affairs practitioners and faculty have adopted these concepts to apply them to inclusive programming and pedagogies. When planning workshops and programs, I center various intersecting marginalized identities, thus yielding more inclusivity and representation of various identities.

Through each of the shared experiences we provide, our work highlights how to avoid replicating the three forms of intersectionality (structural, political, representational). Additionally, we offer tangible suggestions to avoid further marginalizing students in higher education, while working to create spaces and programming that uplifts all aspects of their identity. The combination of critical thought turned into action shows myriad ways practitioners can change their approach to doing the work.

IMPLICATIONS FOR PRACTICE

Within this section we provide specific ways practitioners doing equity and inclusion work can support the experiences of intersectionally marginalized students. As opposed to the traditional ways that implications are written, typically in a paragraph form, we would like to provide a list of what practitioners may consider. It is important to note this list is not exhaustive and requires deep intentionality and thought. There is no one-size-fits-all approach to equity work; what works for some students, communities, regions, and campuses may not for others. It is therefore essential for practitioners to consider their demographics, population, institutional culture and current campus climate. Educators must always work in collaboration with students, as alleviating challenges and barriers should not be the responsibility of students to manage.

- Self-education is critical. There is always something you don't know and need to explore further. Take time to participate and engage in self-education and reflexivity.
- Assess and engage individuals within the community you work with on how the center or program can better serve individuals at the

intersection of identity. Do not just do this as a formality. Be sure to find ways to effectively weave in their feedback and communicate the ways you have made efforts towards better serving them.
- Engage and collaborate with students in the development of programs, content, and events. Be cautious of exploiting students solely for their perspectives and find ways to appreciate and recognize them.
- Determine the role you need to serve in a given context: leader, advocate, supporter, cheerleader, champion.
- Build relationships with students outside of your events and programs. This might mean going to other center events or student organization events not under your purview.
- Consider how your events might change if you were speaking to individuals with intersectional-marginalized identities and change the content or structure based on this information.
- Use your social networks and campus connections to support students' goals and efforts.
- Collaborate and consult with your colleagues who also support students with intersectional-marginalized identities. We all want to provide the best student experience possible, so learn from and with each other on promising practices.

CONCLUSION

Whether developing programs and initiatives, administering diversity education, executing events, or thinking about the aesthetics and structure of your center, creating equitable conditions for those with intersecting-marginalized identities is crucial. Those doing equity, inclusion, and diversity work need to be conscious of how they potentially recreate oppressive conditions and should be intentional when doing this work. Inevitably, our passion and commitment to this work does not exempt us from oppressing others and practitioners should be constantly reflecting on and improving their practice.

REFERENCES

Alimahomed, S. (2010). Thinking outside the rainbow: Women of color redefining queer politics and identity. *Social Identities: Journal for the Study of Race, Nation and Culture, 16*(2), 151–168. https://doi.org/10.1080/13504631003688849

Beltrán, C. (2010). *The trouble with unity: Latino politics and the creation of identity*. Oxford University Press on Demand.

Bengiveno, T. A. (2000). Feminist consciousness and the potential for change in campus based student staffed women's centers. *Journal of International Women's Studies, 1*(1), 1–9. https://vc.bridgew.edu/jiws/vol1/iss1/1

Berger, M. T., & Radeloff, C. L. (2014). *Transforming scholarship: Why women's and gender studies students are changing themselves and the world.* Routledge.

Christian, B. (1989). But who do you really belong to–Black studies or women's studies? *Women's Studies: An Inter-Disciplinary Journal, 17*(1–2), 17–23. https://doi.org/10.1080/00497878.1989.9978786

Chu, J. (1986). Asian American women's studies courses: A look back at our beginnings. *Frontiers: A Journal of Women Studies, 3,* 96–101. https://doi.org/10.2307/3346381

Crenshaw, K. (1989). Demarginalizing the intersection of race and sex: A Black feminist critique of antidiscrimination doctrine, feminist theory, and antiracist politics. *University of Chicago Legal Forum, 139*(1), Article 8. https://chicagounbound.uchicago.edu/cgi/viewcontent.cgi?article=1052&context=uclf

Crenshaw, K. (1991). Mapping the margins: Intersectionality, identity politics, and violence against women of color. *Stanford Law Review, 43*(6), 1241–1299. https://doi.org/10.2307/1229039

Crenshaw, K. (2016, October). *The urgency of intersectionality* [TED video]. https://www.ted.com/talks/kimberle_crenshaw_the_urgency_of_intersectionality?language=en

Croom, N. N., Beatty, C. C., Acker, L. D., & Butler, M. (2017). Exploring undergraduate Black womyn's motivations for engaging in "sister circle" organizations. *NASPA Journal About Women in Higher Education, 10*(2), 216–228. https://doi.org/10.1080/19407882.2017.1328694

DeFreece, M. T. (1987). Women of color: No longer ignored. *Journal of College Student Personnel, 28*(6), 570–571. https://psycnet.apa.org/record/1988-37394-001

Delgado-Guerrero, M., Cherniack, M. A., & Gloria, A. M. (2014). Family away from home: Factors influencing undergraduate women of color's decisions to join a cultural-specific sorority. *Journal of Diversity in Higher Education, 7*(1), 45–57. https://doi.org/10.1037/a0036070

Delgado-Guerrero, M., & Gloria, A. M. (2013). La importancia de la hermandad Latina: Examining the psychosociocultural influences of Latina-based sororities on academic persistence decisions. *Journal of College Student Development, 54*(4), 361–378. https://doi.org/10.1353/csd.2013.0067

Goode-Cross, D. T., & Tager, D. (2011). Negotiating multiple identities: How African-American gay and bisexual men persist at a predominantly White institution. *Journal of Homosexuality, 58*(9), 1235–1254. https://doi.org/10.1080/00918369.2011.605736

Greyerbiehl, L., & Mitchell, D., Jr. (2014). An intersectional social capital analysis of the influence of historically Black sororities on African American women's college experiences at a predominantly White institution. *Journal of Diversity in Higher Education, 7*(4), 282–294. https://doi.org/10.1037/a0037605

Guy-Sheftall, B., & Wallace-Sanders, K. (2002). Building a women's center at Spelman College. In S. L. Davie (Ed.), *University and college women's centers: A journey toward equity* (pp. 79–89). Greenwood Press.

Harris, J. C., & Patton, L. D. (2017). The challenges and triumphs in addressing students' intersectional identities for Black culture centers. *Journal of Diversity in Higher Education, 10*(4), 334.

Hernandez Rivera, S. (2020). A space of our own: Examining a womxn of color retreat as a counterspace. *Journal of Women and Gender in Higher Education, 13*(3), 327–347. https://doi.org/10.1080/26379112.2020.1844220

Hill Collins, P. (2002). *Black feminist thought: Knowledge, consciousness, and the politics of empowerment.* Routledge.

Jennrich, J., & Kowalski-Braun, M. (2014). "My head is spinning:" Doing authentic intersectional work in identity centers. *Journal of Progressive Policy & Practice, 2*(3), 199–210. https://caarpweb.org/wp-content/uploads/2014/12/Jennrich-Kowalski-Braun-2014.pdf

Kumashiro, K. K. (2001). Queer students of color and antiracist, antiheterosexist education: Paradoxes of identity and activism. In K. K. Kumashiro (Ed.), *Troubling intersections of race and sexuality: Queer students of color and anti-oppressive education* (pp. 1–25). Rowman & Littlefield.

Lenzy, C. D. (2019). Navigating the complexities of race-based activism. In S. Evans, D. Domingue, & T. Mitchel (Eds.), *Black women and social justice education: Legacies and lessons* (pp. 261–274). State of New York Press.

Linder, C., & Rodriguez, K. L. (2012). Learning from the experiences of self-identified women of color activists. *Journal of College Student Development, 53*(3), 383–398. https://doi.org/10.1353/csd.2012.0048

López, S. A. (1997). The role of the Cicana within the student movement. In A. M. García (Ed.), *Chicana feminist thought: The basic historical writings* (pp. 131–136). Routledge.

Lorde, A. (1984). The uses of anger: Women responding to racism. In *Sister outsider: Essays and Speeches* (pp. 124–133). Crossing Press.

Martínez Alemán, A. M. (2000). Race talks: Undergraduate women of color and female friendships. *The Review of Higher Education, 23*(2), 133–152. https://doi.org/10.1353/rhe.2000.0006

Mitchell, D., Jr., & Sawyer, D. C., III. (2014). PREFATORY: Informing higher education policy and practice through intersectionality. *Journal of Progressive Policy and Practice, 2*(3), 195–198. https://caarpweb.org/wp-content/uploads/2014/12/Mitchell-Sawyer-2014.pdf

Moraga, C., & Anzaldúa, G. (1983). *This bridge called my back: Writing by radical women of color.* Kitchen Table, Women of Color Press.

Museus, S. D., & Griffin, K. A. (2011). Mapping the margins in higher education: On the promise of intersectionality frameworks in research and discourse. *New Directions for Institutional Research, 2011*(151), 5–13.

Negrete, N. A., & Purcell, C. (2011). Engaging sexual orientation and gender diversity in multicultural student services. In D.-L. Stewart (Ed.), *Multicultural student services on campus: Building bridges, re-visioning community* (pp. 81–93). Stylus Publishing.

Noriega, M. (2015). Creating spaces to break the circle of silence and denial. In U. Quesada, L. Gomez, & S. Vidal-Ortiz (Eds.), *Queer Brown voices: Personal narratives of Latina/o LGBT activism* (pp. 139–150). University of Texas Press.

Parker, J., & Freedman, J. (1999). Women's centers/women's studies programs: Collaborating for feminist activism. *Women's Studies Quarterly, 27*(3/4), 114–121. https://corescholar.libraries.wright.edu/womensctr_bib/29

Patton, L. D. (2006). The voice of reason: A qualitative examination of Black student perceptions of Black culture centers. *Journal of College Student Development, 47*(6), 628–646.

Patton, L. D. (2010). *Culture centers in higher education: Perspectives on identity, theory, and practice.* Stylus Publishing.

Renn, K. A., & Patton, L. D. (2011). Do identity centers (e.g., Women's Centers, Ethnic Centers) divide rather than unite higher education faculty, students, and administrators? If so, why are they so prevalent on college campuses? In P. M. Magolda & M. B. Baxter-Magolda (Eds.), *Contested issues in student affairs: Diverse perspectives and respectful dialogue* (pp. 244–261). Stylus Publishing.

Revilla, A. T. (2005). Raza womyn engaged in love and revolution: Chicana/Latina student activists creating safe spaces within the university. *Cleveland State Law Review, 52*(1), 155–172. https://engagedscholarship.csuohio.edu/clevstlrev/vol52/iss1/11

Revilla, A. T. (2010). Raza womyn—making it safe to be queer: Student organizations as retention tools in higher education. *Black Women, Gender & Families, 4*(1), 37–61. https://doi.org/10.5406/blacwomegendfami.4.1.0037

Saia, T. A. (2022). Disability cultural centers in higher education: A shift beyond compliance to disability culture and disability identity. *Journal of Postsecondary Education & Disability, 35*(1), 17–30.

Sanlo, R., Rankin, S., & Schoenberg, R. (2002). *Our place on campus: Lesbian, gay, bisexual, transgender services and programs in higher education.* Greenwood Press.

Vaccaro, A., & Mena, J. A. (2011). It's not burnout, it's more: Queer college activists of color and mental health. *Journal of Gay & Lesbian Mental Health, 15*(4), 339–367. https://doi.org/10.1080/19359705.2011.600656

Wing, A. K. (Ed.). (1997). *Critical race feminism: A reader.* NYU Press.

CHAPTER 10

RESISTING INTERLOCKING STRUCTURES AND RELATIONS THROUGH SOCIAL JUSTICE PRAXIS

Insights From a Dialogic Exchange Between Three Black Women Academics

Talia R. Esnard
Deirdre Cobb-Roberts
Devona F. Pierre

ABSTRACT

Despite efforts to diversify the academy, there are many interlocking structures of power that continue to affect the professional identities, journeys, and trajectories for Black women. Findings from this intersectional and dialogic work center the importance of social justice praxis within the context of resistance, critical consciousness, and change.

Although steady gains have been made by Black women in academe, their struggles with systemic injustices within higher education remain. In fact, one can argue there is a clear pattern and history of institutional oppression and marginalization within the academy (Turner Sotello-Viernes & Myers, 2002; Winkler, 2000). In such cases, acts of racism, sexism, and microaggressions manifest as (un)intended barriers faculty of color face in antagonistic (Harley, 2008; Wallace et al., 2012), and unwelcoming or hostile academic environments (Hill et al., 2005). Oftentimes, these forms of institutional oppression remain steeped in White male privilege and patriarchy (Aguirre, 2000; Esnard & Cobb-Roberts, 2018), and can affect the tenure, promotion, and advancement for women of color (August & Waltman, 2004; Diggs et al., 2009). Inadvertently, these oppressive structures reproduce and/or sustain the underrepresentation, disfranchisement, and oppression of women of color in academe (Gutierrez y Muhs et al., 2012).

In such contexts, Black women faculty are forced to resist systematic forms of oppression and social injustices within systems of higher education (Esnard & Cobb-Roberts, 2018; Mabokela & Green, 2001). At the heart of such resistance are questions around—and contestations over—existing claims of inclusivity and diversity within academic contexts (Avery et al., 2007). Oftentimes, reported or observed acts of resistance rest on the incongruences between institutional claims of inclusivity and diversity, vis-à-vis struggles associated with systemic forms of oppression within academe (Ferguson, 2012); a reality that fails to reform, disrupt, or dismantle prevailing systems of power (Musser, 2015). As such, the argument in the literature is that despite efforts to diversify the academy, structural policies and practices within institutions of higher education continue to affect the relative positionalities (Milem & Umbach, 2003) and relational experiences for women of color (Solorzano et al., 2000; Turner Sotello-Viernes & Myers, 2002). In fact, social justice scholars contend even where diversity structures exist within institutions of higher education, many remain nested within distributive models or notions of social justice that center on issues of access and participation. However, there is little attention within this body of literature to the systemic processes and social relations that sustain ongoing forms of injustice within that space (Brennan & Naidoo, 2008; Furlong & Cartmel, 2009; Gale & Densmore, 2000; Gewirtz, 1998; Young, 1990).

Where such distributive models fall short of addressing systemic and institutional forms of oppression, more is needed to move the needle that defines and situates what has been achieved in relation to social justice agendas within institutions of higher education. Moving beyond these limitations within the academy therefore requires us to center conversations and solutions that shift the boundaries of social engagement and mobility; particularly for marginalized groups of women within academe. Advancing inclusive excellence also calls for explorations that tease through the extent to which the university and institutional praxes (around teaching, supervision, and research) can serve as "possible site[s and points of reference] for [understanding] social justice action" (Nixon & Comber 1995, p. 63). This empirical gap, however remains less interrogated. In fact, researchers assert that while there is growing attention to issues of social justice in education (Darling-Hammond et al., 2002), fewer scholars delve into the thinking, practices, and experiences of social justice advocates (Atweh, 2011; Zollers et al., 2000). There is also scant research that documents the professional development and persistence strategies Black women utilize within academe to combat and speak back to the intertwined and muddled systems of power they confront (West, 2018). Advancing such work calls for scholars to tease through the nature of this empirical gap, explore the relative significance of structural and relational axes of power within academe (as experienced), and the extent to which these factors affect the prospects and possibilities of social justice agendas at individual and collective levels. Our work extends the discussion.

SOCIAL JUSTICE, HIGHER EDUCATION, AND CRITICAL PRAXIS

While social justice emerges as a necessary counteraction to persistent forms of social and economic inequities, the concept remains undertheorized and indefinable, with diverse conceptualizations and multiple contentions around the nature, direction, and scope (Brennan & Naidoo, 2008; Gewirtz, 1998). Rizvi (1998) for instance argued that

> the immediate difficulty one confronts when examining the idea of social justice is the fact that it does not have a single essential meaning, [and that] it is embedded within discourses that are historically constituted and that are sites of conflicting and divergent political endeavors. (p. 47)

Gewirtz (1998) deliberated on the importance of distributive and relational nature of social justice, and the extent to which these forms of social justice center issues of power located within micro and macro structures. The central point of reference in this conceptualization was on the need to factor in the relative significance of the "interconnections between individuals in society, rather than [solely on] how much individuals get" (Gewirtz, 1998, p. 471). Gale and Densmore (2000) extended such conceptualization to include the three core aspects of social justice: distributive, redistributive, and recognitive. While the former deals with the extent to which "freedom, social cooperation, and compensation" is distributed to individuals, redistributive touches on the "liberty and protection of rights" (p. 27). Recognitive justice on the other hand involves the creation of opportunities for persons to exercise and reach their fullest potential/capacities. In this case, the notion of social justice remains embedded within related complexities surrounding concerns for social and economic mobility, human rights and dignity, and opportunities for self-actualization.

Despite these ongoing contestations, the need for social action that challenges ongoing expressions of (in)difference, (dis)privilege, (in)equality, and (in)equity remain central to social justice agendas. In this sense, Gewirtz (1998) asserted notions of social justice remain grounded in the act of disrupting and subverting existing structures (distributive) and processes (relational) that marginalize individuals. Here, social justice becomes situated in practices and political dialogues (Young, 1990), and rooted within acts of resistance that seek to deconstruct structures, relations, identities, positionalities, and social experiences. Others call for resistance that speaks to issues of equality and fairness in structures and processes that exist at individual and collective levels (Singh, 2011). In many cases, acts of social justice make visible the realities of marginalized or underprivileged groups, while bringing to the fore the many strategies they employ in their attempt to reclaim and sustain alternative systems that promote basic human rights and freedoms for all (Brennan & Naidoo, 2008; Furlong & Cartmel, 2009; Goldfarb & Grinberg, 2002). Even there, many questions remain when constructing narratives and calls for action around how to become a socially just society.

When such discourses are applied to the study of higher education, it raises many questions, inter alia, as to the nature of institutional oppression and the extent to which institutional actors push back against such systems of power (Armstrong & Bernstein, 2008; Giroux, 2007). In many cases, these discourses have translated into related discussions that center the relevance and impact of affirmative action policies, equal opportunity programs, or other initiatives within higher education that communicate fairness and equity (see Massey & Fisher, 2005; Sowell, 2004). For instance, Furlong and Cartmel (2009) called for social justice programs that meet the needs of all stakeholders without prejudice or favor, and that foster an environment wherein everyone can access opportunities for social mobility and successful engagement. Other scholars narrow their attention to the everyday experiences and praxes of institutional stakeholders (including faculty members, students, administrative personnel, and other active groups) who challenge ongoing forms of privilege or inequities (Giroux, 2004; Winkle-Wagner & Locks, 2014). In both instances, scholars draw on the struggles of resisting and on the challenges of pushing radical solutions that diversify institutions of higher education, while shifting institutional structures, practices, and relations. Where they exist, these acts of advocacy and resistance become social justice praxis, where there is a deliberate attempt to transform institutional contexts and to promote institutional cooperation and respect (Baillon & Brown, 2003).

Critical pedagogy emerges to foster a sense of hope, activism, and commitment to transforming oppressive structures or systems of power within the academy. At the heart of this pedagogical framework is the need for transformative institutional praxes built on the critical, collaborative, and innovative systems of change (Giroux, 2004; hooks, 1994). Here, a central goal becomes that of understanding the relationship between power and knowledge, how this relationship is established and reproduced, and how it can challenge and democratize the relationship between teaching and learning in the classroom (Hytten, 2006). In speaking to this phenomenon, Hackman (2005) called for teachers to demonstrate strong mastery of content, ability to historicize and situate contemporary social issues, to be critically inclined, to be committed to improving their broader society, and to be reflective in these processes. Bettez (2008) advanced the need for students to develop key skills, dispositions, and practices that promote "(1) a mind/body connection, (2)...critical thinking, (3)...discussions of power, privilege, and oppression, (4)...compassion for students, (5)...[a] belie[f] that change toward social justice is possible, (6)...self-care, and, (7) [that] build critical communities" (p. 276). Enterline et al. (2008) contend teaching for social justice requires complex ways of measuring, speaking to, and enacting agendas built around its very premise and/or intentions. This argument is likened to Berila's (2016), who called for mindfulness within teaching and learning that moves students to a place where they can critically contemplate and embody their commitment to change key issues affecting themselves and broader societies. The central premise here is the need to reframe students' resistance as mindful dissonance where they are able to recognize, unlearn, and dismantle existing forms of oppression. Still, other scholars argue such transformation remains dependent on the extent to which exemplary leadership and/or mentoring practices communicate critical consciousness and the need for advocacy around social justice agendas (Jean-Marie, 2006; Tillman et al., 2006).

THEORETICAL FRAMEWORK

As a theoretical framework, intersectionality highlights the importance of connecting interlocking systems of power (racism, sexism, classism, ageism, colorism, just to name a few), to the experiences and broader realities of marginalized groups (Choo & Ferree, 2010; MacKinnon, 2013; Wilkins, 2012). As Hill Collins (1995) noted, race, class, and gender emerge as structures of power that influence or shape the broader social positions we occupy. Central points of reference within this framework are those of socially constituted forms or categorizations of identity used to establish structures and relations of power, while situating individuals relative to where they are located along various axes of power. It is important for us to recognize the contextual and situational nature of identity markers, their meanings, everyday manifestations, and effects on those who remain most vulnerable (Esnard & Cobb-Roberts, 2018). It is critical therefore, that even as we seek to address the domains and relations of institutionalized forms of power, we recognize the spatial and temporal nature of the inequalities and injustices resulting from these corrective efforts.

Activist agendas around social justice remain core aspects of intersectionality theory (Carbado et al., 2013). In part, these expressions of advocacy unfold as active forms of questioning and destabilizing complex structures that promote inequality, discrimination, and oppression wherever they exist (Weldon, 2008). Crenshaw (1991) specifically noted political intersectionality calls for examinations of the radical strategies and activist agendas marginalized groups employ to counteract multiple systems of oppression. Here, the use of intersectionality offers a critical lens through which one can investigate the impact of converging identities on human rights, freedoms, and possibilities. This use of intersectionality can advance social justice agendas that unpack and dismantle nodes of power which denigrate marginalized groups. Within higher educational contexts, such practices of resistance remain critical to how we move beyond sociopolitical expressions of power and privilege that affect ongoing attempts to diversify and equalize social contexts (Ross, 2014). It is imperative in such cases for scholars to connect the dots between these intersectional domains of power, subsequent acts of resistance, the need for advocacy, and social justice. While we recognize the elusive nature of social justice conceptualizations (Brennan & Naidoo, 2008), we support the notion that social justice offers a means for naming while disrupting the structures of power within systems of higher education in ways that provide meaningful change to those who remain affected by acts of injustice (Jean-Marie, 2006).

As a way of exploring the nexus between the intersectionality and social justice, this chapter centers the relational and structural dynamics of power that exist within the academy and the ways two Black women faculty (across different contexts, institutions, and at different stages of their careers) and one Black woman administrator push back as a necessary aspect of advancing social justice agendas. In particular, this chapter shows how our struggles with systematic and structural forms of inequalities politicize not just the everyday academic space, but also, our own resistance and actions around the need for social justice. By so doing, the chapter situates the university as a site of oppression, resistance, and activism. The goals of this work are therefore threefold: (a) to underscore the belligerent nature of the academic space, (b) to illuminate the role Black women faculty and administrators bring to bear as social justice advocates, and (c) to demonstrate the potential for collaborative autoethnography to unpack the complexities and risks embedded in working towards social justice within an environment of systemic and structural inequalities.

METHODOLOGY

As a way of working through such theoretical and empirical concerns around social justice within institutions of higher education, we embraced the use of a collaborative autoethnography approach that is "simultaneously collaborative, autobiographical, and ethnographic" (Chang et al., 2013, p. 17). The uniqueness of this approach is in the extent to which it allows a group of researchers to collectively engage in researcher subjectivity, while deepening opportunities for learning about the phenomenon in question and strengthening the relations between researchers. We use collaborative autoethnography to explore the thinking, practices, and experiences around social justice for three Black women within the academy. We do so by collaboratively delving into a dialogic exchange around our lived experiences, understanding ourselves as Black women in relation to others in academe, the significance of axes of power on our positionality, and the extent to which we are able to advance social justice agendas.

A critical aspect of this analysis includes the interrogation of our own academic profiles and experiences: as two faculty members (at different levels—one assistant and the other associate), and across different disciplines (sociology and education). The other researcher remains substantively in an administrative position, directly addressing issues related to diversity and inclusion in higher education. Between these researchers, there are different research interests, different years of experiences, professional roles, disciplines, and institutional contexts. Despite these differences, these stories offer not just portraits of injustices, but also narratives and dialogic exchanges that tease through structural, relational, and situated challenges of confronting social injustices within higher education. Such a qualitative framework allows us to speak to the multiple and varied markers of our social identity, how our identities unfolded within and across institutional contexts, and how these milieus shape specific points of contestations and points for resistance.

It is through our dialogic conversations that we were able to investigate tensions, connections, insights, and opportunities for praxis (Sawyer & Liggett, 2012). In particular, the work brings into light the tensions between the need for social interventions and the act of doing; particularly the practical and often risky nature of responding to (in)justices within higher education. It is this view that allowed for a new perspective and framing for analysis of the relational and structural facets of social justice struggles and the extent to which praxes can be developed to circumvent these struggles. This phenomenon is examined through a critical dialogue, which was guided by the following questions:

1. How would you describe your overall experience in academe and have these varied across institutional types?
2. How would you describe the organizational climate/culture of your institution?
3. How would you describe your positionality within your institution?
4. What are the tensions and challenges within academe that impact your experiences?
5. What are the strategies you have employed to resist the challenges in academe?
6. Do you enact social justice as part of that resistance? If yes, how and why?
7. What has your resistance achieved?

Our 1-hour-long dialogue was audiotaped, transcribed, manually coded, discussed by all researchers, and thematically processed to address the inherent theoretical and research foci of the chapter. This collaborative process allowed for an interpretative narration of the data (Ellis & Brochner, 2000), and the stories of our collective selves. Our conversation provided a foundation for discussing critical social justice incidents and the relational aspects in higher education. Such work creates a necessary space where our shared stories around social justice advocacy in higher education can be situated in structural and relational terms. Our dialogue also explored the implications for ushering diversity, equity, and inclusion from a critical standpoint. The sections that follow therefore situate the relevance of (a) institutional contexts and interlocking structures, (b) breaking the silence, and (c) promoting critical consciousness and action, as three major themes within this work. These themes are explored and contextualized.

Institutional Contexts: Interlocking Structures and Relations

Theoretically, intersectionality calls for examinations of the multiple nodes of power that interface to affect the identities and lived experiences for marginalized groups. When we use this lens to reflect on our own experiences within academia, the chilly and contentious nature of our institutional climates remains central to that discussion. In this regard, both Devona and Deirdre spoke on the challenges around working within predominantly White institutions, and the extent to which institutionalized structures and expressions of power affected their experiences as African American women within academia. As an administrator, Devona remained troubled by the "close-minded" nature of her White academic colleagues who bought into "broader narratives and stereotypes about African Americans in academe." In this case, she underscored the ways in which these racial stereotypes structured the identities and positionalities of African American women within the academy. She focused on the expectation that one should suffer indignities in silence in order to maintain status in a manner that constrains African Americans in academe. She spoke of her own observations around gendered racism within the academy, the injustices around the negative framing of African Americans, the power relations that both produce and sustain injustices, and the implications for how African Americans respond to such oppressive experiences. In elaborating on this, she also spoke to the observations that some African Americans like herself—who have been negatively affected by these socially constructed labels—are seen as troublemakers for challenging the system in order to make it better for those who, like her, experience gendered racism. For her, these encounters with racial stereotypes unfold as a consequence of systemic axes of power that marginalize Black women within academe, even when they are authentically attempting to improve existing structures. For other scholars in the field, these reflections speak to the antagonistic nature of academic institutions; particularly for Black women who work on the margins and against racial stereotypes (Aguirre, 2000; Hill et al., 2005; Winkler, 2000).

In expanding on challenges for African Americans, Deirdre pointed to the lack of a critical mass and the struggles this introduces, whether for faculty or students. At the level of faculty, she touched on the presence of "networks within a network" that exist and operate to the benefit of White colleagues, mainly males, and on the peculiar positionality of African American women who work within such spaces. Higher education in this sense is constructed as a site is fraught with networks, where individuals socialize in exclusive spaces, share stories, opportunities, information, and resources. Similar to an "old boys club," membership is secretive and based primarily on race, gender, and socioeconomic status. A related position for Deirdre was that African American women are not seeking to join these clubs, but instead are working to demystify those spaces, make the information shared transparent and to ameliorate microaggressive environments.

In speaking to her personal experiences around these injustices, Deirdre reasoned "it was a combination of race, gender, and maybe at that time, age; [particularly because] they figure I looked a lot younger." In the classroom, she spoke to questions around how she was perceived, called, or referred to. In many instances, she noted her White colleagues were referred to as Dr. and she was either nameless, called by her first name, or asked, "Exactly how should we (students) address you?" Like Devona, Deirdre shared her concerns for the relational forms of injustices that exist and the negative effects they have on the academic engagement of African Americans. She underscored the intensification of already existing "tensions...about [issues] of diversity" were prevalent. She stressed these tensions were particularly visible within the practice of hiring faculty of color and sitting on search committees. In this case, she elaborated:

> You may work...to have a qualified and diverse pool...but the "diverse pool" only represents window dressing...because your colleagues can say with authority...we had candidates in the pool that fit these particular demographics..., but you are not seeing the same diversity reflected in three people that they bring on campus to actually interview.

The issue here is one of implicit bias, disenfranchisement, and the lack of access to opportunities for already marginalized groups within academe. When these issues emerged, Deirdre spoke to the lack of redress, of a space to deconstruct these practices, and of a "place to go and seek accountability for the inequitable practices and the lack of change." It was particularly problematic when "the people that are...stopgaps are leaders or administrators within your colleges and within your institution." Such cases of inequality and inequity bring to bear both (a) the need for dialogue around notions of equality of opportunity versus equality of outcome (Atweh, 2011; Gewirtz, 1998; Goldfarb & Grinberg, 2002) and (b) the importance of leadership to institutional reform within higher education (Jean-Marie, 2006; Tillman et al., 2006).

When considering students, Deirdre suggested the struggle becomes associated with whether the university responds to, and addresses, the injustices experienced by African American students. She opined that "there is a very chilly effect where we're having issues recruiting and retaining students on campus; meaning we have African American students that are currently not being admitted to the university." She noted "we have outside organizations that are asking those questions, we have people with inside the university that are asking those questions...but nothing is really being done." In making sense of these realities, she suggested the tensions are situated between the centrality of diversity issues within the broader mission of the university and the day-to-day practices that affect the lived realities of

Black students and Black women in academe. Deirdre touched on distributive and recognitive notions of social injustice, where overriding concerns are for the lack of representation and voice that result from related issues of access and freedom. She stressed the situation becomes very tense when "people don't want to have that conversation [and] then they wonder why you're becoming so particular [about diversity] in your discussion." She insisted however, that "if we're going to be honest about diversity and who's coming to the university...who is being allowed and having access, then we need to really talk about which groups are...being disenfranchised." Such contentions draw attention to the politics of color and its resultant effects for already marginalized groups in academe (Gutierrez y Muhs et al., 2012).

Talia's reflection, however, troubled the expectations around working within institutionally diverse contexts. In this case, she stressed her own experiences working within academic contexts that are racially and ethnically diverse and, where there is a lack of common interest and shared experiences between the respective social groups. In particular, she spoke to the lack of a collective community, the presence of extensive individualism, and a lack of "collegiality and feeling [of]...belonging in that space." She elaborated:

> It's highly individualized...with a lack of respect for comrades or colleagues, but also, a deliberate effort to dismiss rather than to recognize the works of others. So, in a space like this achievement is not really celebrated at an individual [or collective] level...primarily because of professional jealousy, other professional issues, [personal grievances]...[and because] of [what it takes to work] in a competitive space where everybody thinks that they're going to lose.

The emphasis was on academic tribalism; where faculty members, even though they may be diverse socially and professionally, maintain the exclusionary and individualistic status quo of the organization (Becher & Trowler, 2001; Sutherland & Markouskaite, 2012). In such contexts, she noted the "emphases on research, tenure, and promotion, have people on edge." She stressed negativity surrounded how persons are (or are not) promoted within the university "fostered a high sense of animosity and lack of collegiality [and] lack of support" for other colleagues. In such competitive academic contexts, she alluded to the tendency for persons to "dismiss rather than to pull someone up." She also weighed in on the tendency for such dismissal to coincide with the use of socially constituted categorizations of persons to informally deflect attention away from their individual strengths and/or achievements. In citing or speaking to her own experiences, she spoke to lurking questions around her age, size, maturity, length of time in the institution, and emerging positionality within her institutional context.

Here, she insisted these categorizations and reins of power are used to construct narratives and judgements around one's institutional credibility or legitimacy. What emerged in Talia's reflection was an attention to the nature of the rules of engagement, and the competitive basis of their connectivities; a reality that closely connects to concerns for the retributive and recognitive forms of injustices, which may unfold within institutional contexts (Gale & Densmore, 2000).

Breaking the Silence

Both Talia and Deirdre also spoke to the need for breaking the silence or pushing back against injustices within the academy as critical aspects of social justice praxis. Deirdre and Talia embraced the notion of social justice praxis as an act of actively questioning, challenging, and highlighting institutional forms of injustice (Baillon & Brown, 2003). In speaking to her practices around social justice, Talia articulated the following:

> I recognize [the need to open up the conversation; [particularly] where there's a silence around either the use or abuse of power. [I see this as] a way of enacting social justice. So that whether it be among colleagues among students. I will open the conversation around how are things...perceived...received...experienced...and have really authentic conversations about issues of power...[and how it manifests within] the...environment.... So, by doing that it's not just a way of disrupting, but it's also a way of sensitizing others around that circle of power so that they have [the ability to] recognize the way in which [it is being used]...and [perceived by others]...

She stressed the need for such conversations to "create a sense of consciousness around, 'this is what's happening'...and...to bring [issues related to structures of power] to the center..." For her, this was a way of "creating spaces where we could have open conversations around things that have been silenced within our own context." She also saw this as a critical way of undoing institutional messages surrounding acceptable types of research, discussions, and scholarly engagement. This was particularly important given that in her contexts, "students have the perception that you cannot research about things that are personal...about experiences related with various types of abuse...with being divorced or being a single parent." Conversations on positionality emerge as social experiences are stigmatized and personalized and where the dominant narrative is one that communicates that persons cannot speak to the specifics around these stories and experiences. She insisted, "Why not?!" While Talia's positionality and thinking can be considered as acts of social justice, she remains conscious of the broader social constructions and structures of power that (re) produce a silence around personal experiences with acts of injustice. She noted that pushing back requires the freedom to

> Speak very openly and freely and without any sense of shame or regret... in other words to speak to it and just speak through the struggle... but [also] to recognize that the struggles are part of my own journey to success and I share that with my students and colleagues so that they move away from the shame that is constructed around their personal and professional experiences.

While Deirdre echoed the need to make "the invisible visible," she noted, "Once you break that silence then people aren't able to hide and manipulate and engage in unfair and unjust practices, because you've pulled that cover back." She also called for caution in how this is enacted within that space. For instance, in her reflection, she noted, "I like that notion of... breaking silence but when I think about... social justice... I am always cognizant of... [what happens when and how you] open up spaces." In this case, Deirdre recorded the need to be self-reflective, strategic, and to avoid emotionally driven thinking or action in that process. She insisted:

> The minute you come at them emotionally your argument falls, it fails... and when you talk about issues of legitimacy that is one of the quickest ways to deem somebody illegitimate... so I make sure that I'm coming from a position of knowledge.

In applying this principle, she also asserted the impact "legitimacy" has on research:

> You can tell me that my work is not legitimate or that I'm doing too much race work, but I'm going to show you what the research says about what it means for a Black woman to seek tenure at a predominantly white institution. So, it's not going to be just me telling my particular narrative... that's going to be a part of it. But another part is... the cornerstone of academia... research... I'm going to show you five other scholars [that] have said exactly the same thing that I'm saying. Because now you're not just challenging me... one is challenging colleagues in the field, and it makes it a little more difficult for them to do that. So I'll draw my strength from there because it's one thing to tell my story which is an important one. But let me give you something else... if you try to dismantle me [my work] then you have to dismantle them [their work]. And you're not going to dismantle them... then they really have to be very careful with how they respond to what it is that I'm doing and what it is that I'm talking about.

Here, she accentuated the need for strategic resistance where one employs the value accorded to certain scholars and uses that as a foundation to make the case for work that would otherwise be dismissed as race research or work that is limited in scope. As a scholar who may be deemed as residing at the margins, she can employ the "master's tools to dismantle the master's house," thus understanding the importance of knowing one's environment and how to navigate within. Even with this attention to one's strategic engagement within the academy, Deirdre acknowledged the need for one to constantly "watch yourself... [to be conscious of] who you align with... to be very strategic about how you share information... what [professional] relationships you are involved in... [even as you remain] collegial with everyone." From a social justice perspective, such experiences speak to the sociopolitical dynamics of academic contexts, and the effects of these contexts on how marginalized groups, such as Black women, are challenged; particularly in how they give voice to their own experiences with social injustices. The act of breaking silence remains framed within and by the broader political and social landscapes that pervade within institutional contexts. This double-edged sword also raises more pointed questions around politics of social justice; specifically, the realities surrounding whether, and to what extent, institutions of higher education promote principles of liberty, fairness, and recognition that extend to all social groups.

Promoting Critical Consciousness and Action

Inspired by the work of Paulo Freire, Torres (2009) called for social justice learning as one that is "social, political, and pedagogical... [and that] take[s] place when people reach a deeper, richer, more contextualized, and more nuanced understanding of themselves and their world" (p. 92). To a large extent, institutionalizing such practices calls for teachers, faculty members, and learners to employ critical consciousness in confronting the complex structures and relations that exist within their everyday existence. Our findings centered on this discussion.

In fact, both Deirdre and Devona spoke to the importance of institutional networks and programs that support marginalized women as critical forms of praxis. Deirdre called for a "critical mass of Black individuals in leadership positions on the campus." She reiterated the need for Black scholars—whether they are in a position of leadership or moving along the professional ladder—to "speak back from a position of knowledge and not emotions" to avoid being labeled illegitimate. For Deirdre, this kind of strategic response calls for examinations of "people... institutions... how they become successful" and how African American women in leadership can create "additional spaces for other people [students and faculty] to have conversations that they may not have had." This sense of responsibility around the professional pathways of Black women within the academy emerges as a critical form of praxis that is nested within the parameters of mentoring networks (Cobb-Roberts & Esnard, 2020). For Devona and Deirdre, the consciousness around mentoring networks becomes significant to the distributive aspects of social justice where we work towards building capacity. Deirdre noted that mentoring networks provided open spaces to "engage in critical listening" and to figure out "strategically what direction to go in." Devona saw these mentoring networks as fundamental to how women of color "make [their] own connections" and succeed in "fighting against the power structures" that exist within the academy.

Talia extended this discussion to the need to speak through students, to sensitize them around the injustices that occur and foster critical thinking and listening within that process. Here, she expressed:

> I promote a sense of critical listening, particularly among my students critical questioning of what is heard of what is received... It really is important for me for students [and colleagues] to have that sense of critical listening... not just to listen to the story, but, also of how the story is being told by others, by who? I think it's important for them to recognize how the story... could [emerge as] an expression and a manifestation of power between two individuals.

Talia spoke to the use of her own story, the speaking up of her own experiences within social and institutional forms of injustice, and of using these experiences to teach transformative thinking and action. She insisted on the need for critical listening skills that empower students to deconstruct what is being told, how it is being told, and why it is being told. She also contended such transformative praxis is not without its challenges. She wondered, "How do you move through those struggles and get them [students] to understand that we are not to judge, but rather to understand, the purposes through which we are all subjects, [being] subjected." These questions therefore speak to the processes of teaching resistance and of centering subjected knowledge (Giroux, 2007). For Talia, this type of teaching likens to hooks' (1994) notion of transgressive practice, where students are encouraged to critically reflect on structures and practices to empower themselves in the process. This type of praxis empowers students with "a lens to look in and to look out, [and to] constantly go back and forth between the two." The important point of reference in this case is the need for transformative praxis that allows one to become conscious of the "politics of truth; not [as a process of] changing people's consciousness... or what's in their heads... but [as one through which they become sensitive to] the political, economic, institutional regime of the production of truth" (Rabinow & Rose, 2003, p. 317).

CONCLUSION

Marginalization, racism, sexism, and microaggressions manifesting as unintended barriers are presented as a few of the impediments faculty of color face in academe. These same Black women faculty members are often more likely than their White counterparts to incorporate diverse perspectives into curriculum and practice (Harley, 2008; Wallace et al., 2012); a strategy, which can impact their tenure, promotion, and advancement (Diggs et al., 2009). Further, they are vulnerable to, and victims of, systemic injustice and oppression in higher education (Esnard & Cobb-Roberts, 2018; Mabokela & Green, 2001). Using an intersectional analysis of a dialogical exchange, we explored the interlocking structures of power and its effects on three Black women in academe (faculty and administrator) and their social justice praxis approach. This work further addressed the gaps in the literature surrounding a clear definition of social justice and the role of Black women in higher education, exemplifying social justice praxis as critical strategy in addressing, speaking back to, and reforming higher educational unjust practices.

Our findings around the interlocking systems of power support many marginalizing and troubling effects of such oppressive structures. We believe that ending oppression and domination means working toward equitable policies and practices that challenge the exploitation, marginalization, powerlessness, cultural imperialism, and violence experienced by marginalized groups (Young, 1990). One interesting and complicated result of this oppression—and acknowledgement of such—is the creation of space for discourse around this issue. However, this aim is complicated by the ways the university recognizes diversity and diverse perspectives. Often, space is created for the acknowledgment of difference (i.e., offices of diversity, university lecture series, clubs/organizations that support diversity and inclusion) and the university can tout this as progress while simultaneously employing diversity as a "tool to discipline subjects." Awareness facilitates the idea of openness and progress by acknowledging the difference and avoiding further marginalization under the illusion of creating change.

However, that change is problematized by Ferguson (2012) who says the systemic oppression of the institution is not upended and reformed at the nexus of change is fabricated by admitting marginalized identities into the space without disrupting or dismantling the prevailing system of power (Musser, 2015). Through our conversation, we stressed the many contradictions of those narratives, as well as the need for constructive thinking and action that advances social justice agendas within everyday interactions throughout higher education. While our institutional and contextual nuances varied, our dialogue highlighted the relative importance of naming systems of power within academe, of breaking the silence or speaking out on these systems, of promoting critical thinking and action within higher education, and of seeking and receiving critical systems of support necessary to engage in acts of resistance and advocacy.

Theoretically, these findings provide important points for advancing empirical examinations of how Black women within academe experience and respond to intersecting domains of power within the academy. Further, we examined how we constructively attempt to dismantle the very structures and processes that (re)produce oppressive and antagonistic institutional climates. On a practical level, our dialogic exchange also strengthened the call for more authentic discussions and strategic responses that fundamentally problematizes and address issues related to institutionalized oppression, resistance, and change. Our narratives offer a reflective and collaborative take on the complexities surrounding intersectional axes of power, institutional resistance, and speak to the importance of critical dialogical exchange as a call to action.

This chapter also grounds the need for ongoing, deliberate, and strategic forms of interventions that simultaneously emerge and operate at individual and institutional levels to subvert institutional forms of oppression for Black women within the academy. At the individual level, the call is for Black women academics to remain critical of the intersections between racialized constructions, and those of the processes through which these representations structure their thinking and actions within the academy. The work also challenges scholars and Black women in academe to speak back to these structures; to question, challenge, and highlight injustices that exist, as a necessary aspect of seeking institutional change. While there is a call for some caution in this process, our work promotes the need for self-reflection, strategic engagement, and evidence-based responses to disrupt institutionalized oppression. We close with a call for critical consciousness and transformative praxis that situates systemic injustices, practices of subversion, and those that promote social justice.

REFERENCES

Aguirre, A. (2000). Women and minority faculty in the academic workplace: Recruitment, retention, and academic culture. *ASHE-ERIC Higher Education Report, 27*(6). https://eric.ed.gov/?id=ED447752

Armstrong, E. A., & Bernstein, M. (2008). Culture, power, and institutions: A multi-institutional politics approach to social movements. *Sociological Theory, 26*(1), 74–99. https://doi.org/10.1111/j.1467-9558.2008.00319.x

Atweh, B. (2011). Reflections on social justice, race, ethnicity, and identity from an ethical perspective. *Cultural Studies of Science Education, 6*(1), 33–47. https://doi.org/10.1007/s11422-010-9305-3

August, L., & Waltman, J. (2004). Culture, climate, and contribution: Career satisfaction among female faculty. *Research in Higher Education, 45*(2), 177–192. https://doi.org/10.1023/B:RIHE.0000015694.14358.ed

Avery, D. R., McKay, P. F., Wilson, D. C., & Tonidandel, S. (2007). Unequal attendance: The relationship between race, organizational diversity cues, and absenteeism. *Personnel Psychology, 60*(4), 875–902. https://psycnet.apa.org/doi/10.1111/j.1744-6570.2007.00094.x

Baillon, S., & Brown, E. (2003). Social justice in education: A framework. In M. Griffiths (Ed.), *Action for social justice in education: Fairly different* (pp. 55–58). Open University Press.

Becher, T., & Trowler, P. (2001). *Academic tribes and territories: Intellectual inquiry and the cultures of disciplines.* Open University Press.

Berila, B. (2016). *Integrating mindfulness into anti-oppressive pedagogy: Social justice in higher education.* Routledge.

Bettez, S. C. (2008). Social justice activist teaching in the university classroom. In J. Deim & R. J. Helfenbein (Eds.), *Unsettling beliefs: Teaching theory to teachers* (pp. 279–296). Information Age Publishing.

Brennan, J., & Naidoo, R. (2008). Higher education and the achievement (and/or prevention) of equity and social justice. *Higher Education, 56*(3), 287–302. https://doi.org/10.1007/s10734-008-9127-3

Carbado, D., Crenshaw-Williams, K., Mays, V. W., & Tomlinson, B. (2013). Intersectionality: Mapping the movements of a theory. *Du Bois Review: Social Science Research on Race, 10*(2), 303–312. https://doi.org/10.1017/S1742058X13000349

Chang, H., Ngunjiri, F. W., & Hernandez, K. C. (2013). *Collaborative autoethnography.* Routledge.

Choo, H. Y., & Ferree, M. M. (2010). Practicing intersectionality in sociological research: A critical analysis of inclusions, interactions, and institutions in the study of inequalities. *Theory & Society, 28*(2), 129–149. https://doi.org/10.1111/j.1467-9558.2010.01370.x

Cobb-Roberts, D., & Esnard, T. (Eds.). (2020). *Mentoring as critically engaged praxis: Storying the lives of Black women.* Information Age Publishing.

Crenshaw, K. (1991). Mapping the margins: Intersectionality, identity politics, and violence against women of color. *Stanford Law Review, 43*(6), 1241–1299. https://doi.org/10.2307/1229039

Darling-Hammond, L., French, J., & Garcia-Lopez, S. P. (Eds.). (2002). *Learning to teach for social justice.* Teacher College Press.

Diggs, G. A., Garrison-Wade, D. F., Estrada, D., & Galindo, R. (2009). Smiling faces and colored spaces: The experiences of faculty of color pursuing tenure in the academy. *The Urban Review, 41*(4), 312–333. https://doi.org/10.1007/s11256-008-0113-y

Ellis, C., & Bochner, A. P. (2000). Autoethnography, personal narrative, reflexivity. In N. K. Denzin & Y. S. Lincoln (Eds.), *Handbook of qualitative research* (2nd ed., pp. 733–768). SAGE.

Enterline, S., Cochran-Smith, M., Ludlow, L. H., & Mitescu, M. (2008). Learning to teach for social justice: Measuring change in the beliefs of teacher candidates. *The New Educator, 4*(4), 267–290. https://doi.org/10.1080/15476880802430361

Esnard, T., & Cobb-Roberts, D. (2018). *Black women, academe, and the tenure process in the United States and the Caribbean.* Palgrave Macmillan.

Ferguson, R. A. (2012). *The reorder of things: The university and its pedagogies of minority difference.* University of Minnesota Press.

Furlong, A., & Cartmel, F. (2009). *Higher education and social justice.* SRE & Open University Press.

Gale, T., & Densmore, K. (2000). *Just schooling: Exploration in the cultural politics of teaching.* Open University Press.

Gewirtz, S. (1998). Conceptualizing social justice in education: Mapping the territory. *Journal of Educational Policy,* 13, 469–484. https://doi.org/10.1080/0268093980130402

Giroux, H. A. (2004). Cultural studies, public pedagogy, and the responsibility of intellectuals. *Communication and Critical/Cultural Studies, 1*(1), 59–79. https://doi.org/10.1080/1479142042000180926

Giroux, H. (2007). *The university in chains: Confronting the military-industrial-academic complex.* Paradigm.

Goldfarb, K. P., & Grinberg, J. (2002). Leadership for social justice: Authentic participation in the case of a community center in Caracas, Venezuela. *Journal of School Leadership, 12*(2), 157–173. https://doi.org/10.1177/105268460201200204

Gutierrez y Muhs, G., Niemann, G. F., Gonzalez, G. C., & Harris, P. A. (Eds.). (2012). *Presumed incompetent: The intersections of race and class for women in academia.* State University Press.

Hackman, H. (2005). Five essential components for social justice education. *Equity & Excellence in Education,* 38, 103–109. https://doi.org/10.1080/10665680590935034

Harley, D. A. (2008). Maids of academe: African American women faculty at predominately white institutions. *Journal of African American Studies, 12*(1), 19–36. https://doi.org/10.1007/s12111-007-9030-5

Hill, N. R., Leinbaugh, T., Bradley, C., & Hazler, R. (2005). Female counselor educators: Encouraging and discouraging factors in academia. *Journal of Counseling & Development, 83*(3), 374–380. https://doi.org/10.1002/j.1556-6678.2005.tb00358.x

Hill Collins, P. (1995). The social construction of Black feminist thought. In B. Guy-Sheftal (Ed.). *Words of fire: An anthology of African American feminist thought* (pp. 338–358). The New Press.

hooks, b. (1994). *Teaching to transgress: Education as the practice of freedom.* Routledge.

Hytten, K. (2006). Education for social justice: Provocations and challenges. *Educational Theory, 56*(2), 221–236. https://doi.org/10.1111/j.1741-5446.2006.00013.x

Jean-Marie, G. (2006). Welcoming the unwelcomed: A social justice imperative of African-American female leaders at historically black colleges and universities. *Educational Foundations, 20*(1–2), 85–104. https://eric.ed.gov/?id=EJ751762

Mabokela, R., & Green, A. L. (Eds.). (2001). *Sisters of the academy: Emergent Black women scholars in higher education.* Stylus.

MacKinnon, C. (2013). Intersectionality as a method: A note. *Signs: Journal of Women in Culture and Society,* 38, 1019–1039. https://doi.org/10.1086/669570

Massey, D. S., & Fischer, M. J. (2005). Stereotype threat and the academic performance: New findings from a racially diverse sample of college freshmen. *Du Bois Review, 2*(1), 45–67. https://doi.org/10.1017/S1742058X05050058

Milem, J. F., & Umbach, P. D. (2003). The influence of precollege factors on students' predispositions regarding diversity activities in college. *Journal of College Student Development, 44*(5), 611–624. https://doi.org/10.1353/csd.2003.0056

Musser, A. J. (2015). Specimen days: Diversity, labor, and the university. *Feminist Formations, 27*(3), 1–20. https://doi.org/10.1353/ff.2016.0006

Nixon, H., & Comber, B. (1995). Making documentaries and teaching about educational disadvantage: Ethical issues and practical dilemmas. *Australian Educational Research, 22*(2), 63–84. https://doi.org/10.1007/BF03219593

Rabinow, P., & Rose, N. (Eds.). (2003). *The essential Foucault: Selections from the essential works of Foucault, 1954–1984*. New Press.

Rizvi, F. (1998). Some thoughts on contemporary issues of social justice. In B. Atweh, S. Kemmis, & P. Weeks (Eds.), *Action research in practice: Partnerships for social justice in education* (pp. 47–56). Routledge.

Ross, S. N. (2014). Diversity and intergroup contact in higher education: Exploring possibilities for democratization through social justice education. *Teaching in Higher Education, 19*(8), 870–881. https://doi.org/10.1080/13562517.2014.934354

Sawyer, R. D., & Liggett, T. (2012). Shifting positionalities: A critical discussion of a duo-ethnographic inquiry of a personal curriculum of post/colonialism. *International Journal of Qualitative Methods, 11*(5), 628–651. https://doi.org/10.1177/160940691201100507

Singh, M. (2011). The place of social justice in higher education and social change discourses. *Compare: A Journal of Comparative and International Education, 41*(4), 481–494. https://doi.org/10.1080/03057925.2011.581515

Solorzano, D., Ceja, M., & Yosso, T. (2000). Critical race theory, racial microaggressions, and campus climate: The experiences of African American college students. *Journal of Negro Education, 69*(1–2), 60–73. https://www.jstor.org/stable/2696265

Sowell, T. (2004). *Affirmative action around the world: An empirical study*. Yale University Press.

Sutherland, L., & Markauskaite, L. (2012). Examining the role of authenticity in supporting the development of professional identity: An example from teacher education. *Higher Education, 64*(6), 747–766. https://doi.org/10.1007/s10734-012-9522-7

Tillman, L., Brown, K., Campbell-Jones, F., & Gonzalez, M. L. (2006). Transformative leadership for social justice: Concluding thoughts. *Journal of School Leadership, 16*(2), 207–209. https://doi.org/10.1007/978-94-007-6555-9_19

Torres, C. A. (2009). *Education and neoliberal globalization*. Routledge.

Turner Sotello-Viernes, C., & Myers, S. (2002). Snapshots from the literature: Elements influencing the workplace environment. In C. Turner Sotello-Viernes, A. Antonio, M. Garcia, B. Laden, A. Nora, & C. Presley (Eds.), *Racial and ethnic diversity in higher education* (2nd ed., pp. 222–247). Pearson Custom Publishing.

Wallace, S. L., Moore, S. E., Wilson, L. L., & Hart, B. G. (2012). African American women in the academy: Quelling the myth of presumed incompetence. In G. y Muhs Gutiérrez, Y. Flores Niemann, C. G. González, & A. P. Harris (Eds.), *Presumed incompetent: The intersections of race and class for women in academia* (pp. 421–438). University Press of Colorado.

Weldon, L. S. (2008). The concept of intersectionality. In G. Goertz & A. Mazur (Eds.), *Politics, gender, and concepts: Theory and methodology* (pp. 193–218). Cambridge University Press.

West, N. M. (2018). In the company of my sister-colleagues: Professional counter spaces for African American women student affairs administrators. *Gender and Education, 31*(4), 543–559. https://doi.org/10.1080/09540253.2018.1533926

Wilkins, A. C. (2012). Becoming Black women: Intimate stories and intersectional identities. *Social Psychology Quarterly, 75*(2), 173–196. https://doi.org/10.1177/0190272512440106

Winkler, J. A. (2000). Faculty reappointment, tenure, and promotion: Barriers for women. *The Professional Geographer, 52*(4), 737–750. https://doi.org/10.1111/0033-0124.00262

Winkle-Wagner, R., & Locks, A. M. (2014). *Diversity and inclusion on campus: Supporting racially and ethnically underrepresented students.* Routledge.

Young, I. M. (1990). *Social justice and the politics of difference.* Princeton University.

Zollers, N. J., Albert, L. R., & Cochran-Smith, M. (2000). In pursuit of social justice: Collaborative research and practice in teacher education. *Action in Teacher Education, 22*(2), 1–14. https://doi.org/10.1080/01626620.2000.10463000

CHAPTER 11

THE JOURNEY MATTERS

Examining the Paths and Lived Experiences of African American Males for STEM Success

Latara O. Lampkin
Adrienne Stephenson
Andria Cole
Jonathan Townes
Marquise L. Kessee

ABSTRACT

There are a number of nuanced challenges that disproportionately impact the recruitment, persistence, and success of African American males in the STEM training pipeline and the scientific workforce. Evidence suggests that in addition to developing positive campus environments, community colleges and 4-year institutions can advance Black male student success by identifying and addressing the factors (academic, societal, psychological, and environmental) that enhance or impede success. In this chapter, the authors share insights from African American male students matriculating through STEM pathway programs, as well as from those who have successfully completed their academic programs. Specifically, we share findings from a case study where we explore factors that enhance the success of African American males pursuing STEM degrees at one of the few community colleges designated as a historically Black college and university (HBCU). The authors provide considerations that can potentially enhance the recruitment, persistence, and success of African American males pursuing STEM degrees.

The idea that the science, technology, engineering and math (STEM) pipeline is leaky—described by some as the unintended loss of trainees in the field—has long been recognized and is uncontested, particularly for underrepresented minorities, including African American males. Among the remedies to address this issue are intervention programs at the K–12 and postsecondary levels to increase the recruitment, retention, and success of underrepresented groups. In both K–12 and postsecondary settings, these programs vary in terms of forms, purposes, programmatic features, and timing based on a students' degree path and/or employees' career track or stage in their career. Evidence suggests higher education institutions can play a role in advancing the STEM pipeline for underrepresented groups, specifically Black males, by creating positive campus environments and identifying facilitators and addressing barriers to success (Amechi et al., 2015; Wood et al., 2016).

Minority-serving institutions (MSIs)—which typically provide a culturally immersive, culturally-responsive environment—are uniquely situated to design and implement programs to broaden participation for underrepresented groups to enhance STEM diversity. These institutions can also serve as models and lead efforts for disseminating and scaling-up programs tailored for these groups. MSIs account for approximately 14% of degree-granting colleges and universities in the United States, eligible to award Title IV federal financial aid (Espinosa et al., 2017), and are fairly geographically dispersed throughout the nation.

Historically Black colleges and universities (HBCUs)—which are designated MSIs—have documented history and unparalleled success in conferring degrees for underrepresented student groups and preparing them to diversify the STEM workforce. HBCUs play a critical role in the institutional pathways for Black STEM degree recipients for undergraduate and graduate degrees, including those earning PhDs (Upton & Tannenbaum, 2014). In examining the role of HBCUs as pathway providers, Upton and Tannenbaum (2014) found that most Black STEM PhD recipients took predominantly White institutional pathways to the doctorate. However, Black PhD recipients among the most underrepresented groups (i.e., U.S. citizens, women, first-generation college students) in the STEM academic and broader workforce, earned at least an undergraduate degree—if not both undergraduate and doctoral degrees—from an HBCU.

There has been an increase in policy efforts geared towards addressing racial inequities in STEM for Black students, as well as students from other racially marginalized groups (NSF, n.d.). Legislation and federally funded initiatives that support STEM academic programming (e.g., FUTURE Act) and research (e.g., National Science Foundation Racial Equity in STEM Education) at HBCUs, emphasize the integral role MSIs continue to play in broadening STEM participation. Industries have also recognized the value of partnering with MSIs to train and diversify the STEM workforce. For example, programs like the Future of STEM Scholars Initiatives (FOSSI) are partnering with HBCUs and leading efforts to create STEM career pathways for underrepresented groups to excel in STEM careers.

Notably, Gasman and Nguyen (2016), asserted HBCUs do a better job of socializing and cultivating talent to improve students' chances of succeeding in the sciences. Evidence suggests STEM pathway programs, which are prevalent at many HBCUs, provide early exposure to STEM opportunities and STEM professions. These programs designed to introduce and socialize students to STEM include undergraduate and graduate summer bridge programs and Research Experiences for Undergraduates (REUs). Pathway programs also provide internships in academia, government, and industry to prepare and train STEM scholars. Intentional modeling for STEM programming of this nature arguably increases STEM interest for students from underrepresented groups—who oftentimes can be excluded from STEM exposure and related STEM experiences—as well as their likelihood to pursue undergraduate STEM degrees, persist academically, and succeed in the STEM workforce.

There has also been a growing awareness of the role of community colleges and their capacity to increase the STEM pipeline, particularly for underrepresented student populations. Community colleges serve as a major entry point for postsecondary studies among underrepresented minority populations (Stage et al., 2013). Evidence suggests these institutions also play a critical role in serving as the gateway to STEM for these students (Palmer & DuBord, 2013).

Few studies have examined the factors that influence outcomes for African-American males at 2-year community colleges (Strayhorn, 2012). In fact, extant literature on the exploration of African-American males attending community college is generally sparse (Strayhorn, 2012; Wood et al., 2016). With the lack of readily available data, there is limited evidence to inform programming and practice relative to the recruitment and matriculation of African-American males in the community college setting or their transitions to 4-year institutions.

As part of a larger case study, we examined the experiences of Black males who participated in a federally funded STEM program at one of the few community colleges in the nation designated as a HBCU. Specifically, we explored participants' perceptions of and experiences in a National Science Foundation funded, STEM-UP program while enrolled at the Community College Campus.[1] To our knowledge, no study to date has examined the collegiate experiences of Black males pursuing STEM degrees at a historically Black community college. This is a gap this current study seeks to fill.

One key question guided our thinking for the study: "What factors enhance the success of Black males matriculating through post-secondary academic STEM programs and pursuing STEM degrees?" And while this is not a new question, we amplify the voices and needs of the "end-user"—Black men—sharing what *they* deem "matters" for *their* STEM journey at each juncture along way (i.e., pursuing and transitioning from each degree level through workforce entry). First, we briefly consider the factors that can influence the academic success of Black males and their postsecondary experiences. Drawing on prior research and later focus group findings, we then highlight factors Black males in our study deemed salient to *their* academic experiences and success as Black men in pursuit of STEM degrees. Lastly, guided by the participants' voices, we situate the findings as opportunities for higher education stakeholders to enhance experiences and support more equitable postsecondary outcomes for Black men.

FRAMING IDEAS TO EXPLORE STEM SUCCESS FOR BLACK MALES: THE JOURNEY ENVISIONED

As early as ninth grade, students formulate strong opinions of their own potential for success beyond high school, often to the extent of preferring to end their journey prematurely. In laying the foundation for academic success for Black males, Howard and Lyons (2021) noted the need to *empower* them by adhering to the following mechanisms:

1. increasing the number of African American teachers and mentors in our schools,
2. increasing opportunities via pipeline initiatives,
3. offering relevant and engaging curricula,
4. listening and connecting to the African American male experience,
5. building positive relationships between students and stakeholders,
6. acknowledging their diverse experiences and histories, and
7. devoting attention to their mental health circumstances.

In terms of the STEM pipeline, Howard and Lyon's (2021) mechanisms for Black male success align with research highlighting the importance of identifying tailored interventions and ways to eliminate systemic barriers for Black males to increase STEM participation and success (Burt & Johnson, 2018). And while there are myriad factors that can impact the outcomes of Black males' pursuing STEM degrees, their collegiate experiences in higher education settings are arguably one of the most critical factors that can enhance (or impede) their postsecondary success.

In gauging and illuminating the experiences of Black males entering and matriculating through STEM undergraduate programs, it is important to understand the factors that inform their collegiate experiences. Researchers have identified a number of institutional factors that influence Black male success in higher education settings, including the types of institutions Black males attend (Fries-Britt et al., 2012; Freis-Britt & White-Lewis, 2020) and how institutional stakeholders interact and engage with these students outside and in the classroom. Here, we briefly highlight research that sheds light on institutional factors that can hold promise for enhancing Black male STEM success in postsecondary environments.

Institutions

The types of institutions Black males pursue STEM degrees from are among the factors identified to strengthen their retention in the sciences (Freis Britt & White-Lewis, 2020; Fries-Britt et al., 2012). Evidence suggests MSIs implement holistic initiatives to support STEM success for Black males in higher education (Gasman et al., 2017; Pascarella & Terenzini, 2005). Researchers have noted the commitment of HBCUs in developing the whole individual by attending to other cultural dimensions, such as moral and ethical responsibilities to the Black community, as well as character, spiritual, and leadership development (Jett, 2013).

Academic environments on campuses and within classrooms can be critical to their persistence and overall outcomes. Researchers have highlighted the role faculty play as "essential institutional agents" (Fries-Brit & White-Lewis, 2020, p. 522) in promoting student success for minority students (Burt et al., 2019; Hurtado et al., 2011; Museus et al., 2011). In this context, faculty members play a key role in creating welcoming and supporting environments on college campuses. Evidence suggests faculty members that set high expectations while demonstrating care and concern for students both inside and outside the classroom have an impact on students' sense of belonging and determination to persist (Fries-Britt & White-Lewis, 2020). This demonstrated care and concern, oftentimes with faculty "centering students' needs over their own needs," is particularly evidenced at MSIs (Fries-Britt & White-Lewis, 2020, p. 524; Gasman & Nguyen, 2016).

Intentional Programming and Program Models

Several studies highlight the salience of program models tailored to meet the needs of minority students. For example, researchers have noted the importance of opportunities for socialization in models (Bertrand Jones & Osborne-Lampkin, 2013; Bertrand Jones et al., 2016) and social communities (Mondisa & McComb, 2015). Opportunities such as faculty–student interactions, mentoring, and social community have been identified as key elements of intentional programming that facilitate academic, personal, and professional growth in Black males majoring in STEM.

Because STEM fields usually involve a great deal of time working and learning together, Black male students benefit when they can establish meaningful relationships with other students and faculty. Efforts to establish these relationships can be challenging due to the competitive nature of STEM; however, forming meaningful relationships and models that facilitate these relationships can contribute tremendously to the persistence of Black males in STEM fields (Boyd & Mitchell, 2018).

It is, indeed, important to highlight the individual benefits of social communities for Black males in STEM at the postsecondary level. Community building fosters a sense of belonging and emphasizes the importance of developing relationships that provide intellectual and emotional support, while building confidence in the ability to succeed. This mindset builds resilience and mental fortitude and supports scholarly development where challenges and failure are not viewed negatively. Social community empowers Black male STEM scholars to show up as themselves and put their best foot forward, understanding that challenges, struggles, adversity, and failure are factors that exist throughout the STEM journey (Mondisa & McComb, 2015). In this context, mentors play a pivotal role in Black male success by serving as role models, introducing Black males to educational and professional opportunities, guiding them through intricate institutional mazes, and motivating them to persevere (Scott & Sharp, 2019).

Models that incorporate meaningful activities and experiences to provide exploration and exposure beyond the institution have also been found to support STEM success for Black males. Exposure to research, national conferences, internships, and advanced academic degrees extend the development of interest and acquiring skill sets beyond the classroom. Such exposure is critical to the development of STEM talent and preparation for lifelong enrichment in STEM careers. These experiential learning opportunities encourage training that expands skill sets and connects academic learning to real-life experiences (Hrabowski & Maton, 2009), allowing scholars to make informed decisions about academic and career choices. These types of experiences also set the stage for scholars to interact with professionals and experts in government, industry, and academia. This intentionality in programming extends exploration and engagement in STEM learning beyond the academic setting and serves as a critical support for Black male STEM scholars throughout the undergraduate journey and into STEM careers.

Lastly, institutional initiatives and interventions that support the recruitment and prime the pipeline can also be critical for STEM success. For example, pre-major courses for incoming students and summer boot camps provide opportunities for enrollment into STEM programs and successful degree completion (Premraj et al., 2021). These initiatives provide early STEM exposure, support socialization, and can be critical levers for institutions seeking to enhance the recruitment, retention, and overall success of Black males pursuing STEM degrees.

METHODS FOR EXPLORING AN INSTITUTIONAL MODEL FOR STEM SUCCESS

This qualitative study draws on focus group interviews with Black men who attended the Community College Campus and participated in the STEM-UP Academy—a program designed to increase the pipeline and preparation of students to complete associate's degrees and pursue bachelor's degrees in STEM disciplines. The Community College Campus is one of the few community colleges in the nation officially designated as an HBCU preparing students to transfer to baccalaureate institutions. Located in the southeast in a small, rural community, the institution serves approximately 420 students annually. Since 2015, institutional faculty and staff have served over 2,000 academic, career, and technical certificate students, many of whom have been required to spend their first two to four semesters in remedial courses to enhance and support preparation in mathematics and science at the college level. This context is noteworthy given research highlighting the role HBCUs play in providing encouragement to students to persist in STEM, even when additional academic support or remedial education is needed.

The Program Model

Funded by the National Science Foundation (NSF) in 2010, the *Cohesive Community College STEM Institutional Transformation Academy—STEM-UP Academy* program is designed to increase the number of minority students completing an Associate of Arts degree at the institution and pursuing a Bachelor of Science degree in STEM areas at 4-year colleges or universities. The goal of the program is to strengthen students' community college academic experiences by developing bridges and transitional points that support students' matriculation from one education level to the next.

The core strategy foci for *STEM-UP* include: (a) challenging students to achieve the highest level of intellectual and personal development in math and science, (b) enhancing students' problem-solving and critical-thinking skills, (c) enhancing STEM students' ability to use technology in content-specific and general areas, (d) introducing students to STEM research, (e) providing students with a headstart on their STEM college career, and (f) facilitating student success and transfer to 4-year institutions.

Employing a cohort model, students can pursue majors in science (biology, chemistry, physics), technology (aerospace technology, computer science), engineering (chemical, civil, computer, environmental), and mathematics (actuary, mathematician, statistician). In addition to full financial support, key components of the STEM-UP program include enrollment in a 2-week boot camp prior to entering the fall semester, tutoring for intervention and enrichment, summer internships, mentoring, and one-on-one guidance into STEM related fields.

In conjunction with the STEM-UP program, the institution offers enrichment and intervention programs that span K–12 and postsecondary settings to enhance enrollment and STEM success. For example, the HBCU-UP targeted infusion project supports intervention and enrichment in STEM for K–12 and postsecondary students, with an emphasis in mathematics. In the context of this study, this program is designed to increase the student's developmental knowledge and interest in STEM education and careers. This program also supported math faculty working to enhance teaching and learning in order to improve student performance in math courses.

Internal and external advisory committees support all programs. These committees are comprised of administrators and staff in the Office of Institutional Research, Science, and Math faculty, high school administrators, personnel from 4-year institutions, and industry leaders. Previous graduates also serve on both internal and external committees, availing themselves as essential stakeholders and enabling the institution to leverage their experiences as "end-users" (Tseng, 2012).

Exposure and Exploration Beyond the Institution

With the implementation and success of the STEM-UP Academy, the institution has seen a growth in partnerships and external funding pertaining to STEM. This includes securing funding for the NSF Innovative Technology Experiences for Students and Teachers (ITEST) project, NSF Louis Stokes Alliances for Minority Participation (LSAMP) program, Minority Science and Engineering Improvement Program (MSEIP), and NASA Community

College Aerospace Scholars (NCAS) program. The institution has also developed research agreements with neighboring institutions to provide additional enrichment, exposure, and mentoring to STEM students at the college.

Participants

Participants included 10 Black males who were enrolled in, and completed, the STEM-UP Program at the selected community college between 2017 and 2020. Employing a purposeful sampling strategy, participants were recruited and selected to participate in the study based on their gender, entering cohort year, and their undergraduate majors. Participants' entering cohort years and the majors pursued while at the community college varied (e.g., biology, biology-pre-med, chemistry, environmental science, physics, mechanical engineering, agricultural engineering, math), as did the subsequent level of degrees pursued/earned in their respective fields (ranging at the time of data collection from bachelors to doctorates). For example, 4 of the 10 participants were currently pursuing their bachelors' degrees at 4-year institutions, while other participants (6/10) previously earned bachelors' degrees and were pursuing master's or doctoral degrees and/or were working as STEM professionals. All participants elected to continue their undergraduate degrees at either an in-state PWI-Research 1 institution or a HBCU-High Research institution.[2]

Data Collection and Analysis

Focus group interviews were conducted to gather insights into participants' experiences and their perceptions of factors that enhanced their success in pursuing STEM degrees. To explore the research question, participants responded to questions about factors and salient experiences that influenced their decisions to pursue undergraduate degrees in STEM generally, and in the case institution specifically. Central to the research question, participants responded to questions about their experiences in the STEM-UP program and factors that potentially enhanced their experiences in the pursuit of their STEM degrees. Guided by the literature, the semi-structured protocols focused on institutional factors we know can influence the persistence of Black males pursuing STEM degrees. For example, participants were asked, "Describe any formal precollegiate STEM-related programs you participated in prior to entering your undergraduate program." The protocols also included questions to gather insights about the institutional context and program aspects that participants deemed salient to enhancing their STEM success. For example, we asked: "What aspect of the STEM-UP program would you say contributed most to your STEM success?" A total of two focus group interviews, which included 4–6 participants, were conducted for the study. Interviews lasted 60–90 minutes, were tape-recorded to accurately capture participants' responses, and subsequently transcribed verbatim for analysis.

We employed a systematic, multi-stage, iterative approach for coding and analyzing the data. We employed pattern coding to identify central constructs in the data (Miles et al., 2014; Yin, 2013). Using the a priori coding framework, coding was initially theory-driven, followed by a more in-depth examination of the data. Strategies were used to test and confirm findings, including checking for representativeness from the data prior to drawing final conclusions.

Limitations of the Study

As with all research investigations, this project is not without methodological limitations. Using focus-group interviews as a method of data collection, we were able to gather detailed information and in-depth insight into participants' experiences and how they made sense of those experiences (McMillan & Schumacher, 2010). While the use of focus groups provided an opportunity for participants to reflect on their experiences in a forum designed to facilitate in-depth discussion and mutual reflection, individual interviews might have potentially enhanced disclosure of information perceived too personal to share in a group setting. Focus group data is also self-reported and relies on participant's honest and accurate reflections. Finally, while the study provides insight into the experiences of participants included in the sample, the findings cannot be generalized to all program participants or Black males. Although these limitations are important, the study provides valuable information about the collegiate experiences of African-American males who have been prepared and matriculated through STEM degree programs, specifically at a 2-year community college designated as an HBCU.

THE JOURNEY REALIZED: ILLUMINATING WHAT "REALLY MATTERS" FOR BLACK MALE STEM SUCCESS

Black males who participated in the study conveyed what they perceived as factors that enhanced their collegiate experiences and academic success as they pursued STEM degrees. Although the focus was on their experience while attending the Community College Campus and enrolled in the STEM-UP Academy, they were prompted to "go down the road" to share "what mattered" as they persisted and earned degrees along the entire path of their academic journey.

Consistent with prior research, evidence from this study suggests that indeed, *institutions matter* for Black males pursuing STEM degrees, particularly those who acknowledge and use targeted approaches to meet their needs. Overwhelmingly, participants highlighted the importance of "institutional fit" (i.e., community college, HBCU) explaining it is important that "institutions differentiate themselves" from other institutions. Participants expounded by emphasizing that the individual "recruiting us [them], came after us," emphasized "why the institution would be a good fit for us [Black males]," and explained "what was in place to support our [added emphasis] academic success." As one participant explained, "We [Black males] are different and sometimes have different issues." The men participating in this particular focus group, confirmed this participant's statement with elaborating—"from other students."

Notably, the vast majority (8 of 10) of participants also reported being encouraged to attend a community college as a step towards obtaining a bachelor's degree. In fact, apart from two participants, participants reported being strongly encouraged to attend a community college. In fact, several of the Black men "had planned to go to—[named another institution], a 4-year institution," but "decided to go to the Community College Campus, due to an administrator's targeted recruitment efforts and the fact that it is also a HBCU."

In this context, our findings were consistent with prior findings that *academic environments matter* and can influence Black males' perceptions of themselves and their ability to thrive in higher education settings. Participants in the study highlighted the importance and value of the nurturing environment at the institution, and the "HBCU environment," noting it was critical to their overall academic success. Participants explained the "nurturing environment was across the entire institution." As one participant explained, the "nurturing environment extended beyond traditional advising support you might get at 'other' institutions." Elaborating on the response, another participant explained, "We may not always know or want to ask for help." Further probing revealed that this was particularly the case in terms of "*any* support needed." Another participant continued, "But everyone at the institution knew what we needed."

Notably, when asked to identify relevant and critical aspects of the program model that most supported their success, participants returned to discussing the role of the institution in creating a supportive academic environment, noting that the "wrap around support of the entire institution" and the "intentionality" in the program model were "key (i.e., mattered) to students' success and our [their] success as Black men." Opportunities for socialization, tailored professional development, and mentorship were the top three aspects of the model participants highlighted. All participants referenced the "cohort model" as key in their ability to matriculate through their programs. As they explained, "the support you have made a difference and doing it together with other people like you is important." The built-in scholarly development also played a significant role in their growth as the Black male scholars while at the case institution, transfer institutions, and their professional careers. Participants highlighted the importance of the "tailored" professional development opportunities, such as "internships," "opportunities to meet and talk with people in the industry" that while not in all cases, but in many cases, "looked like us [them]."

The Black men in the study also valued the intentional mentorship that was embedded in the STEM pathway program. Overwhelmingly, participants expressed their gratitude for the mentorship provided by the then STEM director, who was Black male, and explained how his mentorship significantly enhanced their collegiate experiences. In fact, participants shared the director was "critical in us [referring to Black males] persisting through our programs." As one participant notably shared, "Seeing him do it, made me believe that I could also do it." Other participants vehemently nodded as the participant spoke about the directors' influence on their academic experiences.

Finally, and not surprising, findings from the study revealed that "money matters." Financial support was one of the primary factors that weighed into the decisions and ability of the participants to pursue postsecondary education in STEM. All participants indicated that financial aid, specifically the amount of "financial support being offered by the *institution*" was among the criterion used for college selection. Seven out of the 10 participants indicated that the financial support provided by the community college was the primary factor in their decisions, which "would lessen the financial stress and enable us [them] to focus on our studies."

THE JOURNEY FORESEEN AND MODELS FOR BLACK MALE STEM SUCCESS: OPPORTUNITIES AND CONSIDERATIONS

For Black males, choosing to pursue a college education is an undertaking that must be precisely navigated, and whether fluid, deviating, or direct, the journey matters. The question is, "Will they stay the course?" This question can undoubtedly yield positive results with on-time, on-purpose, dedicated, and guided attention to the journey. The question then becomes, "How do we develop a path forward to facilitate success and mitigate barriers along the journey to help them stay the course?" To answer this question, we must

The Journey Matters • **227**

begin with the "end-user" in mind—Black male students. This study brings to the forefront the voices of Black males, illuminating what they deemed the most valuable of experiences in their STEM journey as they matriculated through STEM programs, and in a few cases, into the STEM workforce.

Informed by the voices of Black men, we situate the experiences and "what matters" to the men in this study to provide considerations for supporting equity and inclusion in higher education settings. We seek to provide actionable steps that will foster more equitable outcomes for Black men on the STEM journey.

Perhaps most critical to this discussion is the acknowledgment that "Black men matter—their voices matter." Higher education institutions must create opportunities that allow Black men the freedom and flexibility to guide their narrative to enhance their success and provide an ability to mentor and guide others along the journey. Institutions can play a key role in ensuring they have in place institutional structures, systems and supports that acknowledge the voices and needs of Black male students, tailoring interventions to meet their specific needs. Below we highlight opportunities and considerations grounded in the premise that institutions, intentional modeling, money, and research all matter for Black male STEM success in higher education settings.

Historically, HBCUs have provided Black students with learning environments that affirm their talents and potential (Gasman et al., 2008). It is not surprising that STEM Pathway programs at HBCUs, in this case the STEM-UP Academy, are strategic in providing nurturing environments that support academic achievement, scholarly development, and student success. In this study, the Black men participants touted the importance of the collective institutional community in their persistence and academic success. To some extent, all of the men described how faculty perceptions and their relationships and positive interactions with their instructors (and other institutional stakeholders) increased their academic development and educational aspirations (Fries-Britt & White-Lewis, 2020). Along those lines, findings from this study revealed peer interactions and faculty accessibility (Perna et al., 2009) played a pivotal role in participants' experiences. And while these findings were reflective of the institutional environment created at an HBCU, the ability to create welcoming academic environments for Black men is not relegated to these institutions.

> All postsecondary institutions can and should be intentional about creating spaces and places where Black males can feel valued and supported (Tolliver & Miller, 2018). Inclusive campus spaces are places where minoritized individuals can go to be affirmed in their abilities and accepted

> for who they are instead of stigmatized and marginalized due to their race, gender, socioeconomic status, or other categorizations. On campus, institutions should identify or create dedicated physical spaces where Black men can gather and socialize. The selection or designation of these spaces should be intentional and have permanence (not a random room that could be designated for different use the next semester or funded with discretionary dollars that may not be available from year to year). Examples of safe spaces include Black student unions, residential living and learning communities, multicultural or student success centers, learning centers, minority-friendly administrative offices and designated meeting rooms that are identifiable by signage. These spaces should be well-maintained, located in physically safe areas on the campus, and adequately staffed with individuals that have completed relevant training such as sensitivity, emotional awareness, or diversity awareness.

While we acknowledge challenges and pitfalls experienced by Black men on their STEM journeys, we found more support and evidence of how intentional programming enhanced the experiences and overall success—and reportedly helped to mitigate the challenges—of our participants. For example, evidence of the benefits and the significance engaging in cohorts with like-minded individuals who shared collective perspectives, experience, and knowledge fostered a social community that went uncontested. Aspects of the program model that provided opportunities for socialization, professional development, and mentoring served as essential mechanisms for creating enhanced experiences that supported the ongoing success of Black males in the study, including within prospective STEM degree programs and the workforce.

> In order to enhance student outcomes, higher education institutions can ensure STEM programs incorporate aspects deemed critical to Black male STEM success within program designs. These opportunities include—but are not limited to—establishing cohort models and other opportunities for socialization, professional development, and mentoring Institutions can also provide a variety of opportunities to students within and outside their home institution in varying, accessible formats (i.e., face-to-face, online, hybrid).

Funding for individual students and targeted programs are vital to the success of Black male STEM collegiates. Financial and family resources are a prevalent deterrent to college admissions for minoritized populations, including Black males. These issues impact opportunities to pursue postsecondary education, as well as the amounts of unmet financial need experienced while pursuing postsecondary studies (U.S. Department of Education, Institute of Education Sciences, 2016). Evidence from our study suggests a need for the continued commitment to dedicating incentives and resources towards recruitment and promoting Black males through college. Scholarships and grants can be limited and incurring student loan debt is not desirable. In this instance, federal and other grant funding is essential. Further, administrators will tout the advantages of STEM intervention programs without committing the funds necessary to staff and implement the intervention (Rincón & George-Jackson, 2016).

> Higher education entities and stakeholders can seek funding from nonacademic entities to support funding minoritized individuals pursuing STEM degrees, particularly those committed to increasing equitable outcomes for students from marginalized and underrepresented populations. Higher education administrators can also back up rhetoric with dedicated finances to tailor programs to meet the needs of students.

Evidence also suggests that the greatest barrier to STEM persistence and progression occurs at the "undergraduate–graduate interface" (Allen-Ramdial & Campbell, 2014). As such, there is a need for initiatives to enhance knowledge, skills, and awareness among stakeholders that guide efforts and strategies which ensure access to high-quality, culturally significant education and training experiences at all levels. Culturally significant structures and supports that enhance transitions among Black males from undergraduate education to postgraduate experiences are also critical to all domains of student development, including academic, professional, social, mental, and physical.

> Higher education institutions can work towards identifying and implementing mechanisms to support these transitions, specifically among Black males. Recommendations for training and development of faculty to support culturally responsive developmental experiences consist of: (a) including diversity or sensitivity components in required training modules for new faculty, (b) including themes of diversity in professional development modules for current faculty, (c) providing required social opportunities where faculty can engage with people of minoritized groups, and (d) developing intentional mentor/mentee pairings between individuals with different backgrounds.

Lastly, as we take action to eliminate the persistent disparities in education, our ideas, policies, and practices must be rooted in using evidence to meet educational needs and increase outcomes for all students, particularly for Black males. Findings from this study revealed a number of lessons learned and implications for ongoing research. Further investigation to identify targeted recruitment and retention approaches can inform initiatives that enhance Black male experiences in STEM programs and support the achievement and success for these students. Research that further unpacks aspects of program components most salient to Black males could also provide additional insight into resources that can be used to support and enhance outcomes for these students. Also, studying well-designed, intentional models have the potential to generate research that could be particularly effective for the end-user, in this case Black males. Little is known about the structures and enabling supports required to build, implement, evaluate, and sustain STEM programs intentionally designed to enhance the success of Black males.

> Implementation science can be particularly useful for framing studies to examine factors that might impact the effectiveness of implementing specific interventions in this context. Conducting this research through research practice partnerships where practitioners and researchers co-construct designs and products can potentially hold even more promise (Gasman & Nguyen, 2016). Evidence from this study suggests that conducting this work in HBCU settings could be, particularly, informative.

NOTES

1. Community College Campus used to replace the name of the institution.
2. As designated by the Carnegie Classification of Institutions of Higher Education.

APPENDIX A
Funding Entities and Resources to Enhance and Diversify the STEM Pipeline

This appendix provides examples of entities and resources that can be used to fund and support programs to enhance and diversify the STEM Pipeline.

Department of Defense
    Department of Defense SMART Scholarship

Department of Education
    Minority Science and Engineering Improvement Program (MSEIP)
    GEM Fellowship Program
    HHMI Gilliam Fellowship

Department of Energy
    Office of Science Graduate Research Program
    Portals for Undergrad and Gard Student Opportunities
    Science Undergraduate Laboratory Internships (SULI)
    Visiting Faculty Program (VFP)

The ***Institute for Broadening Participation*** has a website, www.pathwaystoscience.org that houses a Resource Library with funding entities that provide funding support to engage underrepresented youth K-12 and post-secondary in STEM. Several institutions of higher education and federally funded agencies are listed. The website also offers several resources that focus on mentoring underrepresented students in STEM including a Mentoring Manual.

National Institutes for Health F31 and various supplemental grants
    https://www.nigms.nih.gov/training/diversity/

National Aeronautics and Space Administration
    NASA Minority University Research and Education Project MUREP
    NASA Community College Aerospace Scholars (NCAS) Program

National Science Foundation Division of Equity for Excellence in STEM (EES) has quite a bit of funding opportunities under various award types and directorates including but not limited to the Directorate for STEM Education
    Historically Black Colleges and Universities—Undergraduate Program (HBCU-UP)
    Louis Stokes Alliances for Minority Participation (LSAMP)

Innovative Technology Experiences for Students and Teachers (ITEST)
NSF GRFP

Southern Regional Educational Board
Starting a Grant-Funded Community or Campus-Based Initiative: SREB—State Doctoral Scholars Program Webinar Series

United Negro College Fund
UNCF Fund II Foundation STEM Scholars

APPENDIX B
Sample Workshop

Compact22 Program

Compact22 takes place over the course of three days and features a wide variety of engaging, interactive sessions focused on civic engagement, community-engaged research, civic- and service-learning, institutional change, university-community partnerships and more.

Compact22 promises lots of space for learning and networking with faculty, staff, senior administrators, students, and community partners all dedicated to harnessing the power of higher education to achieve a more equitable tomorrow.

Call for Proposals

Campus Compact builds its conference agenda by inviting faculty, staff, students, and community partners to submit sessions for inclusion in this process. The deadline for submission is [insert date]. If you have any questions about our proposals process, please read more below or contact us at conference@compact.org.

We asked that all submitted proposals explore our theme: A Better Way Forward: Innovation with Equity at the Center. Sessions may explore topics such as civic engagement, community-engaged research, civic- and service-learning, institutional chance, university–community partnerships, and more. We welcome proposals representing work undertaken through public, private, two-year, four-year, and graduate colleges and universities, along with organizations outside of higher education, including community-ty-based partners. All sessions should contribute to equity & inclusion goals and represent a multiplicity of perspectives.

Session Types

To ensure the Compact22 virtual conference runs smoothly and is interactive and engaging for participants, we are introducing several new session types. The majority of sessions on the agenda will be 50 minutes in length and follow one of these four formats: (*Note:* A session description has been provided in the program agenda for one of each of the four formats.)

Watch Party
During this session, participants will join as presenters screen a pre-recorded presentation. Presentations will last 20 minutes and participants may use the chat functionality to ask questions during the screening. After the presentation ends, participants will spend the rest of the session time in Q&A and discussion.

Roundtable
Roundtable discussions will be used to discuss workshop ideas, gather feedback, and work collaboratively toward solutions. In small groups of 8–10, participants will discuss an initiative, project, or program that is in development.

Knowledge-to-Action Workshop
Knowledge-to-Action sessions are focused on sharing specific knowledge, theories, skills, or methods for practical application. These sessions will be highly interactive, and all participants will leave with actionable recommendations for practice. Lightning Talks These 5–7-minute prerecorded videos delivered in either Pecha Kucha (https://www.pechakucha.com/) or Ignite talk (http://www.ignitetalks.io/) format will be curated into themed groups of 4-5 videos. After the lightning talks are screened, participants will join presenters of all video creators for Q&A.

Lightning Talks
Lightning talks will also be made available as on-demand content for conference attendees.

Program Agenda

Day 1
11:00 AM–11:30 AM Eastern | General Session
Conference Opening & Welcome
    Session Type: General Session
    Description: We cannot wait to welcome you to Compact22! Join us to learn more about what to expect over the three days of the conference and

get to know a little more about our theme, A Better Way Forward: Innovation with Equity at the Center.

11:30 AM–12:30 PM Eastern | Opening Panels

Centering Equity in Civic Engagement Praxis and Language: Meeting the Moment

Session Type: General Session

Description: "If we get back to normal, we will have failed." This statement, boldly displayed on Campus Compact's conference page, challenges us to seize the moment and build a more just world. This plenary session encourages attendees to take stock and examine how our civic engagement praxis and language center equity and identify the ways our words and our work hold us back from achieving a just and equitable democracy. This plenary and the dialogue sessions throughout the conference help us come together to explore and envision a way forward that ensures we do not return to normal. This is our moment- let's find a better way forward together to create an equitable and inclusive civic engagement praxis.

Equity & Innovation: Building a National Movement

12:30 PM–2:30 PM Eastern | Choose your own Adventure.

2:30 PM–3:30 PM Eastern | Keynote

We Gon' Be Alright, But That Ain't Alright: Abolitionist Teaching and the Pursuit of Educational Freedom

3:40 PM–4:30 PM Eastern | Breakout Sessions

Putting "The U" in HBCU: Building Student Excellence and Community Connections at Hinds-Utica

Session Type: Watch Party

Description: Learn how one HBCU community college in rural Mississippi incorporated service- learning as a cross-curricular program at the institution with students in both academic courses and career-technical programs engaging in community-centered projects. The session will explore the ways we built institutional support and funding for the project, as well as early results from our pilots in English, history, radio/television production, agriculture, business office technology and cosmetology courses. We will also discuss the development of a faculty professional development Summer Institute leveraging the unique background of HBCU community work. We especially invite faculty from smaller institutions and community colleges to join us in imagining service-learning from our unique frameworks.

Tutoring from a Critical Lens

Teaching Civic Engagement across a Network

Moving General Education Forward to Center Equity and Justice

Equity-Centered Community Engagement: Teaching Strategies for Justice, Solidarity, & Advocacy

Abolition as Praxis: An Engaged Research Approach for Confronting Anti-Blackness

Supporting Health through a Return to Traditional Foods Among Michigan Tribal Communities

Engaging the Whole Campus: How Tech and Student Outreach Build Inclusive Civic Engagement Programs

4:40 PM–5:30 PM Eastern | Breakout Sessions
Preparing for the 2024 Carnegie Elective Classification for Community Engagement
   Session Type: Knowledge-to-Action Workshop
   Description: The 2024 Carnegie Elective Classification for Community Engagement framework has been updated to reflect ongoing shifts within our institutions, communities, and how we come together to address community-based public problem solving. This workshop is designed to assist campuses preparing for both first-time applications and campuses that are re-classifying (those classified in 2016). The session will include: 1. an orientation to both the classification and reclassification frameworks 2. an overview of the 2024 process 3. additions and changes to the documentation framework 4. review of the documentation framework and complete application 5. strategies that have been effective for successful applications.

Co-Creating Strategies to Connect K-12 and Higher Education: Partnerships, Programs, Lessons Learned

Where is the Equity in Service-Learning?

Building Community/Life Skills in the Kitchen: A Partnership with Special Olympics & Undergraduates

Lightning Talks
   Session Type: Lightning Talks
   Description: Get flashes of inspiration, ideas, and resources in a series of engaging short talks. In this session, you will hear:

- Correlation between E-Service-Learning and Students' Civic and Academic Learning and Personal Growth
- Student Civic Leadership: Bridging the Gap
- Building a Campus Culture of Engagement: Our Transition from Episodic to Meaningful Opportunities

Neighborhood Civic Engagement Training: Co-creation, Implementation, and Evaluation

Session Type: Round Table

Description: The West Philadelphia Promise Neighborhood, a place-based initiative at Drexel University, is co-creating with university staff, community leaders, and educators a series of civic engagement trainings for community members. The goals of the civic engagement trainings are to educate participants in issues that impact their children's education and community, provide resources and connections to organizations advocating for children and community, and provide tools for advocating on behalf of themselves, their families, and their community. In this roundtable discussion, we will present the curriculum development, recruitment, and first round of implementation. Participants will review successes and challenges to the program launch and provide feedback on ways to improve the program while discussing strategies for university and community civic engagement education.

How to Effectively Teach Social Determinants of Health Through Service Learning

Training for the Times: Educating Faculty on Community-Engaged Best Practices Amidst a Pandemic

Day 2
11:00 AM–11:15 AM Eastern | General Session
Day 2 Opening & Welcome

11:15 AM–12:15 PM Eastern | General Session
Anchors in the Storm

12:25 PM–1:15 PM Eastern | Breakout Sessions

Engaged Scholars Initiative: Looking Back, Moving Forward

Lightning Talks

Our Engaged Department's Path Forward: Establishing "The Collaborative" of Community Partners

Fostering Equity Through Project-Based Community Engagement

Growing the Next Generation: Aiding Graduate Student Development through Cross-Campus Collaboration

Multi-Institutional Perspectives in Higher Education During COVID19: Walk the Walk of Reflection

Orienting Campus-Community Engagement towards Reparations

A Model for Student-Driven Civic Education

1:15 PM–3:00 PM Eastern | Choose your own Adventure.

3:00 PM–3:50 PM Eastern | Breakout Sessions

Educating Students for Democracy: A Practical Guide for Integrating Civic Engagement into the Community College Curriculum and Developing a Guided Pathway for Transfer

Transcending Barriers for Transformative Knowing: STEM Needs Equity

Campuses for Climate Solutions Action Research Network

First-Year Seminars as a Site for Building Just and Equal Campuses-as-Communities Boundary Spanners in Action - Dismantling Institutional Silos

A Developmental Approach to Institutionalizing Community Engaged Learning Moving Beyond Transactions into Transformational Relationships

4:00 PM–4:50 PM Eastern | Breakout Sessions

Better Together

Using Dialogue as a Participatory Evaluation Tool to Promote Cultures of Inclusion and Equity All Together Now: Participatory Techniques for Community-Engaged Learning (CEL)

A Better Way Forward for Faculty Development in Service Learning and Community Engagement

Bridging the Divide: Developing Students Capacity to Navigate Urban/Rural Divides

Action through Policy Pods

Using Digital Learning to Integrate Cross-Campus DEI, Civic Engagement, & Global Learning

5:00 PM–6:00 PM Eastern | General Session
Impact in Action

Day 3
11:00 AM–11:15 AM Eastern | General Session
Day 3 Opening & Welcome

11:15 AM–12:15 PM Eastern | General Session
Full Participation: A Conversation with Juan Salgado

12:25 PM–1:15 PM Eastern | Breakout Sessions

How to "Keep on Keeping on": Interrupting Patterns and Navigating the Challenges of our Time (A dialogue with recipients of the Nadinne Cruz Community Engagement Professional Award)

Plus Side to a Pandemic—Connecting Communities Virtually

Program Evaluation in Civic Engagement: A Case Study of Tisch Summer Fellows Program Culture and Language Centered Engagement

Empathy and Service Learning: Building Connections to Community through Service and Identity

Centering Equity: Who is the "We" that Engages Community

1:15 PM–2:45 PM Eastern | Choose your own Adventure.

2:45 PM–3:35 PM Eastern | Breakout Sessions

Newman Fellows: Reflections

Service, Equity, and Institutional Support in Civic Engagement

Democratic Deliberation in Civic Learning and Democratic Engagement

Growing Cultural Fluency

Achieving Academic, Civic Learning and Personal Growth Outcomes in Electronic Service- Learning

Exploring the Locus of Campus-Community Partnerships: A Roundtable Discussion

Transition and Change from the Perspective of Mid-Career Professionals

REFERENCES

Allen-Ramdial, S., & Campbell, A. (2014). Reimagining the pipeline: Advancing STEM diversity, persistence, and success. *BioScience, 64*(7), 612–618. https://doi.org/10.1093/biosci/biu076

Amechi, M. H., Berhanu, J., Cox, J., McGuire, K., Morgan, D., Williams, C., & Williams, M. (2015). Understanding the unique needs and experiences of Black male subgroups at four-year colleges and universities. In S. R. Harper & J. L. Wood (Eds.), *Advancing Black male student success from preschool through Ph.D.* (pp. 118–146). Stylus Publishing.

Bertrand Jones, T., & Osborne-Lampkin, L. (2013). Black female faculty success and early career professional development. *Negro Educational Review, 64*(1–4), 59–75. https://www.education.pitt.edu/sites/default/files/NER-%20Volume-64-2013-12.pdf

Bertrand Jones, T., Osborne-Lampkin, L., & Wilder, J. (2016). Balancing the call to serve: The costs and benefits of leaving a legacy in the academy. In B. Marina & S. Ross (Eds.), *Beyond retention: Cultivating spaces of equity, justice, and fairness for women of color in U.S. higher education* (pp. 249–266). Information Age Publishing.

Boyd, T., & Mitchell, D. (2018). Black male persistence in spite of facing stereotypes in college: A phenomenological exploration. *The Qualitative Report, 23*(4), 893–913. https://doi.org/10.46743/2160-3715/2018.3124

Burt, B. A., & Johnson, J. T. (2018). Origins of early STEM interest for Black male graduate students in engineering: A community cultural wealth perspective. *School Science and Mathematics, 118*, 257–270. https://doi.org/10.1111/ssm.12294

Burt, B. A., Williams, K. L., & Palmer, G. J. (2019). It takes a village: The role of emic and etic adaptive strengths in the persistence of Black men engineering graduate programs. *American Educational Research Journal, 56*(1), 39–74. https://doi.org/10.3102/0002831218789595

Espinosa, L. L., Turk, J. M., & Taylor, M. (2017). *Pulling back the curtain: Enrollment and outcomes at minority serving institutions.* American Council on Education.

Freis-Britt, S., Burt B., & Franklin K. (2012). Black males majoring in physics: How HBCUs are making a difference. In R. T. Palmer & J. L. Wood (Eds.), *Black men in Black colleges: Implications for diversity, recruitment, and retention* (pp. 71–88). Routledge Press.

Fries-Britt, S., & White-Lewis, D. (2020). In pursuit of meaningful relationships: How Black males perceive faculty interactions in STEM. *The Urban Review, 52*, 521–540. https://doi.org/10.1007/s11256-020-00559-x

Gasman, M., Baez, B., & Turner, C. S. V. (2008). *Understanding minority-serving institutions.* State University of New York Press.

Gasman, M., & Nguyen, T. (2016). Engaging voices: Methods for studying STEM at historically Black colleges and universities. *Journal of Multicultural Education, 10*(2), 194–205. https://doi.org/10.1108/JME-01-2016-0011

Gasman, M., Nguyen, T., Conrad, C., Lundberg, T., & Commodore, F. (2017). Black male success in STEM: A case study of Morehouse College. *Journal of Diversity in Higher Education, 10*(2), 181–200. https://doi.org/10.1037/dhe0000013

Howard, T. C., & Lyons, T. (2021). Enriching the educational experiences of Black males. *Social Education, 85*(3), 133–138. https://www.socialstudies.org/system/files/2021-06/se850321133.pdf

Hrabowski, F. A., & Maton, K. I. (2009). Beating the odds: Successful strategies to increase African American male participation in science. In H. T. Frierson, W. Pearson, & J. Wyche (Eds.), *Black American males in higher education: Diminishing proportions* (pp. 207–288). Emerald Group Publishing.

Hurtado, S., Eagan, M., Tran, M. C., Newman, C. B., Chang, M. J. & Velasco, P. (2011). We do science here: Underrepresented students interactions with faculty in different college contexts. *Journal of Social Issues, 67*(3), 553–579.

Institute of Education Sciences. (2016). *National postsecondary student aid study*. United States Department of Education Sciences. Retrieved from https://nces.ed.gov/surveys/npsas

Jett, C. C. (2013). HBCUs propel African American male mathematics majors. *Journal of African American Studies, 17*(2), 189–204. http://dx.doi.org/10.1007/s12111-011-9194-x

Miles, M. B., & Huberman, A. M., & Saldana, J. (2014). *Qualitative data analysis: A methods sourcebook* (3rd ed.). SAGE.

Mondisa, J., & McComb, S. (2015). Social community: A mechanism to explain the success of STEM minority mentoring programs. *Mentoring & Tutoring: Partnership in Learning, 23*(2), 149–163. https://doi.org/10.1080/13611267.2015.1049018

McMillan, J., & Schumacher, S. (2010). *Research in education: Evidence-based inquiry* (7th ed.). Pearson.

Museus, S. D., Palmer, R., Davis, R. J., & Maramba, D. C. (2011). *Racial and ethnic minority students' success in STEM Education*. ASHE-ERIC Monograph Series. Jossey-Bass.

National Science Foundation. (n.d.). *Racial equity in STEM education*. Retrieved from https://www.nsf.gov/funding/pgm_summ.jsp?pims_id=505910

Palmer, R. T., & DuBord, Z. M. (2013). Achieving success: A model of success for Black males in STEM at community colleges. In R. T. Palmer & J. L. Wood (Eds.), *Community colleges and STEM: Examining underrepresented racial and ethnic minorities* (pp. 193–208). Routledge.

Pascarella, E., & Terenzini, P. (2005). *How college affects students: A third decade of research*. Jossey-Bass.

Perna, L., Lundy-Wagner, V., Drezner, N. D., Gasman, M., Yoon, S., Bose, E., & Gary, S. (2009). The contribution of HBCUs to the preparation of African American women for STEM careers: A case study. *Research in Higher Education, 50*(1), 1–23.

Premraj, D., Thompson, R., Hughes, L., & Adams, J. (2021). Key factors influencing retention rates among historically underrepresented student groups in STEM fields. *Journal of College Student Retention: Research, Theory & Practice, 23*(2), 457–478. https://doi.org/10.1177/1521025119848763

Rincón, B. E., & George-Jackson, C. E. (2016). Examining department climate for women in engineering: The role of STEM interventions. *Journal of College Student Development, 57*(6), 742–747. https://doi.org/10.1353/csd.2016.0072

Scott, L. & Sharp, L. A. (2019). Black males who hold advanced degrees: Critical factors that preclude and promote success. *Journal of Negro Education, 88*(1), 44–61.

Stage, F., John, G., Lundy-Wagner, V. C., & Conway, K. (2013). Minority serving community colleges and the production of STEM associate's degrees. In R. Palmer & L. Wood (Eds.), *Community colleges and STEM: Examining underrepresented racial and ethnic minorities* (pp. 141–155). Routledge.

Strayhorn, T. (2012). Satisfaction and retention among African American men at two-year community colleges. *Community College Journal of Research and Practice, 36*(5), 358–375. https://doi.org/10.1080/10668920902782508

Tseng, V. (2012). *The uses of research in policy and practice* (Social Policy Report, Vol. 26, No. 2). Society for Research on Child Development.

Tolliver, D., & Miller, M. T. (2018). Graduation 101: Critical strategies for African American men college completion. *Education (Chula Vista), 138*(4), 301–308. https://eric.ed.gov/?id=EJ1180204

U.S. Department of Education, Institute of Education Sciences. (2016). *National postsecondary student aid study.* Retrieved from https://nces.ed.gov/surveys/npsas

Upton, R., & Tanenbaum, C. (2014). *The role of historically Black colleges and universities as pathway providers: Institutional pathways to the STEM PhD among Black students.* American Institutes for Research. https://www.air.org/sites/default/files/downloads/report/Role%20of%20HBCUs%20in%20STEM%20PhDs%20for%20Black%20Students.pdf

Wood, J. L., Harrison, J., & Jones T. K. (2016). Black male's perceptions of the work-college balance: The impact of employment on academic success in the community college. *Journal of Men' Studies, 24*(3), 216–343. https://doi.org/10.1177/1060826515624378

Yin, R. K. (2013). *Case study research: Design and methods.* SAGE.

CHAPTER 12

"NOT A THING THAT WE TALK ABOUT"

Recommendations for Supporting and Engaging LGBQ+ Identified Caribbean Heritage Students

Louise Michelle Vital
Mike Hoffshire

ABSTRACT

This chapter provides insight on Caribbean heritage students' intersecting cultural, ethnic, and sexual orientation identities as they navigate campus environments. Drawing from the conceptual model—students as partners in learning and teaching in higher education (Healey et al., 2014)—this chapter offers implications for professionals working in higher education settings.

United States' higher education has become increasingly diverse, with a large amount of scholarship emphasizing themes of diversity, equity, and inclusion with respect to ethos and practice (Chang, 1999; Gurin et al., 2002; Harper et al., 2009; Harris et al., 2015; Hu & Kuh, 2003). The increased focus on issues of diversity, equity, and inclusion can be attributed to higher numbers of historically marginalized and underrepresented student groups at higher education institutions, and external pressures related to institutional outcomes including retention, persistence, and graduation rates. The attention to issues of diversity, equity, and inclusion has also influenced institutional policies, programs, and practice and related language has been embedded in the mission of many institutions (Wilson et al., 2012). A major theme included in recent scholarship on diversity and inclusion in institutions is the concept of intersectionality. First introduced by Crenshaw (1989), intersectionality refers to the notion that social identities overlap, and offers a lens from which to observe and raise to consciousness the multiple systems of social stratification (race, ethnicity, class, gender, sexual orientation) that influence individuals' identity and lived experiences (Peek et al., 2016). Individuals do not experience their identities separately but rather, they are experienced simultaneously and "experiences can vary in magnitude and direction depending on time, place, and circumstance" (Peek et al., 2016, p. 679). This chapter focuses on lesbian, gay, bisexual, queer, and other non-heteronormative sexual orientations (LGBQ+[1]) Caribbean students' intersecting identities related to culture, ethnicity, and sexual identity orientation.

The Caribbean is composed of 28 territories with a population of over 35 million people (Baldacchino, 2015) and estimates suggest that 20% of the population identify themselves as non-heterosexual (McDonald, 2012). While some countries have legalized same-sex marriage, some islands across the Caribbean region criminalize acts of homosexual behavior (Hickling et al., 2009; Human Rights Watch, 2004; Taylor, 2018). Many LGBQ+ individuals in the Caribbean face "legal, religious, and social discrimination" (Arcus Foundation, 2018, para. 1), and, consequently, many of the region's LGBQ+ residents conceal and suppress their sexual identity to prevent social exclusion or criminalization (Grey & Attai, 2020; Hickling et al., 2009; Shaw, 2023). Thus, many LGBQ+ people in the Caribbean have long struggled for social, cultural, and legal acceptance and tolerance (Coates, 2010; Smith, 2011). This chapter consists of three parts. Part 1 of this chapter provides a contextual understanding of the LGBQ+ experience in U.S. higher education and the Caribbean, as well as the framework and methods of the research study we conducted from which this chapter derives. In Part 2, we discuss the conceptual model of students as partners in learning and teaching in higher education (Healey et al., 2014) that we adapted to our study. We conclude by drawing from the findings of our study and the adapted model (see Figure 12.1) to offer strategies, interventions, and initiatives that can serve as practical implications for professionals working in higher education settings.

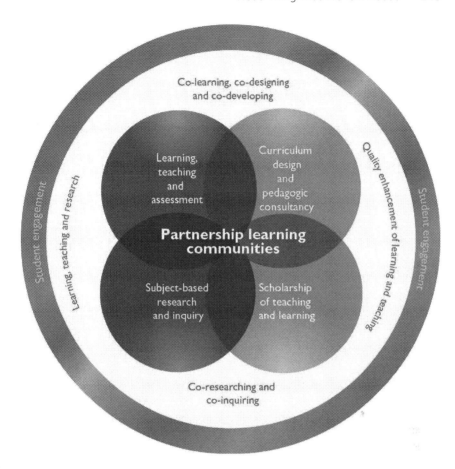

Figure 12.1 Model of students as partners in learning and teaching in higher education (Healey et al., 2014).

LGBQ+ EXPERIENCES IN HIGHER EDUCATION

As a result of homosexuality being removed from the *Diagnostic and Statistical Manual of Mental Disorders (DSM-IV;* American Psychiatric Association, 1994), Supreme Court rulings such as *Romer v. Evans* (1996), *Lawrence v. Texas* (2003), *United States v. Windsor* (2013), *Obergefell v. Hodges* (2015), and a major shift in public opinion, many institutions have welcomed the idea of having LGBQ+ students on their campus. Despite this increased awareness and support of LGBQ+ populations through visibility, resource centers, and ally training programs, significant challenges and obstacles remain. LGBQ+ students on college campuses continue to face harassment, discrimination, and microaggressions. Studies of the experiences of LGBQ+ students have indicated that college campus climates continue to be negative and non-inclusive (Brown et al., 2004; Gortmaker & Brown, 2006; Rankin, 2003; Rankin et al., 2010; Tomlinson & Fassinger, 2003; Woodford & Kulick, 2015). Additionally, studies continue to find the existence of heterosexism in schools, which often include social isolation and interpersonal discrimination (Sherriff et al., 2011; Silverschanz et al., 2008; Woodford et al., 2015). In a national study of 5,149 LGBT college students, 25% reported being harassed on campus due to their sexual orientation, 30% felt uncomfortable with their overall climate, and 30% seriously thought about withdrawing from their institution (Rankin et al., 2010).

Despite the negative climate found in U.S. institutions, it stands to reason that students of Caribbean heritage often face higher levels of acceptance of their LGBQ+ identity in U.S. higher education institutions than they do in their home countries, where they can face jail time or even death. However, greater acceptance at U.S. colleges and universities does not alleviate the challenges that LGBQ+ Caribbean heritage students experience because of their cultural upbringing. Nor does the acceptance lessen the complexities of having these intersecting identities that undergraduate students experience on their respective campuses. Little is known about the experience of LGBQ+ Caribbean heritage students studying at higher education institutions in the United States, which served as the impetus for this study. Findings from the research revealed cultural markers, media, religion, silence/avoidance, politics, threats of violence, positive/negative messages, and the campus community impacted participants' sexual identity development. These findings were utilized to develop the supplemental materials found in the final section of this chapter.

INTERSECTIONALITY

Intersectionality can be defined as a process in which individuals negotiate competing and harmonious social identities (Choo & Ferree, 2010; Few-Demo, 2014). Examples can include race, religion, class, and sexual orientation. These intersections shape the way an individual views and operates in today's society (Crenshaw, 1989). The theoretical underpinning of intersectionality contributes to the assumption that identities cannot be experienced and/or studied in silos due to interactions with systems of power and privilege. Findings from our study uncovered LGBQ+ Caribbean students' acute awareness of possessing multiple, often competing, identities. Intersectional approaches in research reveal and address multiple identities, exposing different types of discrimination and disadvantages that occur because of the combination of identities. The intersections of sexual orientation, culture, and ethnic identity were discussed throughout the semi-structured interviews conducted with our participants.

As higher education professionals with academic training in student affairs administration and multiple years of practical experience in the profession, we were struck by how candid our participants were about the intersections of their cultural and sexual identities. They were quite thoughtful about how their higher education experiences, as students who receive education and as students who contribute knowledge to their institutions in their capacities as student leaders, helped to shape their self-concepts as LGBQ+ students of Caribbean heritage. Participants were clear about their double consciousness (Du Bois, 1994) among groups of individuals of Caribbean descent in various spaces and how their level of outness was dependent on how accepting their home and school community members were. For instance, one participant noted she was more "out" and "masculine presenting" at her LGBQ+ student organizations meetings and less so when attending Caribbean student meetings. They also shared how the very notion of music as a cultural marker of their regional Caribbean or country-specific affiliation created a paradox, such that lyrics themselves conveyed an incongruence between being both Caribbean and gay or lesbian. In other words, such a thing did not or could not exist. These examples can provide insight for future higher education professionals seeking to support students with multiple, intersecting identities.

METHODS

During the Spring of 2018, we conducted 60-minute semi-structured interviews with 9 LGBQ+ Caribbean heritage students representing the Dominican Republic, Haiti, Jamaica, Trinidad and Tobago. Participants represented a variety of sexual orientations, ranged between 18–24 years old, and attended either historically Black colleges and universities, predominantly White institutions, or community colleges. Participants were either born in the Caribbean, or one or both of their parents were born in the Caribbean. Furthermore, we conducted a review of relevant documents, databases, and media reports documenting laws, policies, practices, and experiences related to LGBQ+ individuals in the region (Glesne, 2015). These methods are consistent with qualitative research designs for a phenomenological study (Moustakas, 1994).

PARTNERSHIP LEARNING COMMUNITIES FRAMEWORK: STUDENTS AS PARTNERS IN LEARNING AND TEACHING IN HIGHER EDUCATION

The conceptual model of students as partners in learning and teaching in higher education (Healey et al., 2014) is offered as a tool for all members of the university community to use to reflect on, inspire, and enhance practices and policies that relate to partnerships in learning and teaching. We adapted this framework to describe the key challenges experienced by students possessing intersecting marginalized identities, discuss implications for higher education practice, and offer suggestions for university members who support undergraduate student populations. We believe that university members can learn directly from the voices and lived experiences of historically marginalized students and draw from that learning to develop initiatives and interventions to support students on their respective campuses. As such, the adapted model will allow readers of this text to draw from the experiences of the participants who inspired this chapter to develop student support strategies that may prove effective. The four components of the conceptual model (see Figure 12.1) are (a) learning, teaching, and assessment; (b) subject-based research and inquiry; (c) scholarship of teaching and learning; and (d) curriculum design and pedagogic consultancy.

Learning, Teaching, and Assessment

According to Healey et al. (2014), engaging students in partnership means acknowledging students as "active participants in their own learning" (p. 8). Furthermore, the authors noted, "Although not all active learning involves partnership it does mean engaging students in forms of participation and helps prepare them for the roles they may play in full partnership" (p. 8). Thus, engaging students as both "teachers and assessors in the learning process is a particularly effective form of partnership" (p. 8) and will allow them to educate their campus communities on how best to support them. This is critical because the students in our study were clear about how their marginalized identities impact and influence their lived experiences in the collegiate environment.

Subject-Based Research and Inquiry

Hearing our participants discuss their roles as student-leaders and the activities they created to support the development of their fellow students greatly contributed to our research study. Healey et al. (2014) indicated that involving selected students in work with faculty and staff on research projects or on a course engaging in inquiry-based learning, is "an [effective] approach in stimulating deep and retained learning" (p. 8). This is critical because as the authors conveyed, "students have extensive autonomy and independence and negotiate as partners many of the details of the research and inquiry projects that they undertake" (p. 8). As such, purposefully including students in developing projects is an appropriate strategy to leverage their lived experiences as a means for them to contribute to applied research and the development of evidence-based best practices.

Scholarship of Teaching and Learning

Healey et al. (2014) explained that conducting projects in partnership with students is a principle of good practice in the scholarship of teaching and learning. They emphasized "there are an increasing number of effective initiatives of engaging students as change agents in institutions" (p. 9) where they could draw from the research activities they participate in to develop and contribute tangible strategies to leverage the learning and teaching that occurs at their respective higher education institutions. Thus, focusing on the scholarship of teaching and learning conveys an "intention of enhancing the quality of student learning" (p. 9), such that the learning students receive, and arguably the institution at large, is directly tied to the research contributions of students engaged in collaborative activities with institutional decision-makers.

Curriculum Design and Pedagogic Consultancy

As administrators and faculty members, we recognize that students are often engaged in end-of-year course evaluations and may hold representative positions in departmental or institutional committees. However, as noted by Healey et al. (2014), it is rare for institutions to "go beyond the student voice and engage students as partners in designing the curriculum and giving pedagogic advice and consultancy" (p. 9). Yet, as we learned from conducting our study, students have a lot to say about their lived experiences, how universities could support them better with regard to their sexual orientation, and what they wish university staff knew to better support them. Thus, we argue students can offer voice to curricular decisions related to course resources that center the voices of marginalized voices traditionally at the periphery, a first step to educating university members on the notion of intersectionality and the complexities of having a cultural identity that is seemingly at odds with one's sexual identity. As the authors concluded, "where institutions have implemented such initiatives they have seen significant benefits for both students and staff" (p. 9).

APPLICATION OF THE FRAMEWORK: PRACTICAL IMPLICATIONS FOR HIGHER EDUCATION PROFESSIONALS

As researchers and educators, we are drawn to the questions of (a) "How can we better support LGBQ+ students with intersecting identities?" and

(b) "How can we create a more equitable and inclusive environment?" Drawing from the data gathered from this study and the model highlighted in this chapter, we have developed material that institutions, administrators, and faculty can use or modify to suit their unique needs.

Training Faculty and Staff: Partnership Learning Community Framework

No model can become institutionalized without a commitment from administrators, faculty, and staff to educate the campus community, as well as assist in offering mechanisms for implementation. We offer the following training agenda (see Appendix A) as a starting point for any institution looking to implement the conceptual model of students as partners in learning and teaching in higher education (Healey et al., 2014). Additionally, we have provided practical examples below for implementation with each of the four components of the model for use amongst college students.

Learning, Teaching, and Assessment

Incorporating a student-centered approach to teaching and assessment is a way of engaging students as partners (Healey et al., 2014) in their own learning. There are possibilities for faculty to leverage the expertise of students, particularly student leaders, by partnering with them to contribute to classroom learning. Student leaders often participate in student leader training opportunities that, together with their own lived experiences, enhance their knowledge on a variety of topics that can be translated into the learning that occurs in the classroom. By including them as facilitators in the classroom, faculty provide students with an opportunity to deepen their understanding and awareness of a particular topic as they contribute to teaching during class sessions. Likewise, actively involving students as both "teachers and assessors in the learning process is a particularly effective form of partnership" (Healey et al., 2014, p. 8). Finally, by involving students in assessment, faculty help to foster the development of these skills in students while concurrently leveraging student perspectives during data analysis, interpretation, organization, and discussion.

The participants in our study described their campus communities on a continuum in terms of how they perceived identity-based organizations or how relevant administrators supported their identities on campus. For instance, one participant explained that their campus' LGBTQ+ center was 2 years old, implying it was nascent in the larger campus community. Other students indicated the LGBTQ+ entity at their institution did not appear to

"Not a Thing That We Talk About" • 251

be culturally responsible as it was perceived to exclusively support White students. Some participants, however, happily noted LGBT student organizations that were specific to students of color. All participants expressed that they felt their campuses could do a better job, in both curricular and co-curricular experiences, supporting LGBQ+ students and believed their institutions should consider partnering with student leaders to do so.

Partnering with student organizations to teach in the classroom could be a useful strategy for addressing information gaps on the part of faculty and working with students who are better connected to topics of interest. For instance, Yves, the president of her campus LGBT organization, explained her college needed to do a better job supporting students in their identity development in the classroom. In one example, she noted that during a gender studies class presentation, students often had a slide that listed their ethnic or racial background, but they would then "breeze over it in 10 seconds." This was a misstep in Yves' opinion because "there's that one kid in that class who's like, 'oh, that's me,' and it's like you've totally just deleted who I am." However, when class discussions arise on topics that students know how to—or have been trained to—address, they—together with faculty—can enrich the conversation. Faculty members could consider partnering with student affairs professionals (i.e., those in student involvement and leadership) to share upcoming opportunities or invite members of a student organization to speak to their class. Appendix B offers examples of such emails to begin the conversation.

Involving students as assessors in their own learning process provides opportunities and obstacles and will require additional planning on the part of the faculty member. As noted above, involving students in assessment can produce positive outcomes. In addition, engaging students in this way allows them to participate in a component of teaching and learning they are traditionally receivers of. An example of this interaction includes involving students indesigning formative and summative assessment instruments. Furthermore, students will be able to provide critical feedback on the congruency between various assessment mechanisms and actual classroom learning that faculty themselves can learn from. Conversely, to be effective in such a student–teacher learning partnership, faculty will need to be aware of the obstacles of such an endeavor. Students may be wary of providing feedback on assessment tools because they are not sure what information they could offer that would be useful, or if they have the skills to offer input at all. Students may believe designing assessment tools is not their responsibility and solely the purview of faculty. Finally, students may believe that focusing on assessment feedback will take away from instruction that should be devoted to class material. To address these potential obstacles and concerns, faculty will have to incorporate student partnership on assessment in the course objectives and devote time throughout the course to train students on this facet of the course experience.

As noted by Falchikov (2004), "The balance of power in education today appears to be swinging away from the lecturer as infallible expert with total decision-making power, to a more democratic position where students are partners in the education process" (p. 106). Healey et al. (2014) appear to support this premise with an emphasis on including students as partners in co-learning, co-designing, and co-developing in higher education. Including students in self, peer, and collaborative assessment and design prioritizes students in learning and teaching practice. In one such example, faculty could include students in collaborative syllabus design, a process by which students help develop learning objectives while identifying the skills they need to learn. Furthermore, faculty and students alike could have a meaningful discussion on course expectations, including assessment and grading practices. While designing a course in this manner may certainly take more time and effort on behalf of the faculty member, students are more likely to have a favorable view of the course and be active participants in the learning process. Partnering with students in this way contributes to their development as students and enhances their skill set beyond the institution.

Subject Based Research and Inquiry

Inquiry-based learning stimulates deep and retained learning for students (Healey et al., 2014). With this understanding, participatory action research (PAR) can serve as an approach for students to take part in subject-based research while working collaboratively to identify and address an issue in their campus communities. PAR is grounded in community participation (Torre et al., 2012) and contrasts with other research methods that emphasize controlled experimentation, statistical analysis, and reproduction of findings. As emphasized by Freire (1968/1970), the inquiry process can bring positive change that students seek in their collegiate environments through critical reflection and solidarity. As all students can take electives as a component of their program of study, a PAR-informed project embedded in a social justice-minded course will allow students, like those reflected in our study, to provide evidence-based solutions to some of the challenges they experience or observe on campus.

There are several benefits to engaging students in a PAR project. Strode (2013) shared that through the process of organizing and leading, the PAR activity can foster the development of students' professional knowledge and skills. In turn, "the objective of students' individual development is influenced by his/her life experience, values, and attitudes" (p. 84). Many of the students reflected in our study spoke about their lived experiences on campus, both from having a broader societal marginalized sexual orientation identity, and in the context of their institutional environment. Each participant was able to identify some of the practices and attitudes they faced or observed that further marginalized students, especially students of color, who identified as LGBQ+. Likewise, each participant was able to identify strategies or interventions that could alleviate some of the burden experienced by students. While engaging in a PAR-informed project, students will be able to draw from their life experiences, values, and attitudes (Strode, 2013) while conducting research they can later present to campus senior administrators as evidence of the changes that need to occur.

Pain et al. (2011) developed a PAR toolkit that includes seven themes and accompanying critical questions they describe as central to each stage of the PAR process. The themes are collaboration, knowledge, power, ethics, building theory, action, emotions, and well-being and speak to the transformative inquiry that students can be engaged in throughout a course. By following this process, educators and student researchers can ensure their project reflects the planning, action, and reflection that is embedded in PAR research.

PAR-informed projects can include those related to the student experience or their academic discipline. For example, research can focus on understanding how students are making sense of an institutional policy and its implications to them, specifically. Additionally, course faculty can allocate time in their course to engage students in PAR projects that allow them to partner with local communities and organizations related to their majors or disciplines; for instance healthcare, business, youth-serving, criminal justice, among others. Early in the semester, the faculty will need to explain what PAR entails. Next, together with course students, the professor can decide to have one class project or several smaller scale projects. After, the PAR groups will need to determine a focus and follow the steps outlined by Pain et al. (2011) to conceptualize, implement, and evaluate their projects.

Engaging students in a PAR project can be complex in the confines of one semester-long course, which is why we emphasize a PAR-informed project. Implementing a PAR model, particularly in a non-research-based course, can reveal both challenges and benefits. Strode (2013) shared there are limitations to implementing a PAR process including, "insufficiency of student's experience and pedagogical skills, inadequate student's self-evaluation, lack of motivation, and insufficiency of support and encouragement during practice" (p. 88). These limitations can be compounded when the comprehensive PAR activity occurs alongside the other aims of the course. Despite these factors, we believe a PAR-informed approach allows room for flexibility that considers these limitations, while leveraging student's interest in engaging in community action and research.

When discussing subject-research and inquiry, Healey et al. (2014) explained "students have extensive autonomy and independence and negotiate as partners many of the details of the research and inquiry projects that they undertake" (p. 8). For instance, when asked about their reaction to learning about the study conducted by the authors of this chapter, Ari said:

> I was like, oh, wow. That's me. That's who I am. In my room I have a Tobago flag and a Pride flag right next to each other. These are two very important aspects of my personality and my identity. And I think it's important for people to hear what it's like to be both of these things.

Participating in a PAR-informed research project will enhance students' academic skills and have two important outcomes. First, students will design projects that utilize their own institutions as research sites where they can potentially serve as change agents. Second, they will develop research and analysis skills that can be useful post-graduation. An elective course, or a core course that has the flexibility to infuse a PAR project, can reflect the critical pedagogy and action that students in our study are seeking.

Scholarship of Teaching and Learning

When faculty and staff are engaged in intersectional approaches and critical pedagogies in their scholarship, they may have a better understanding of the lived experiences and the unique advantages/disadvantages experienced by the students they serve. Taking an intersectional approach to research challenges the notion of essentialism, which defines social groups as homogenous categories. Instead, intersectional researchers argue that an individual or social group is positioned at the intersection of multiple identity axes. Under this approach, training and educational instruction is multifaceted, presenting various layers, which can then present complexities and differences, often within the same social group. Intersectional analysis recognizes the multidimensional and relational nature of social locations, which are often overlooked in scholarship studying identity. It specifically delves into power relationships that exist at the level of interpersonal relationships; power is used by dominant groups to obtain and maintain economic and social control. Non-intersectional research may be less likely to be confirmed in representative samples reflective of real-world diversity.

Utilizing Healey et al.'s (2014) model, we argue faculty and staff should conduct research projects in conjunction with students. In addition to practical research skills, students can "build on 21st century skills such as collaboration, communication, critical thinking, and the use of technology, which will serve them well in the workplace and life" (Larmer & Mergendoller, 2010, p. 3). While no students in our sample discussed opportunities for research during their interviews, several were keenly aware of our work as researchers undertaking critical and intersecting approaches to our research. Kdot stated, "[This is] an interesting study and I think it's important to talk about, and hopefully it advances it." This quote not only speaks to several of the participants' desire to be involved in studies undertaking an intersectional approach, but the necessity for researchers to engage in such topics.

When students bear witness to researchers engaged/involved in intersectional-related project designs, a sense of validation towards their identity becomes evident. No longer are students pigeonholed into a sense of self where they feel competing interest between their lived experience and the theories that suggest the way they experience the world. For those who want to engage in intersectional strategies, Warner (2008) provided a guide for researchers choosing to engage in intersectional inquiry. We also offer suggestions on how college students can become key players in these processes.

Researchers may experience difficulty in expanding their scope to include multiple dimensions of social identity when seeking to incorporate intersectional perspectives in their research (McCall, 2005). Critics argue that it is impossible to account for all intersecting identities because the diversity of humanity does not allow it. Additionally, it makes data analysis more complex. However, as researchers, we articulate a strong desire to account for those identities, which is possible when considering a research design. This allows us to gain a closer understanding of the phenomenon under investigation in relation to the identity memberships the participants possess. As humans, we are complex, multifaceted individuals and should be examined as such.

Examples of intersectional research could include examining phenomena from multiple identities, including, but not limited to race, gender, sexual orientation, ethnic heritage, cultural background, age, religious affiliation, physical size, and political perspective, among others. Conducting such a project will require an inquiry lens. When developing research projects, reflexive questions to ask include:

> Whose perspective is included or excluded by the research question(s)? What body of work will be reviewed to offer a contextual and culturally responsive understanding of the scholarship surrounding the research topic and questions? What is the critical framework, theoretical or conceptual, that is guiding this work? What are the methodological approaches utilized in this project and whose knowledges (TED, 2020)—epistemological, ontological, and axiological stances—will be reflected in the design of the research and influence the analysis and interpretation of the data? Whose experience will be privileged or marginalized by the potential findings? What nuances will be embedded in the discussion?

Curriculum Design and Pedagogy

When faculty and staff incorporate Healey et al.'s (2014) learning partnership model, the result is an engaged classroom where curriculum and design is student-centered and provides rich materials representing a wide variety of intersecting identities. Ari stated, "Honestly, if I'm paying $45,000 for tuition, then I feel like I should have a say in my education." As discussed, an intersectional approach acknowledges the diverse perspectives and experiences of individuals in a social group based on the intersections of differing identities along with access to power, privilege, and resources (Hankivsky & Cormier, 2011). In current classroom, workshop, and training structures, a traditional, one-size-fits-all competency approach, is typically utilized, which fails to recognize complexity of individual experience(s). Therefore, we argue for intersectional teaching and learning approaches to engage students in critical and intersectional discussions, assignments, and research.

In addition to utilizing readings and materials that represent diverse perspectives, faculty and student affairs practitioners should utilize self-reflection, critical reflexivity, and discussion practices that allow students the opportunity to delve deeper into related topics (Vital, 2020). Fostering activities such as these allow for transformative learning experiences amongst all in the learning environment. Additionally, it allows for individuals to challenge long-held beliefs and assumptions surrounding a particular group of individuals.

With a goal of incorporating an intersectionality approach into daily practice, we propose incorporating a short "intersectionality statement" in course syllabi and implementing the following 50-minute lesson plan.

Syllabus

The concept of intersectionality will be utilized throughout this [course, workshop, training session]. Intersectionality operates under the assumption that individuals possess multiple, layered identities, and the way these identities intersect affect individuals' realities and lived experience (Crenshaw, 1989). As such, it is important for us to acknowledge the ways in which an individual may experience privilege and oppression given their identity. Intersectionality can prove to be a powerful lens for us to critically examine the topics covered in this [course, workshop, training session]. Examples include both biological and social identities, including but not limited to sex, gender, national origin, race, and religious affiliation.

Activity

After completing readings on the topic of intersectionality, students should be given the opportunity to apply their knowledge. A helpful tool is the contextual lens protocol (Jackson, 2019) that helps students to gain deeper insight and engage in reflective, evidence-based discourse about any given topic. The following example could be adapted and utilized in a leadership training course for student leaders.

PART 1: STUDENTS ARE BROKEN APART INTO SMALLER GROUPS AND ASKED TO DISCUSS THE FOLLOWING CASE STUDY.

You are the vice president of Pride, the LGBQ+ organization on campus and identify as a White, lesbian female. At a recent off campus planning retreat meeting, some other members of the executive board complained they felt their voices were being silenced when it came to participating in general membership meetings as well as program implementation plans. You cannot possibly understand how they are feeling as they are present at almost every meeting and event.

Guiding Questions:
- What may be the cause of the students' feelings?
- What do you propose to be done to rectify the problem?
- How do you acknowledge multiple identities within the same group?

Part 2: Students are provided the opportunity to hear responses from each group, answer questions, and offer feedback.

Part 3: Students are randomly assigned an identity within the group. Students are encouraged to roleplay how the conversation involving these students may manifest itself. Possible identities include an Asian American gay male in his 20s, a Black pansexual female in her early 40s, and a White gender nonconforming individual in their late teens.

Part 4: Students are asked to reflect, either verbally or through writing, how their identities impacted the lens in which they viewed the problem. Students are also asked to visually draw how multiple, often overlapping identities, represented their experience in this case study. This activity should conclude with ensuring that students have a thorough understanding of how identities play an important role in shaping an individual's experience.

As educators, we have a responsibility to not make assumptions and generalize in curriculum and pedagogy design. Utilizing an intersectional design approach limits the possibility of assumptions and fosters an environment where students are at the center. Educators and scholars must be held accountable for exposing structures of both power and privilege, acknowledging the historical roots of intersectionality in the scholarship, lived experiences of marginalized individuals on college campuses, and foregrounding and unpacking structures of inequality in intersectional analysis.

CONCLUSION

We learned a great deal by interviewing our participants on their intersecting LGBQ+ Caribbean identities in ways that our individual identities as a scholar of Caribbean descent and a queer scholar may have missed independently. While the participants were quite candid in their conversations with us, we expect that *they* may have had more success in reaching a wider student population than we could have as student-researchers with insider positionalities and gatekeepers of this student population. We hope that by utilizing Healey et al.'s (2014) model of students as partners in learning and teaching in higher education will develop practical strategies and approaches that provide educators with the skills to confidently implement intersectional approaches to their research and classroom instruction. As a result, student's social identities and rich lived experiences will be brought to the forefront of their educational experience where their identity would no longer be, as said by Ari, "not a thing we talk about."

APPENDIX A
Sample Training Agenda for Conceptual Model of Students as Partners in Learning and Teaching in Higher Education (Healey et al., 2014)

Welcome: Setting the Stage
Characteristics of Today's Students
Student Engagement Theory and Application
Intersectionality Theory and Application
Lunch
Student Partnership Model
- Learning, Teaching, and Assessment
- Subject Based Research and Inquiry
- Scholarship of Teaching and Learning
- Curriculum and Pedagogy

Implementation of Ideas
Self-Reflection
Closing: Next Steps

APPENDIX B
Sample Emails

To: Student Involvement and Leadership

Greetings!

My name is [name] and I teach [course name and section] on [day] at [time]. One of my main course objectives is [course objective that aligns with request]. In order to enhance the learning experience of those students enrolled in my course, I write today to request a list of upcoming seminars or programs that would be conducive to share with my students to further develop their understanding of course materials and/or themselves. I would love the opportunity to discuss my objectives further.

To: Student Organization

Greetings!

One of my main course objectives is [course objective that aligns with request]. While as a faculty member I can present this information through lecture and course activities, I am limited in scope based on what I have researched and experienced. Therefore, I am writing to your student organization today in the hope that you may be able to discuss some ways that we can enhance the knowledge acquisition of students enrolled in my course. Perhaps you are able to send a few members of your organization to my class to speak about their experiences or have developed some activities and/or assessments that would complement my coursework? I would love the opportunity to discuss this further.

NOTE

1. We did not include the letter "T" of the commonly utilized acronym LGBTQ+ to denote trans* identities because our research study was conceptualized to focus on sexual orientation rather than gender identity. Understanding that sexual orientation terminology shifts over time alongside cultural and social awareness and expectations, we utilize the acronym "LGBQ+" to collectively refer to our study participants who described their sexual orientations as lesbian, gay, bisexual, queer, pansexual, and asexual. When citing our participants directly, we include the acronyms they shared in their interviews, which may differ from our own.

REFERENCES

American Psychiatric Association. (1994). *Diagnostic and statistical manual of mental disorders, 4th edition, text revision (DSM-IV-TR)* (4th ed.).

Arcus Foundation. (2018). *The safety, legal protections, and social inclusion of LGBTQ people in the Caribbean in 2018.* https://www.42d.org/2020/07/15/the-safety-legal-protections-and-social-inclusion-of-lgbtq-people-in-the-caribbean-in-2018-2/

Baldacchino, G. (2015). *Entrepreneurship in small island states and territories.* Routledge.

Brown, R., Clarke, B., Gortmaker, V., & Robinson-Keilig, R. (2004). Assessing the campus climate for gay, lesbian, bisexual and transgender (LGBT) students using a multiple perspectives approach. *Journal of College Student Development, 45*(1), 8–26. https://doi.org/10.1353/csd.2004.0003

Chang, M. J. (1999). Does racial diversity matter?: The educational impact of a racially diverse undergraduate population. *Journal of College Student Development, 40*(4), 377–395. https://psycnet.apa.org/record/1999-03332-005

Choo, H. Y., & Ferree, M. M. (2010). Practicing intersectionality in sociological research: A 151 critical analysis of inclusions, interactions, and institutions in the study of inequalities. *Sociological Theory, 28,* 129–149. https://www.ssc.wisc.edu/~mferree/documents/Choo&Ferree0610-published.pdf

Coates, R. (2010). *The rough guide to Jamaica.* John Wiley & Sons.

Crenshaw, K. W. (1989). Demarginalizing the intersection of race and sex: A Black feminist critique of antidiscrimination doctrine, feminist theory, and antiracist politics. *University of Chicago Legal Forum,* Vol. 1989, Iss. 1, Article 8. http://chicagounbound.uchicago.edu/uclf/vol1989/iss1/8

Du Bois W. E. B. (1994). *The souls of black folk.* Dover.

Falchikov, N. (2004). Involving students in assessment. *Psychology Learning & Teaching, 3*(2), 102–108. https://doi.org/10.2304/plat.2003.3.2.102

Few-Demo, A. L. (2014). Intersectionality as the "new" critical approach in feminist family studies: Evolving racial/ethnic feminisms and critical race theories. *Journal of Family Theory and Review, 6,* 169–183. https://doi.org/10.1111/jftr.12039

Freire, P. (1970). *Pedagogy of the oppressed* (M. B. Ramos, Trans). Seabury Press. (Original work published 1968)

Glesne, C. (2015). *Becoming qualitative researchers* (5th ed.). Pearson.

Gortmaker, V., & Brown, R. D. (2006). Out of the college closet: Differences in perceptions and experiences among out and closeted lesbian and gay students. *College Student Journal, 40*(3), 606–619. https://eric.ed.gov/?id=EJ765359

Grey, C., & Attai, N. A. (2020). LGBT rights, sexual citizenship, and blacklighting in the Anglophone Caribbean: What do queers want, what does colonialism need? In M. J. Bosia, S. M. McEvoy, & M. Rahman (Eds.), *The Oxford handbook of global LGBT and sexual diversity politics* (pp. 249–266). Oxford University Press.

Gurin, P., Dey, E., Hurtado, S., & Gurin, G. (2002). Diversity and higher education: Theory and impact on educational outcomes. *Harvard Educational Review, 72*(3), 330–367. https://doi.org/10.17763/haer.72.3.01151786u134n051

Hankivsky, O., & Cormier, R. (2011). Intersectionality and public policy: Some lessons from existing models. *Political Research Quarterly, 64*(1), 217–229. https://doi.org/10.1177/1065912910376385

Harper, S. R., Patton, L. D., & Wooden, O. S. (2009). Access and equity for African American students in higher education: A critical race historical analysis of policy efforts. *The Journal of Higher Education, 80*(4), 389–414. https://repository.upenn.edu/gse_pubs/205/

Harris, J. C., Barone, R. P., & Davis, L. P. (2015). Who benefits?: A critical race analysis of the (d)evolving language of inclusion in higher education. *Thought & Action,* 21–38. https://eric.ed.gov/?id=EJ1086865

Healey, M., Flint, A., & Harrington, K. (2014). *Engagement through partnership: Students as partners in learning and teaching in higher education.* HEA. https://www.advance-he.ac.uk/knowledge-hub/engagement-through-partnership-students-partners-learning-and-teaching-higher

Hickling, F., Matthies, M., & Gibson, G. (2009). *Perspectives in Caribbean psychology.* University of the West Indies Press.

Hu, S., & Kuh, G. D. (2003). Diversity experiences and college student learning and personal development. *Journal of College Student Development, 44*(3), 320–334.

Human Rights Watch. (2004). *Hated to death: Homophobia, violence, and Jamaica's HIV/AIDS epidemic.* Human Rights Watch.

Jackson, A. J. (2019). *Contextual lenses protocol.* MindUTeach. https://minduteach.org/resources-open-access

Larmer, J., & Mergendoller, J. R. (2010). Seven essentials for project-based learning. *Educational Leadership, 68*(1), 34–37. https://www.ascd.org/el/articles/seven-essentials-for-project-based-learning

Lawrence v. Texas, 539 U.S. 558 (2003)

McCall, L. (2005). The complexity of intersectionality. *Signs, 30*(3), 1771–1800. https://doi.org/10.1086/426800

McDonald, N. (2012, March 8). Gays say 'We are here to stay!' *The St. Lucia STAR.* http://stluciastar.com/gays-say-we-are-here-to-stay

Moustakas, C. (1994). *Phenomenological research methods.* SAGE.

Obergefell v. Hodges, 576 U.S. 644 (2015)

Pain, R., Whitman, G., & Milledge, D. (2011). *Participatory action research toolkit: An introduction to using PAR as an approach to learning, research, and action research.* Durham University. https://www.durham.ac.uk/media/durham-university/research-/research-centres/social-justice-amp-community-action-centre-for/documents/toolkits-guides-and-case-studies/Participatory-Action-Research-Toolkit.pdf

Peek, M. E., Lopez, F. Y., Williams, H. S., Xu, L. J., McNulty, M. C., Acree, M. E., & Schneider, J. A. (2016). Development of a conceptual framework for understanding shared decision making among African-American LGBT patients and their clinicians. *Journal of general internal medicine, 31*(6), 677–687. https://doi.org/10.1007/s11606-016-3616-3

Rankin, S. R. (2003). *Campus climate for gay, lesbian, bisexual, and transgender people: A national perspective.* The National Gay and Lesbian Task Force Policy Institute.

Rankin, S. R., Weber, G. N., Blumenfeld, W. J., & Frazer S. J. (2010). *State of higher education for LGBT people: Campus pride 2010 national college climate survey*. Campus Pride.

Romer v. Evans, 517 U.S. 620 (1996)

Shaw, A. (2023, January 25). *LGBTI victories in the Caribbean and a turning point for LGBTI rights in the Americas*. Global Americans. https://theglobalamericans.org/2023/01/lgbti-victories-in-the-caribbean-and-a-turning-point-for-lgbti-rights-in-the-americas/

Sherriff, N. S., Hamilton, W. E., Wigmore, S., & Giambrone, B. L. (2011). "What do you say to them?" investigating and supporting the needs of lesbian, gay, bisexual, trans, and questioning (LGBTQ) young people. *Journal of Community Psychology, 39*(8), 939–955. https://doi.org/10.1002/jcop.20479

Silverschanz, P., Cortina, L. M., Konik, J., & Magley, V. J. (2008). Slurs, snubs, and LGBQ+ jokes: Incidence and impact of heterosexist harassment in academia. *Sex Roles, 58*(3), 179–191. https://doi.org/10.1007/s11199-007-9329-7

Smith, F. (2011). *Sex and the citizen: Interrogating the Caribbean*. University of Virginia Press.

Strode, A. (2013). Participatory action research for development of prospective teachers' professionality during their pedagogical practice. *Journal of Discourse and Communications for Sustainable Education, 4*(1), 80–90. https://eric.ed.gov/?id=EJ1121128

Taylor, J. (2018). *Homosexuality is still illegal in these 9 Caribbean countries*. NewNowNext. http://www.newnownext.com/homosexuality-illegal-caribbean-countries/04/2018/

TED. (2020, April 24). *Indigenous knowledge meets science to take on climate change | Hindou Oumarou Ibrahim* [Video]. YouTube. https://youtu.be/z3d_UsYgt1c

Tomlinson, M. J., & Fassinger, R. (2003). Career development, lesbian identity development, and campus climate among lesbian college students. *Journal of College Student Development, 44*(6), 845–860. https://doi.org/10.1353/csd.2003.0078

Torre, M. E., Fine, M., Stoudt, B. G., & Fox, M. (2012). Critical participatory action research as public science. In H. Cooper, P. M. Camic, D. L. Long, A. T. Panter, D. Rindskopf, & K. J. Sher (Eds.), *APA handbook of research methods in psychology, Vol. 2. Research designs: Quantitative, qualitative, neuropsychological, and biological* (pp. 171–184). American Psychological Association.

United States vs. Windsor, 570 U.S. 744 (2013)

Vital, L. M. (2020). Understanding self to engage with the 'other': Pedagogical approaches to teaching about identity and belonging in graduate education. In T. S. Jenkins (Ed), *Reshaping graduate education through innovation and collaborative learning* (pp. 147–166). IGI Global.

Warner, L. R. (2008). A best practices guide to intersectional approaches in psychological research. *Sex Roles, 59*(5/6), 454–463. https://doi.org/10.1007/s11199-008-9504-5

Wilson, J. L., Meyer, K. A., & McNeal, L. (2012). Mission and diversity statements: What they do and do not say. *Innovative Higher Education, 37*(2), 125–139. https://eric.ed.gov/?id=EJ959991

Woodford, M. R., Chonody, J. M., Kulick, A., Brennan, D. J., & Renn, K. (2015). The LGBQ microaggressions on campus scale: A scale development and validation Study. *Journal of Homosexuality, 62*(12), 1660–1687. https://doi.org/10.1080/00918369.2015.1078205

Woodford, M. R., & Kulick, A. (2015). Academic and social integration on campus among sexual minority students: The impacts of psychological and experiential campus climate. *American Journal of Community Psychology, 55*, 13–24. https://doi.org/10.1007/s10464-014-9683-x

CHAPTER 13

CONCLUSION

Tamara Bertrand Jones
Shawna Patterson-Stephens

American higher education has not changed drastically since its inception in the 1600s. However, since that time, those who participate in higher education have changed considerably. More women, Black, Latinx, and other minoritized students are enrolling, matriculating, and graduating from a variety of higher education institutions, some at the highest rates for their group in decades. Despite the diversity of constituents, higher education's response to this diversity has not been adequate. Policy changes and pressures from a variety of stakeholders has resulted in increased policies, programs, and institutional practices that attempt to accomplish a plethora of ideas and ideals related to diversity, equity, inclusion, and belonging. Unfortunately, these efforts have not resulted in significantly transforming the academy to be truly responsive to the changing demographics of American society or higher education.

In preparing students for higher education, we continue to rely on invalid assessments and other poor measures of aptitude and potential, when research has shown us that these tools are not accurate predictors of student success, particularly for Black and Latinx populations. By continuing to use these tools, they become gatekeepers reinforcing that Black and Latinx students, for example, will continue to be found lacking and deemed not worthy of a college education. As a result of hostile racial climates, lesser expectations of success, and a host of other issues experienced by minoritized students, faculty, and staff, evidence suggests that these individuals experience feeling not welcomed or supported at many predominantly White institutions. The isolation, microaggressions, bias, and prejudice extend beyond individual treatment to policies with disparate impact for minoritized students, faculty, and staff.

FROM DIVERSITY IMPERATIVE TO INCLUSIVE EXCELLENCE

There have been mixed outcomes related to higher education's embracing of diversity. Some higher education institutions were open to change and recognized the benefits to their students and the institution if they embraced the inevitable changes. Others required more convincing, which led higher education leaders to develop a diversity imperative to help persuade leaders and institutions of diversity's importance. This imperative included several arguments in support of diversity, many of which are not grounded in structural diversity at all. Much of the diversity imperative in higher education has focused on the contributions to institutional prestige or student learning and avoids talk of moral imperatives inherent in social justice dialogue. Some arguments of the diversity imperative include:

- Diversity contributes to institutional excellence.
- Diversity contributes to better disciplinary study.
- Diversity is integral to the work of the institution.
- Diversity helps prepare students to work in a global society.
- Diversity improves student learning.

The diversity imperative encouraged higher education leaders to act in several ways. Higher education leaders recognized that as their institutions became more diverse, the structural diversity changed, and they needed to develop an actual plan for diversity. Formal structures and dedicated personnel were needed to implement diversity; simply providing minoritized communities access to the institution proved insufficient for their success. Many developed institutional policies, practices, and programs related to diversity that had both individual and institutional implications.

Broad scale policies for recruitment, retention, and promotion of diverse populations were developed. Some institutions also monetized/incentivized diversity through policy. Higher education practices solidly seemed focused on individuals with implications for institutional culture. In disaggregating the success data, we identified specific populations of people, particularly Blacks and Latinx, who needed remediation, or "fixing." Innovative programs designed to target the needs of these students and faculty, like professional development and mentoring, became magic bullets designed to target these areas for individual improvement and lessen institutional shortfalls.

POSITIONALITY IN ADVANCING INCLUSIVE EXCELLENCE

Ironically, despite the lack of a relevant and impactful response to these experiences, minoritized populations continue to thrive despite higher education's shortcomings. As evidenced by the authors in our volume, many of higher education's students advance to become faculty or administrators and must decide how to participate in a system that was not created for them or their students. Through engagement with policy, programs, and institutional practices, higher education institutions, and those who work in them, grapple with bigger ideals than simply "diversity" and "inclusion." These issues center on changing our institutions and the entire system in ways that truly transform higher education for all students.

As we discussed in the Introduction, the authors in this volume represent a variety of positions in higher education, and cultural identities and positionalities related to diversity, equity, inclusion, and belonging. Not intentional, but most of the authors represent at least one minoritized identity. We recognize the unique perspectives those that live in or have lived through marginalization bring to understandings about diversity, equity, inclusion, and belonging. Each chapter, while grounded in practical implications for higher education, addressed directly, or indirectly, the ways that positionality influences our approaches to this work.

We hope—through the examples presented in this book—the importance between research and praxis has been highlighted. We encourage readers to consider how we can enhance communication between faculty, scholars, and practitioners to further inclusive excellence.

We ask institutions that espouse a commitment to inclusive excellence to consider who leads and implements the work of diversity, equity, and inclusion on campus. If this work falls largely on the backs and shoulders of minoritized individuals, "Are they adequately resourced to advance this work?" Is adequate compensation, allocation of time, and institutional resources, and autonomy provided to ensure success of the initiatives and the individuals who facilitate them?

EPILOGUE

ADVANCING INCLUSIVE EXCELLENCE IN HIGHER EDUCATION

Implications for Moving Beyond Diversity to Create Equitable and Anti-Racist Institutions

Frank A. Tuitt

For more than a decade, higher education institutions in this country—and more recently around the world—have been utilizing Inclusive Excellence (IE) as a guiding framework to advance their diversity equity and inclusion commitments. However, the continued existence of student activism on college campuses suggests the results of these efforts have been mixed at best. Part of the reason traditionally White institutions (TWIs) have not experienced more sustainable success is the manner in which TWIs have operationalized IE which has decentered a focus on race and racism as a central component of their diversity and inclusion efforts (Tuitt, 2016, 2022). Specifically, they have been unable to avoid three traps related to:

- believing IE programs would transform institutional systems, structures, and overall campus culture;
- being seduced by the "happy talk" of IE and forgetting to focus on access and racial justice (Ahmed, 2012); and
- believing the hype of the magical diversity professional and failing to develop accountability structures that engage all stakeholders in organizational transformation efforts (Tuitt, 2016).

Fortunately, the chapters in this book provide some guidance for educators to avoid making the same mistakes by exposing some of the challenges that serve as barriers and by outlining specific strategies for moving beyond diversity to create inclusive, equitable, and anti-racist institutional environments.

MOVING BEYOND IE PROGRAMS TO TRANSFORM SYSTEMS AND STRUCTURES

Several of the chapters in this volume acknowledge that though IE initiatives can address the needs of racially minoritized students who participate in them, these efforts are rarely successful in transforming institutional culture because they are not usually linked to institutional structures and systems. Specifically, the authors in this volume point to the realization that amidst superficial and performative enactments of diversity there are still oppressive structures leading to silencing and deficit narratives impacting racially minoritized people. In Chapter 2, Bhattacharya, Liang, and Lander explore how higher education institutions and structures continue to perpetuate oppression, silencing, and deficit narratives through their leadership, training, and curriculum. Moreover, Dee Mosby-Holloway and Furr interrogate in Chapter 3 how TWIs perform diversity because it is "just," though these performances fall short because these efforts rarely include discussions of systemic and structural change. They argue that while there has been significant movement towards cultivating more diverse and inclusive college campuses, seldom is there discussion around dismantling and changing systems and power structures. Taken together, these chapters remind us that the adding additional programs without changing educational systems and structures, is the equivalent of putting band-aids on cuts but leaving the sharp instrument that created the cuts in place (Tuitt, 2016).

MOVING BEYOND THE HAPPY TALK OF IE TO CREATE JUSTICE ORIENTED AND ANTIRACIST CAMPUS ENVIRONMENTS

In addition to making the case that changes need to be at the system and structural level, multiple chapters in this volume provide guidance as to how TWIs can move beyond what Ahmed (2012) refers to as the happy talk of diversity by implementing strategic diversity plans, shifting the nature of conversations, or creating spaces for marginalized communities. For example, Davis, Lewis, and William's Chapter 4 provides insight as to how TWIs can use diversity plans to hold themselves accountable in providing access, equity, and inclusivity in student and faculty recruitment and instructional practices. Their discussion of how an urban research institution's creation and implementation of their diversity plan to shift the diversity infrastructure on campus caused administrators to reflect upon their procedures in engaging with America's multicultural communities. The importance of centering the lived experiences of minoritized communities in TWIs is further reinforced by McElderry, Hernandez Rivera, and Ashford (Chapter 9) who make a compelling case for practitioners to reflect on the ways their spaces also perpetuate ideologies of dominance through their functioning and support. They warn that if campus administrators are not careful, their IE efforts can undermine their good intentions and instead, disempower and invisibilize students with multiple-marginalized identities. As a strategy, McElderry et al. (Chapter 9) advocate for the use of theoretical concepts and frameworks practitioners can employ to create intersectional spaces and programming to practice intentionally in supporting students experiencing multiple-marginality on their campuses. Recognizing that the IE efforts must focus on closing equity gaps, Colomé (Chapter 8) offers a practical example of how one institution partnered with campus and community members to operationalize a social justice framework in the recruitment, hiring, and ongoing practice of a confidential advisor.

As a collective, these chapters call for TWIs to move beyond superficial enactment of IE efforts that are not grounded in social justice frameworks centering the lived experiences of minoritized communities. Even though IE may have replaced its predecessors' diversity and multiculturalism as a seemingly palatable term for driving equity and inclusion efforts, the widespread adoption of IE on college campuses throughout the country should not be disconnected from a focus on access and equity as a central component of institutional change, goals, and outcomes (Tuitt, 2016). Inclusive excellence efforts must resist the temptation to center the institution and instead center the voices of those who are doing—and impacted by—the diversity work. Accordingly, several of the chapters, in different ways, thus call for the recentering of narratives and voices of those doing diversity work and remind us that making the advancement of IE is everybody's business, where all segments of the campus are actively involved is a top priority (Tuitt, 2016).

MOVING BEYOND DIVERSITY BY CENTERING MINORITIZED VOICES AND BEING ACCOUNTABLE

Developing accountability structures that engage all stakeholders in organizational transformation efforts is critical if TWIs have any chance of moving beyond diversity to create equitable and antiracist institutions (Tuitt, 2016). When all employees on campus view themselves as IE champions and work together to form accountability structures, TWIs are more likely to experience real change outcomes that impact institutional culture, reduce institutional stress, and improve the lived experiences of minoritized populations (Tuitt, 2016). For example, Dee Mosby-Holloway and Furr's chapter (Chapter 3) posits that diversity is ultimately dictated by the institution. They argue that institutional leaders should hold as a high priority, a commitment to avoiding the tendency to want to silence or usurp, and instead listen to the voices of those responsible for doing diversity work. Specifically, their chapter convincingly demonstrates the narratives of those doing diversity work should be treated as critical elements required to successfully reimagine what diversity and inclusion can and should look like on college and university campuses. Esnard, Cobb-Roberts, and Pierre in Chapter 10 reiterate the importance of leveraging the lived experiences of those doing the work by illuminating the integral role that Black women faculty and administrators play on institutional transformation by being social justice advocates. Specifically, they show how collaborative autoethnography can unpack and explicate the risks in working towards social justice in an environment already systemically and structurally inequitable.

The taxing nature of doing diversity work—particularly among those who are impacted by it—is another issue addressed in this book. For example, Esnard et al.'s chapter (Chapter 10) critically analyzes the precarious dilemma of having to navigate TWIs while attempting to serve as advocates for institutional change, and the extent to which such activism often places diversity champions in a vulnerable position. Traversing this landscape requires DEI champions to expend significant emotional and physical labor to respond to campus needs during a crisis (Tuitt, 2022). Often, this labor exists outside of their formal responsibilities, and racial battle fatigue can be intensified when this labor does not result in sustainable change or goes unrecognized by campus leadership (Anthym & Tuitt, 2019; Tuitt, 2022). Moreover, this exploited labor has historically landed on the backs of women of color (Griffin et al., 2011). Readers in search of guidance on how to navigate this bind will want to heed the advice offered in Battacharya et al.'s chapter (Chapter 2), which discusses "negotiation and coping strategies" regarding oppression faced by women of color in higher education.

Overall, the chapters in this volume make a compelling argument for TWIs to move beyond diversity to create inclusive, equitable, and anti-racist campus environments. Specifically, two themes emerged that indicate how TWIs can move beyond the happy talk of inclusive excellence included: (a) utilizing social justice frameworks that center the voices and experiences of minoritized communities, and (b) developing accountability structures that support the dismantling of oppressive policies and practices. Due to the recent Supreme Court decision on affirmative action, the use of race in admissions has been severely restricted. This decision is not an opportunity for institutions and practitioners to move away from anti-racism work. In these challenging times, there is an urgent imperative for TWIs to double down on their efforts to create anti-racist institutional environments by advancing institutional policies and practices that produce equitable outcomes for racially minoritized communities. TWIs' ability to embrace the aforementioned considerations as critical components of their IE efforts will increase the likelihood that their process of identifying, addressing, and eliminating policies, practices, traditions, norms, and organizational culture that impede meaningful systemic and structural change, is effective.

REFERENCES

Ahmed, S. (2012). *On being included*. Duke University Press.

Anthym, M., & Tuitt, F. (2019). When the levees break: The cost of vicarious trauma, microaggressions and emotional labor for Black administrators and faculty engaging in race work at traditionally White institutions. *International Journal of Qualitative Studies in Education, 32*(9), 1072–1093. https://doi.org/10.1080/09518398.2019.1645907

Griffin K. A., Bennett, J. C., & Harris, J. (2011a). Analyzing gender differences in Black faculty marginalization through a sequential mixed-methods design. *New Directions for Institutional Research, 151,* 45–61. https://doi.org/10.1002/ir.398

Tuitt, F. (2016). Making excellence inclusive in challenging times. *Liberal Education, 102*(2), 64–68. https://dgmg81phhvh63.cloudfront.net/content/magazines/Archive/LE_SP16_Vol102No2.pdf

Tuitt, F. (2022). More than a hashtag: Nurturing Black excellence in traditionally White institutions. *Journal of Minority Achievement, Creativity, and Leadership, 1*(2), 274–300. https://doi.org/10.5325/minoachicrealead.1.2.0274

ABOUT THE CONTRIBUTORS

Shannon Ashford is an educator and facilitator whose passion is to develop and connect individuals in order to create inclusive and equitable environments. She currently serves as the director of diversity, equity, and inclusion at Duke University in the Office for Institutional Equity. In this role, she is responsible for the management and delivery of the enterprise-wide educational engagement portfolio for faculty, staff, and students with respect to diversity, equity, and inclusion. She has more than a decade of professional experience in the areas of diversity, equity, and inclusion; leadership and identity development; campus activities and K–12 college access initiatives. Shannon holds a BS in journalism (public relations) from Ohio University and a MEd in higher education administration from Kent State University.

Kakali Bhattacharya, PhD, is a multiple award-winning professor at University of Florida housed in the research, evaluation, and measurement program. She is the 2018 winner of AERA's Mid-Career Scholar of Color Award and the 2018 winner of AERA's Mentoring Award from Division G: Social Context of Education. Her coauthored text with Kent Gillen, *Power, Race, and Higher Education: A Cross-Cultural Parallel Narrative* (Sense Publishers, 2016) has won a 2017 Outstanding Publication Award from AERA (SIG 168) and a 2018 Outstanding Book Award from International Congress of Qualitative Research. She is recognized by *Diverse* magazine as one of the top 25 women in higher education.

Tamara Bertrand Jones, PhD, is an associate professor of higher education in the Department of Educational Leadership and Policy Studies (ELPS), as well as associate director at the Center for Postsecondary Success at Florida State University (FSU). She served as interim department chair for ELPS and program coordinator for the higher education program and in both roles brought attention and informed policy related to matters of diversity, equity, and inclusion. With colleague Rhea Lathan, she created CONNECTIONS, a mentoring and scholarly writing accountability program for faculty of color at FSU. In her research, she uses qualitative methods and critical and feminist theories to examine the sociocultural contexts that influence the education and professional experiences of underrepresented populations, particularly Black women, in academia. Dr. Bertrand Jones' previous work as a student affairs administrator and program evaluator also influenced her other research interests in assessment and evaluation, particularly culturally responsive evaluation. She is a founder and past president of Sisters of the Academy Institute, an international organization that promotes collaborative scholarship and networking among Black women in academia. With fellow scholars, she collaborated on *Pathways to Higher Education for African American Women* (Stylus, 2012) and *Cultivating Leader Identity and Capacity in Students from Diverse Backgrounds* (Jossey-Bass, 2015), among other peer-reviewed journal article, book chapters, policy briefs, and research reports.

Deirdre Cobb-Roberts, PhD, is an associate professor in the Department of Educational and Psychological Studies at the University of South Florida and a former McKnight Junior Faculty Fellow. She earned her PhD from the University of Illinois at Urbana-Champaign. Her research focuses on historical and contemporary examinations of equity, treatment, and social justice in American higher education. Dr. Cobb-Roberts has published in journals such as the *American Educational Research Journal*, *History of Education Quarterly*, and the *Journal of Teacher Education*. She has coedited a book, *Schools as Imagined Communities: The Creation of Identity, Meaning, and Conflict in U.S. History (Palgrave Macmillan, 2006)*, and just completed her second coauthored book, *Black Women, Academe, and the Tenure Process in the United States and the Caribbean* (Palgrave Macmillan, 2018).

Andria Cole is the bureau chief for the Bureau of Family and Community Outreach at the Florida Department of Education. Prior to serving as a bureau chief, Andria worked as a program specialist for the Nita M. Lowey 21st Century Community Learning Centers. She is also a professional educator certified in math, science, and gifted education and taught for 17 years in Georgia, Texas, Maryland, and Florida. Her educational journey has resulted in degrees from Texas A&M University, Mercer University, and Kennesaw State University. Currently, Andria is a doctoral candidate in the educational psychology program at Florida State University. Her area of research is success factors and decision-making processes of Black, male STEM PhDs.

Sarah Colomé, MS, (she/her) is the founder and CEO of Collective Futures LLC, a consulting firm with the mission to build value-driven capacity for community-centered social change. Catalyzed by her commitment to advancing liberatory frameworks, her experience spans nonprofit, corporate, and governmental partnerships. A trained domestic violence and sexual assault crisis advocate, Sarah most recently served as the director of the Women's Resources Center at the University of Illinois Urbana-Champaign. In addition to Collective Futures, Sarah is a senior consultant for Wayfinding Partners, Legislative Landscape & Position Statements co-chair for the Campus Advocacy and Prevention Professional Association, and a member of the editorial board for the *Journal of Women & Gender in Higher Education.*

Alicia W. Davis is a doctoral student in curriculum and instruction: urban education at the University of North Carolina at Charlotte. She holds a bachelor's degree in mathematics and a master's degree in school administration from the University of North Carolina at Charlotte. Her research interests include academic achievement for African American students, school discipline, and education policy reform.

Talia Esnard, PhD, is a sociologist attached to the Department of Behavioral Sciences, University of the West Indies (UWI), St. Augustine campus, Trinidad and Tobago. Prior to her recent position at the UWI, she worked for 8 years as an assistant professor in a nontenured position at the University of Trinidad and Tobago. Her research interests center on issues affecting Caribbean women who work within educational and entrepreneurial spheres. Some of her work has been published in the *Journal of Asian Academy of Management; NASPA Journal About Women in Higher Education; Journal of the Motherhood Initiative; Mentoring & Tutoring: Partnership in Learning; Journal of Educational Administration and History;* as well as, *Women, Gender & Families of Color.* She was also a recent recipient of Taiwan Research Fellowship (2012) and Caricom-Canada Leadership Program (2015). She recently completed a coauthored book on *Black Women, Academe, and the Tenure Process in the United States and in the Caribbean* (Palgrave Macmillan, 2018).

Teara Flagg Lander, EdD, is an adjunct assistant professor in educational leadership at Kansas State University. She received her doctorate from Kansas State University in educational leadership with an emphasis in qualitative research and social justice. Her research agenda uses qualitative methods to investigate the intersection of race, gender, and culture in colleges, universities, and other educational settings.

278 ▪ About the Contributors

Jesse Ford, PhD, serves as an assistant professor of higher education in the Department of Teacher Education and Higher Education at the University of North Carolina at Greensboro. His research explores the historical and social-cultural influences of race and gender to tackle inequity in education. More specifically, his scholarship examines the socialization experiences of underrepresented students, faculty, and their pathways in higher education. Dr. Ford is also co-editing a book titled *Engaging Black Men in College Through Leadership Learning* alongside Dr. Cameron Beatty, which will be released in the spring of 2023.

Sara Furr, PhD, is an alumnus of the University of North Carolina at Chapel Hill and the University of South Carolina. She is the dean of students in the School of Social Service Administration at The University of Chicago. Sara holds her doctorate in higher education from Loyola University Chicago. Her dissertation is titled, *Wellness Interventions for Social Justice Fatigue Among Student Affairs Professionals.*

Ignacio Hernández, PhD, is an associate professor and the EdD Program director in the Department of Educational Leadership at California State University, Fresno. Dr. Hernández engages in research that addresses three areas of the study of higher education: (a) community college leadership, (b) community college transfer students' experiences and community college transfer policies, and (c) graduate education and preparation of student affairs professionals. He currently serves on the editorial board of the *About Campus* journal and previously served on the board of directors for the National Community College Hispanic Council.

Susana Hernández, PhD, is an associate professor of higher education administration and leadership and core faculty in the doctoral program in educational leadership at California State University, Fresno. Dr. Hernández adopts critical frameworks and methods to examine educational opportunity in discourse, policy, and practice. Her research aims to interrogate institutional policies and practices to create more equitable educational experiences for underserved communities with a focus on Hispanic serving institutions, undocumented student experiences, and preparation of educational leaders.

Stephanie Hernandez Rivera, PhD, is a Boricua woman and first-generation college graduate. Hernandez Rivera has worked in the education field in some capacity for over 10 years. In higher education, she has focused her efforts on creating equitable and inclusive campus communities. Her research focuses on the experiences of those who are impacted by intersectional marginalization and she is committed to utilizing critical cultural methodologies to do so. Hernandez Rivera completed her PhD in educational leadership and policy analysis from the University of Missouri and holds a Bachelor of Arts in early childhood education, women's and gender studies, and psychology and a Master of Arts in women's and gender studies. She has and continues to support the creation of initiatives that create intentional and loving spaces for women of color.

Mike Hoffshire, PhD (he/him), is the assistant dean of admissions and student affairs at the Herbert Wertheim School of Optometry and Vision Science at the University of California, Berkeley. A queer scholar and practitioner, their research examines the identity development of LGBQ+ students and student success initiatives. Current projects include qualitative studies of faculty advisors of LGBTQ+ organizations at community colleges and the experience of LGBQ+ identified Caribbean heritage students. In addition to researching and writing, they serve as an adjunct faculty member, consultant, and presenter.

Latara O. Lampkin, PhD, is a senior research associate at Florida State University. As a policy and research scholar, her research spans PreK–12 and higher education and is, largely, conducted through collaborative partnerships with practitioners and policy makers—including those at historically Black colleges and universities. For the past decade, she has been engaged in large-scale, federally funded, multidisciplinary research and technical assistant projects that focus on local implementation of policy and reform efforts to increase educational outcomes for underserved student populations across the PreK–20 continuum. In the higher education context, her scholarship and service focus on diversity policies designed and implemented to increase the recruitment, development, and retention of underrepresented racial/ethnic faculty and graduate students.

Teara Lander, PhD, is the assistant vice president for diversity, equity, and inclusion at the University of Oklahoma (OU). She received a Bachelor of Arts degree from the University of Central Oklahoma in political science, a Master of Education degree in higher education administration from OU and a doctoral degree in leadership, alongside two graduate certificates in qualitative research methods and social justice education from Kansas State University.

Chance W. Lewis, PhD, is the Carol Grotnes Belk Distinguished Professor of Urban Education and the director of The Urban Education Collaborative at the University of North Carolina at Charlotte. Additionally, he serves as provost faculty fellow for diversity, inclusion, and access.

Jia "Grace" Liang, PhD, is an associate professor of educational leadership at the Kansas State University. Beside teaching courses in school/educational leadership, she also engages her scholarship, using qualitative inquiry, and teaches qualitative research methods courses. Her research interests focus on school leadership, teacher leadership, mentoring, diversity and equity in STEM, social justice and equity for women and other minoritized populations, and community engagement. She holds a PhD from the University of Georgia in educational administration and policy. She is the president of the Eastern Educational Research Association and the chair for the AERA special interest group—Research on Education of Asian and PacificAmericans.

Marquise Loving-Kessee, PhD, is an educator, teacher, and diversity education practitioner who has served in administrative, instructional, leadership, research, and supervisory roles with 28 years of experience in higher education. Her journey as an instructional specialist fueled her passion for supporting and creating opportunities for underserved populations. Marquise is an avid teacher of mathematics, and she spends much of her free time tutoring students who may need specialized focus on math learning. As a STEM consultant, she served secondary and postsecondary institutions to offer relevant assessment, development, and strategic guidance for student programs. As a diversity consultant, she conducts training workshops, climate assessments, and coaching forums, and she provides recommendations for institutions seeking more inclusive and diverse spaces. Her research interests include increasing cultural competence in higher education, supporting STEM and mathematics pathways for students of color, navigating hybrid learning, and test anxiety for mathematics students.

Jonathan A. McElderry, PhD, serves as the dean of inclusive excellence at Elon University. His experience in higher education has focused on enhancing diversity, equity, and inclusion on college campuses. Additionally, his research has sought to raise awareness of the experiences of underrepresented students at predominantly White institutions and provide strategies to increase their academic and social success. His experience includes serving as the director of the Gaines/Oldham Black Culture Center at the University of Missouri, as well as the graduate assistant in the Multicultural Center at Ohio University. Jonathan earned a PhD in educational leadership and policy analysis with an emphasis in higher education from the University of Missouri.

Charee Dee Mosby-Holloway is an alumnus of the University of Notre Dame and The Ohio State University, and has been a student affairs practitioner for over a decade with a focus on social justice education and identity development. Charee serves as the director of student diversity and inclusion at Columbia College Chicago.

Shawna Patterson-Stephens, PhD (she/hers), is vice president and chief diversity officer at Central Michigan University. She also serves as faculty in educational psychology and higher education at the University of Nevada, Las Vegas and New England College. Her research interests include Black and Latinx issues in higher education, media influences in the postsecondary sector, and critical theory in higher educational contexts. She experiments with various modes of knowledge dissemination to ensure scholarship remains accessible, evidenced through projects like the podcast, *Scholar Tea*. Patterson-Stephens has published several works on the experiences of Black women in higher education and has collaborated on peer-reviewed articles exploring the state of diversity in higher education. Dr. Patterson-Stephens currently serves as co-PI on the national Black doctoral women study (BDWS). She is also editor of the forthcoming volume, *Dirty Computer: Black Cyberfeminism in the Digital Age*.

Devona F. Pierre, PhD, serves as the director of equity, diversity, and inclusion at Saint Petersburg College. Her research interests include the success of Black women in academia, mitigating barriers for Black women academics, and mentoring Black women in higher education. She also explores the recruitment, retention, persistence, and advancement of marginalized populations in postsecondary institutions. She has taught courses in higher education administration as well as worked as an administrator in higher education. Dr. Pierre earned a bachelor's degree in psychology from Dillard University, a Master of Education in adult education at Auburn University, and a Doctor of Education in administration of higher education from Auburn University.

Jonathan T. Pryor, PhD, is an assistant professor of higher education administration and leadership and core faculty in the doctoral program in educational leadership at California State University, Fresno. Dr. Pryor's work primarily focuses on addressing institutional inequities to advance social justice in higher education. His scholarship has explored topics related to LGBTQ+ equity in higher education, the field of LGBTQ+ student services, leadership in education, campus climate, and the experiences of LGBTQ+ college students.

Adrienne P. Stephenson, PhD, is an assistant dean, director (graduate fellowships and awards), and university liaison (McKnight Doctoral Fellowship program) in The Graduate School at Florida State University (FSU). As a scientist, scholar, and servant leader in higher education and the Tallahassee community, she focuses on student success, scholarly development, and mentoring for all students with a particular interest in traditionally underrepresented groups. In 2016 and 2018, Adrienne was awarded the

William R. Jones Mentor Award and Dr. Tribble Award by the Florida Education Fund for mentorship of Black and LatinX doctoral students at FSU.

Jonathan Townes, is a native of Greenville, MS and currently resides in Jackson, MS. He is a 2012 graduate of Jackson State University as well as 2014 graduate of Mississippi College. He currently works at Hinds Community College as the dean of Technology for Career and Technical Education. Prior to this role, he served as the STEM program director and assistant director of sponsored programs. In these roles, he served as PI/Co-PI for NSF HBCU-UP Targeted Infusion Project, Implementation Project, ITEST, and LSAMP. In addition, he has served as the project director for a Minority Science and Engineering Improvement Program (MSEIP) at the college and site coordinator for the MS NASA Space Grant consortium. He has provided mentorship to STEM majoring students that has led to degree obtainment and job placement.

Frank Tuitt, EdD, is the University of Connecticut's vice president and chief diversity officer and professor of higher education and student affairs in the Neag School of Education. With 25 years of experience as an administrator, academic, and change agent in higher education in the United States (and more recently around the globe), Tuitt is responsible for systems-wide strategic planning and implementation of mission-driven institutional diversity efforts. These responsibilities include overseeing the Office for Diversity and Inclusion and its six cultural centers and programs.

Louise Michelle Vital, PhD (she/her), is director/assistant professor of the international higher education program at Lesley University where she also codirects the Institute for English Language Programs Beyond Borders. Her primary line of inquiry is related to the global dimensions of higher education. Broadly, her interests center on a country and regional focus on Haiti and the Caribbean, student experiences in higher education, scholar/practitioner preparation, and critical reflexive practice in academia. Her teaching, research, and scholarship are driven by key suppositions and questions, including how inequalities in power and privilege exist in society. She asks: "What are the consequences of these realities, and how do they impact experience in educational contexts?" Current projects examine racial (in)equity in global higher education.

John A. Williams, III, PhD, is an assistant professor of multicultural education at Texas A&M University at College Station, in the Department of Teaching, Learning, and Culture. His research focuses on developing and replicating best practices, policies, and personnel to dismantle inequitable discipline outcomes for Black students in K–12 school environments. Additionally, his research investigates how to prepare and support culturally inclusive teachers through the adaptation of multiculturalism.

Varaxy Yi, PhD, is an assistant professor of higher education administration and leadership and core faculty in the doctoral program in educational leadership at California State University, Fresno. As a first-generation Khmer American graduate and faculty, Dr. Yi is committed to advancing knowledge to serve racially minoritized communities. She conducts research to advance equity, access, and opportunity for historically underserved communities, such as racially minoritized, Southeast Asian American, and refugee populations. Her work focuses on building capacity within higher education institutions to advance racial justice and equity to serve diverse students.

Eboni M. Zamani-Gallaher, PhD, is professor of higher education and associate dean for equity, justice, and strategic partnerships at the University of Pittsburgh School of Education. In this role, she advances the school-wide strategy for equitable partnerships, which includes partnering with colleagues to further deepen teaching, strengthen existing and propose new programmatic offerings, and reimagine the school's ongoing engagements. Zamani-Gallaher is also executive director of the Council for the Study of Community Colleges (CSCC), a national organization that supports the advancement of the study and practice of community colleges in the United States. Prior to joining Pitt Education, Zamani-Gallaher was a professor at the University of Illinois Urbana–Champaign College of Education, where she was also director of the Office for Community College Research and Leadership (OCCRL) from 2015–2022, securing $9 million in grants and contracts during her tenure. At Illinois, She previously served as associate head of the Department of Education Policy, Organization, and Leadership and associate dean. Zamani-Gallaher earned her BS in psychology and MS in general experimental psychology from Western Illinois University and holds a PhD in educational organization and leadership from the University of Illinois Urbana-Champaign.

Printed in the United States
by Baker & Taylor Publisher Services